GROWTH AND DEVELOPMENT

The child and physical activity

D1225704

GROWTH AND DEVELOPMENT
The child and physical activity

LEONARD D. ZAICHKOWSKY, Ph.D.

School of Education, Boston University,
Boston, Massachusetts

LINDA B. ZAICHKOWSKY, Ph.D.

School of Education, Boston University,
Boston, Massachusetts

THOMAS J. MARTINEK, Ed.D.

School of Health, Physical Education, and Recreation,
University of North Carolina,
Greensboro, North Carolina

with 148 illustrations

The C. V. Mosby Company

ST. LOUIS • TORONTO • LONDON   1980

Library of Congress Cataloging in Publication Data

Zaichkowsky, Leonard D   1944-
    Growth and development.

    Includes bibliographical references and index.
    1. Child development.   2. Motor ability in
children.   I. Zaichkowsky, Linda B., 1943-
joint author.   II. Martinek, Thomas J., 1943-
joint author.   III. Title.
RJ131.Z34   155.4   79-23443
ISBN 0-8016-5663-X

GW/M/M   9   8   7   6   5   05/B/606

To

Justin **Angela**
Bryan **Tommy**
Anna

PREFACE

In writing *Growth and Development: The Child and Physical Activity* we have sought to provide a new dimension to the teaching of growth and development or "motor development" courses in professional physical education programs. Our experiences as students, teachers, and researchers have led us to believe that most schools of physical education in North America deal only with the physical or motor aspects of human development and leave the other domains to fragmented learning in other college courses or to chance. This statement can be supported merely by looking at the available texts in the area of child development. Those that are written by physical educators deal almost exclusively with *motor* development, while those written by general educators and psychologists deal almost exclusively with cognitive or social-psychological development, with perhaps a chapter set aside for physical-motor development. Most students of physical education fail to learn much about the cognitive and social-psychological development of children, and students in other disciplines fail to learn much about physical-motor development.

The plan of this text is to deal with child development in its totality. We see human development as a process in which psychomotor, cognitive, and affective or social-psychological factors all interact during a life span. Physical activity can have a profound effect on the development of these three domains at every stage of a youngster's development. For practical purposes the life span we have chosen to deal with in this book ranges from birth to adolescence, or that age period in which the parent and educator have the greatest influence. Since sex differences are an important aspect of child development and often interact with age, we will devote considerable discussion to both age and sex differences. Most important, we will attempt to describe the effects physical activity has on the total development of boys and girls at the various stages of development.

This book has been written for undergraduate and graduate students who either aspire to or presently do work with children through the medium of physical activity. We hope, therefore, that the book will be helpful not only for students preparing for careers in physical education, but also for those in elementary and secondary teaching, recreation, child development, medicine, and the allied health professions.

This book has been divided into three parts representing the three domains of behavior. Part One deals with psychomotor development; Part Two, with cognitive development; and Part Three, with affective, or social-psychological, development. We begin each chapter with a theoretical overview of the topic, then describe age and sex differences, and finally discuss implications for physical education.

In each chapter we have described basic ideas and important research related to child development. We sought to cover major concepts while maintaining a balance among theory, research, and practical implications of developmental principles. Obviously it was not possible to cover every developmental concept within the three parts of this book. We trust that our selection fits your perceptions of important developmental concepts. We tried to communicate these concepts in a style that was readable and interesting for a diverse readership.

For those who are novices in the language of child development we hope that the Glossary will facilitate the learning of developmental concepts. We also hope that the student projects at the ends of the chapters will foster an increased awareness of important concepts in child development.

Numerous people need to be thanked for helping to "pull off" this text. We would like to thank those individuals who made the initial reviews and offered recommendations. These include Drs. Elizabeth Umstead and Sandra Powers of the University of North Carolina at Greensboro, Dr. Arthur Miller of Boston University, and Dr. Koenraad Lindner of the University of Manitoba. Special thanks to Margaret Read for writing the chapter on language development and to our patient and expert typists, Kathy and Linda. Finally, our deep appreciation goes to our families who were patient during the time it took to conceive and consummate this project and particularly to our children, who piqued our interest in the subject and to whom this book is dedicated.

Leonard D. Zaichkowsky
Linda B. Zaichkowsky
Thomas J. Martinek

CONTENTS

GROWTH AND DEVELOPMENT

The child and physical activity

Chapter 1

INTRODUCTION

The study of child development is a relatively recent undertaking for many disciplines. Although the medical profession has been concerned with child development since the days of Hippocrates, little systematic research was conducted in the behavioral sciences until the early part of the twentieth century. At about that time psychologists became interested in studying the development of children, and as a result the 1920s and 1930s witnessed the publication of a wealth of normative data related to child development (Ames, 1937; Bayley, 1935; Gesell, 1928; Shirley, 1931). Since that time, however, many other disciplines such as sociology, anthropology, and education have realized the importance of studying the developing child from their own perspectives. Although Espenschade published work as early as 1940, physical educationists have only recently demonstrated a concerted effort to study the child. This evidence is exemplified by the increasing number of research articles and symposia, textbooks, and college courses dealing with child development.

Although progress is being made in teaching physical education students about child development, all too often the curriculum is concerned only with motor development. Child development is more than this; it also encompasses the cognitive or intellectual, as well as the social-psychological, development of the child. The latter two domains, often referred to as cognitive and affective, are generally taught in courses offered in psychology departments. This separation is most unfortunate, since this categorization has been constructed simply for the convenience of discussion and writing and is not due to a real, distinct separation of the domains. In reality these domains of behavior are intricately related and affect or interact with each other. Concentrating attention on only one aspect of development to the exclusion of the others is a serious mistake. This is particularly true for students who are learning about child development for the first time. Studying development in fragments produces a distorted picture of the developmental process.

This text attempts to amend existing practices in teaching about child development, particularly for those students studying movement behavior. How children develop in the three domains and how physical activity or movement experiences contribute to the developing child will be described and explained.

The thrust of this introductory chapter will be to describe the process of studying *total development;* provide some working *definitions* of terms commonly used in child development, a discussion of the more common *theories* of child development, and an explanation about the *methods of studying* child development; and discuss the *importance of studying* child development. An effort will be made to depart from the traditional encyclopedic text and be as informal as possible.

UNITS OF STUDY IN CHILD DEVELOPMENT

As mentioned earlier the area of study of child development is relatively new. Although young, the field has undergone tremendous change during the past decade. It is characterized today by a broadening in focus, from a local and regional focus to a *cross-cultural* one. Further, rather than using a single disciplinary approach (for example, psychology), the trend today is to use a *multidisciplinary* approach, that is, combining the efforts of sociology, anthropology, psychology, education, and medicine. Another significant trend today is to stress *experimental* studies rather than relying heavily on observational and descriptive studies in order to explain why certain changes occur.

Studies in child development differ considerably in terms of their focus; that is, researchers differ with respect to the domains, ages, and perhaps sex studied, as well as the method used to study the behavioral phenomena. The specific focus is generally dictated by the investigator's interest and expertise.

It was mentioned earlier that three domains have been conceptualized to deal with the complexities of human behavior. These include the cognitive, affective, and psychomotor. Generally writers about human behavior refer to the above classification; however, there are sometimes differences in words (for example, social-psychological for affective and physical-motor for psychomotor), and some writers use a fourth category. This fourth category adds the social

Table 1-1. Major developmental domains used in child development

Domain	Examples of types of behavior included
Cognitive (intellectual)*	Thought processes, language, memory
Affective (social-psychological)	Feelings, emotions
Social	Effect of society, institutions, groups
Psychomotor (physical-motor, biological)	Biological and motor processes

*Names in parentheses refer to alternative labels used in classification.

domain to the other three (Singer and Dick, 1974). The choice of classification lies in the author's particular preference and should not be interpreted as being a meaningful distinction, since the classification is used merely to facilitate communication about complex behavior. Table 1-1 shows the classifications.

In dealing with child development this text will use the domain classifications of psychomotor, cognitive, and affective to be consistent with predominant usage. Periodically there will be references to social-psychological development instead of affective because there are occasions when social-psychological is more descriptive of the characteristics being discussed. Once again it should be stressed that these three domains *interact* in the development of the child; that is, they do not operate independently in a vacuum. Fig. 1-1 illustrates our conception of the interactive influence of the domains of behavior on child development.

It has been customary to describe *age-related changes* in development by using stages rather than specific ages. Table 1-2 provides the names of the various stages typically used in human development (from conception to death), as well as the approximate age range of each stage. Since this text is concerned with child development, those stages dealt with will be infancy through adolescence. One exception will be Chapter 2, where there is an overview of prenatal development.

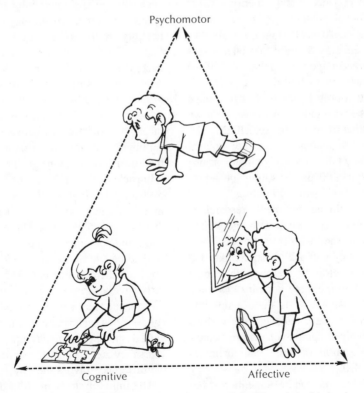

Fig. 1-1. Schematic illustration of interaction between domains of behavior.

Table 1-2. Stages used in human development

Name of stage	Approximate age range
1. Prenatal	Conception to birth
2. Infant	Birth to 2 years
3. Early childhood	2 to 5 years
4. Late childhood	5 to 10 years
5. Adolescent	10 to 18 years
6. Adult	18 to 40 years
7. Middle age	40 to 60 years
8. Old age	60 years and over

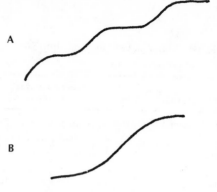

Fig. 1-2. Curve **A** represents stage theory; curve **B** represents theoretical position that growth is continuous and gradual.

A note on the use of stages in this book is in order here since the word has several connotations. Stage theory is used simply to provide suitable age categories in describing the development of children, and it is not advocated as a theory concerning the course of development. In developmental psychology "stage theory versus sequential theory" is a constant source of debate between theoreticians because they represent contrasting views on the nature of development. Proponents of stage theory say that the course of development is segmented, or divided into stages. At each stage new abilities appear. It is generally thought that later stages evolve from preceding ones and that all children go through these stages in the same order, although the rate of progression may differ. Stage theory could be represented by curve *A* shown in Fig. 1-2. Other theoreticians see children developing in a continuous manner by gradual increments. They fail to recognize the existence of definable stages. This view may be represented by curve *B* shown in Fig. 1-2.

In studying child development, researchers in addition to being concerned with age-related changes are concerned with possible *sex differences*. That is, they will ask questions like, Do boys and girls develop differently with respect to specific skills in the three domains? Do they develop at different rates? Is there a possible *interaction* between sex, age, and the various domains in the development of certain behaviors? Our conception of this relationship is shown in Fig. 1-3.

The word interaction has been mentioned before, and since it has a number of different meanings, its various definitions should be clarified. In layman's language interaction usually refers to communicative interaction, for example, we are having an interaction with you. As used in the earlier paragraph interaction meant that several factors combined their influences in affecting behavior. Specifically it was said that the three domains of behavior interacted in the development of human behavior. But suppose we made the statement, "Growth is influenced by several interacting forces." What is being said is that growth may be determined by heredity, nutrition, and exercise, among other factors. The extent of each contribution, however, is unknown. All that is known is that heredity, nutrition, and exercise contribute to growth in some unique pattern.

In speaking of age and sex interactions, it is meant that differences between boys and girls (in physical development or some performance measure) depend upon age. The data in Fig. 1-4 (Hunsicker and Reiff, 1966) show that for the 50-yard dash, boys at 10 years run the distance in 8.3 seconds, while girls at that age run the distance in 8.5 seconds. These values are quite close and for practical purposes could be considered equal. However, at 15 years of age the boys run the distance in 6.9 seconds, while the girls have a time of 8.3 seconds, a substantial difference. Here sex most likely interacts with age, or boys perform better than girls on the 50-yard dash, but *it depends* upon the age. At 10 years they are virtually the same, but at 15 years the difference favors the boys.

The units of study in child development are therefore numerous. Besides the study of age-

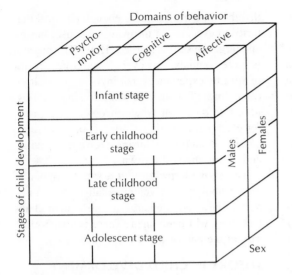

Domains of behavior

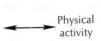

Fig. 1-3. Schematic illustration of significant developmental units of study, their interaction, and their relationship to physical activity.

related changes, scientists may be interested in investigating possible sex differences and quite likely restrict themselves to a particular domain of behavior. The concern in this text is with age and sex differences across all three domains and, most importantly, with how physical activity influences these three factors (age, sex, domains). As Fig. 1-3 illustrates, it is also quite possible that these factors influence one's participation and performance in physical activity.

LANGUAGE OF CHILD DEVELOPMENT

Whenever students are introduced to new subject matter, they usually have the problem of having to learn the vocabulary associated with it. This is true for every specialized field, whether it be medicine, law, agriculture, sports, or child development. Reference has already been made to some important concepts, such as domains of behavior and interaction. Here are some other basic terms and concepts used in child development.

Development is the product of growth, maturation, heredity, and learning.

Maturation refers to changes in body size, shape, and skill throughout a life span. In its pure form maturation determines development without any external influences, such as learning. However, we should point out that there are few cases of pure maturational influences in development. In reality, learning or environmental effects interact with maturation in the

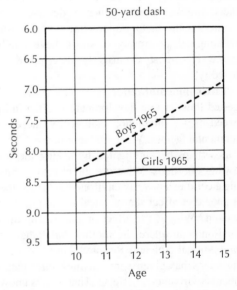

Fig. 1-4. Example of possible interaction between age and sex in motor performance.

development of a child. Probably the closest pure form of maturational effects occurs when the fetus grows in the mother's womb.

Growth is oftentimes used synonymously with maturation; however, they do not mean exactly the same thing. Growth refers to observable step-by-step change in quantity, such as body size. Arms get bigger (growth), and there is growth in skill or even vocabulary. These changes may be due to maturation, but not necessarily. Other effects such as exercise and diet may serve to increase arm size, and learning probably produces the growth in vocabulary.

Heredity refers to a set of qualities that are fixed at birth and hence predetermine certain individual characteristics. Every normal human body is made up of 46 chromosomes arranged in 23 pairs. These chromosomes in turn are made up of thousands of genes that serve to determine eye color, amount of hair, intelligence, personality, and so forth. Heredity thus accounts for many individual traits and characteristics. However, it is also true that these traits and characteristics are modified by the environment. For example, body build is determined by and large by heredity, but it is possible to effect change in this predisposition by working with weights, using steroids, and eating specific diets. Similarly, intelligence is developed by environmental factors interacting with heredity (although there are some who believe intelligence is almost exclusively determined by heredity).

Environmental effects. It has been suggested thus far that development is often influenced by the interaction of heredity and environmental factors. What are these factors? They can perhaps be highlighted by asking the following questions: What are the effects of raising a child in a poverty environment? How does a poor diet affect the physical development of a child? What is the effect of growing up in an environment where the mother and father are professional athletes? Research based on these questions has given some definite information about environmental effects. That is, it is known that a poverty environment and a poor diet can retard development. Similarly, growing up in an athletic environment will probably predispose a child to athletic endeavors.

Although the environment affects development in several ways, its principal effect is through its influence on the *learning* that takes place within each child. Learning is described as a relatively permanent change in the behavior of an individual. Thus, behavioral changes due to disease, drugs, fatigue, and the like are excluded from learned behavior. Following is an example in which learning takes place in the environment. Children learn to throw a ball at a relatively young age (about 2 years). It is true

that the child must possess enough physical maturity to execute the throwing response, but by and large the skill is learned. How? The process is quite complex; however, it could be a result of specific experiences that involve observation (modeling) of another person throwing and positive reinforcement when an object is thrown, for example, "good girl" or "good boy" by a parent, or simply the intrinsic reward of feeling and seeing the ball thrown.

The above terms are but a small number in the vocabulary of developmentalists. When important new terms emerge in subsequent chapters, they will be defined. There is also a glossary at the end of the text (Appendix B).

THEORY IN CHILD DEVELOPMENT

According to Mandler and Kessen, "Theories are sets of statements, understandable to others, which make predictions about empirical events" (Mandler and Kessen, 1959, p. 142). To add to this definition it might be said that theory is usually a summary of known "facts" and conjecture that serves to organize large amounts of information in a meaningful way. It would be chaotic and most frustrating if there were no theory to explain a variety of human behaviors. If a theory was lacking, it would be necessary to constantly describe the many small events that make up behavior. A further function of theory is that it guides additional research. Thus it is possible to gather empirical data that support the theory, suggest modifications of it, or even reject it.

A number of theoretical positions about the development of behavior have been postulated. Five major theoretical views of development will be discussed: the maturational, the cognitive, the psychoanalytic, the humanistic, and the behavioral or learning theory. It is rare that any one theory is accepted by everyone, since in one way or another a given theory is incomplete. This "incompleteness" is due primarily to the desire of the theorist to explain a slightly different facet of child development. For example, psychoanalytic theory concerns itself with the development of personality (primarily), whereas cognitive theory attempts to provide explanatory principles for the development of thinking. Nonetheless, it is important that students of child development be cognizant of the existing theories and their interrelationships so that they can formulate their own perspectives.

Maturational theory

Although maturational theory is not widely accepted today, brief mention of it will be made mainly because it played a significant role in the evolution of the study of child development. In the 1930s Gesell at Yale University advanced his theory of development, which emphasized the role of maturation. Although he recognized that a child's behavior is affected by experience, he argued that a child's development is determined biologically.

Gesell's work prompted a great deal of "normative-descriptive" research. That is, numerous children were observed and assessed during their early years, and from these data developmental norms were established. Thus, although maturational theory receives little support today, it has made a significant contribution to child psychology in that much of the knowledge about early motor skill development comes from research that dealt with maturational theory.

Cognitive theory

Cognitive psychologists who conduct developmental research are primarily interested in the development of intelligence, thinking, and language. In essence their interest focuses on the cognitive section of Fig. 1-1. There is no argument that Piaget is the one researcher who has made the greatest contribution to understanding cognitive development in children. Although Piaget (1952) has been conducting research and writing about child development since the 1920s, it is only recently that North American psychologists have accepted this Swiss psychologist's work. The reason his work was initially frowned upon was that he failed to use methods of "scientific research" that followed an experimental model. Rather, Piaget developed much of his theory from *observing* children. In recent years, however, verification of Piaget's work has been done using experimental methods.

Basically Piaget concerns himself with explaining similarities among children rather than individual differences. He points out that children throughout the world go through the same stages of developing solutions to cognitive problems. Piaget believes that this discovery of solutions occurs largely because of the child's interaction with the environment. Further, according to Piaget, the child is not a passive recipient of events in the environment; rather, the child seeks out experiences. Although Piaget does not downplay the significance of maturation in cognitive development, he does not view all of development as an unfolding of biological processes.

Piaget's views of the developing child have had a significant impact on contemporary research in child development from both a theoretical and practical perspective. For instance, Bruner and others (1966) have made important theoretical contributions that stemmed from Piaget's early work, and Kohlberg (1964) has relied heavily on Piagetian theory to explain moral development in children. From a practical standpoint Piagetian theory has had a significant effect on teaching styles in the classroom. Piaget's emphasis on informal, experiential learning has led to a deemphasis of highly structured, didactic approaches to teaching in many contemporary classrooms. The cognitive theory of Jean Piaget will be discussed in depth in Chapter 6.

Psychoanalytic theory

Psychoanalytic theory concerns itself primarily with explaining the development of personality and changes in interpersonal relationships. The developer of this theory was Sigmund Freud, an Austrian psychiatrist; however, others such as Erik Erikson and Anna Freud have built upon Freud's initial theory. The basic concepts associated with psychoanalytic theory include Freud's personality structure of the *id* (unconscious impulses), *ego* (conscious thinking process), and *superego* (conscious associated with values), as well as stages of development including oral, anal, phallic, latency, adolescence, and maturity.

Freud's interest centered on abnormal functioning in adults, so his theory was concerned with explaining various ways in which these abnormalities could arise. In Freud's view personality followed a fixed developmental pattern with stages brought about in part by maturational changes in the body. Freud believed that the critical factors in the development of a healthy personality were the type of treatment a child received at each stage in development and the type of relationship the child had with the mother.

Erikson (1963) extended Freud's work by proposing eight stages (from birth to death) in the development of personality. Erikson suggests that during each of these stages the individual must resolve an emotional or interpersonal problem. For example, in stage 1 the basic issue is whether the child will develop a sense of trust or mistrust. According to Erikson this development will depend upon the kind of relationship the child has with parents and other adults. The resolution of the conflicts in stage 1 in turn affects the outcomes of the subsequent stages of development.

Psychoanalytic theory has received considerable criticism from its nonproponents mainly because the concepts associated with it are difficult to objectify and as a result are not easily subjected to scientific inquiry. On the other hand, psychoanalytic theory has made significant contributions to knowledge in child development. In addition the theory helped explain that what happens early in life is of utmost importance for the development of a healthy personality. Relationships with parents and significant others help determine ego (self-concept) and superego (conscience).

Humanistic theory

Humanistic psychology is a rather recent theoretical development in psychology. It basically developed from the work of Maslow (1968) and Rogers (1951), who felt that many psychological processes could not be adequately explained either by psychoanalytic theory or learning theory. Included in the list of unexplainable processes were creativity, love, self-concept, autonomy, and identity.

The core feature of humanism is that it is concerned with affection for mankind, man's dignity, man's mental health, respect for individuality, and an intense interest in man's behavior as a human being. It may also be said that humanists are primarily *process* oriented rather than *product* oriented. That is, although they are concerned with the attainment of a goal (product), what matters most is the manner (process) in which they achieve that goal.

Although humanistic psychology is a rather new force, it has produced interesting practical changes in both psychology and education. In psychology humanism brought about new forms of therapy, both individual and group. Further, there has been a shift from animal experimentation and experimentation with pathological subjects to experimentation with "normal, healthy" individuals. This experimentation is also different from that of the behaviorists because the focus in humanism is more on the individual than on average group performance.

Behavioral or learning theory

Learning theory states that all human behavior is governed by laws and therefore can be predicted and controlled. Much of the groundwork for learning theory goes back to the early 1900s; however, the development of concepts used in discussions of modern-day learning theory can be attributed largely to the work of Skinner. Skinner developed what is known as the operant conditioning model for describing human behavior. Operant conditioning basically says that human behavior is under the control of environmental reinforcers (both primary and secondary) and that human behavior can be altered by controlling the type and amount of reinforcement an individual receives.

Several theorists from the learning theory school have focused their attention on child development. Some of these include Bijou and Baer (1961), who use the operant conditioning paradigm to explain behavior in children; Sears and co-workers (1957), who use learning theory principles to account for the development of aggression and dependency in children; and Bandura (1962), who argues on behalf of observational learning. According to Bandura virtually all of what children learn comes from observing others.

Although each learning theorist has somewhat different perspectives on the development of behavior, they have many elements in common. First, they use well-established principles of learning to account for children's behavior. Second, they assume that the laws of learning are the same for everybody. Third, unlike the cognitivists and psychoanalysts, learning theorists place little importance on the stages of development. Because laws of learning are the same for everyone, they argue that there is no reason to believe that these laws change at different stages in the child's development.

METHODS OF STUDYING CHILD DEVELOPMENT

Now that some theoretical underpinnings related to child development have been presented, the question arises, How do researchers test these theories? How do they find out how and why children develop as they do?

The vast majority of research studies in child development are described as cross-sectional. By this it is meant that rsearchers look at age differences in behavior simply by selecting children representing different ages (preferably a large number in each age group) and measuring their behavioral characteristics. For example, in order to study the development of vertical jumping ability in girls from 6 to 10 years, there would probably be a random selection of a large number of girls representing each age group, a measurement of their vertical jumping ability, and then by using statistics make some decision about their differences. The advantage of the cross-sectional technique in this example, in comparison to the longitudinal approach (described below), is that the researcher can describe age differences without having to wait for the 6-year-old girls to become 10 years old, a total of five years.

When research is conducted on the same child or group of children for an extended period of time, the study is termed *longitudinal.* In the above example, if the researcher measured the same group of girls at age 6, then measured them again at ages 8 and 10, it would be a longitudinal study. Although longitudinal studies are necessary in some cases, such as giving us some idea about the consistency of behavior over time, the technique is not popular. The reasons are obvious. First, it takes a great deal of time of find answers to questions; second, the study will usually be more expen-

sive; and third, a considerable number of subjects may be lost during the course of the study through their moving away as well as other reasons.

Cross-sectional and longitudinal methods represent two basic ways in which child behavior is studied. Besides being cross-sectional or longitudinal, studies can also be labeled according to a specific research design or methodology. Several of these strategies will be described briefly; some of them are simple and others complex. A summary of these strategies is included in Table 1-3.

Cross-cultural studies are those studies that compare child development among different cultures. Comparing the throwing ability of girls in the United States and Europe would be one example.

The *survey method* and the *interview method* of gathering data are quite similar. Both techniques depend upon responses to questions that have been developed to look at concepts such as attitudes, opinion, and beliefs—feelings about school, peers, and parents are only a few. The distinguishing characteristic of the interview method is that it is more personal than the written survey. The investigator asks a question, then records the response, generally with the aid of a tape recorder.

The *case history method* provides a detailed analysis of background information on a child. Case studies are used whenever problems require a detailed probe of an individual's history. Because of the detail involved this type of research is limited to a small number of cases. Unfortunately, because of these small numbers, generalization is limited and the experimenter must be cautious in making interpretations.

Systematic *observation* is a very popular method of observing child behavior today. Generally children are viewed at work or play through one-way mirrors in a laboratory or unobtrusively in a natural work or play environment. Trained observers then observe and code their behavior.

The *clinical testing method* provides data regarding intelligence, perceptual-motor ability, personality, interests, and other psychological attributes of individual children. These data generally derive from clinics that function to diagnose and remediate individual problems.

The *correlational method* is a statistical technique that attempts to describe the relationship between two or more variables. These studies are usually considered exploratory because correlation coefficients do not allow the researcher to make causal inferences. Correlation coefficients can range from 0.00 to ±1.00, with a high coefficient indicating a higher relationship. The positive and negative signs merely indicate the direction of the relationship and do not imply that a positive relationship is necessarily better than a negative one. For example, if the correlation between self-concept scores and high jumping performance was +.30, the conclusion might be that there was a low positive relationship between one's self-concept and high jumping ability—those with a higher self-concept tended to jump higher. What cannot be said, however, is that the high self-concept caused one to jump higher. Although the two variables in this hypothetical example are related, there are alternative causal explanations of high jumping performance.

The *experimental method* uses carefully designed procedures for data collection. This method seeks to provide answers to troublesome problems by selecting groups through randomization and carefully controlling all other possible explanatory variables. In order to get this control experimental studies use what is called an experimental group(s) and a control group(s). For example, suppose you were interested in determining whether organized physical activity improves the self-concept of 8-year-old children. The first step would be to obtain a group of 8-year-old children and, in order to control for possible sex differences, divide them according to sex. Next you would randomly assign the boys and girls either to a group that receives organized physical activity (experimental group) or to a group that does not receive physical activity (control group). On the assumption that this was all logistically possible, the necessary criteria for an experiment have been met, that is, randomization and control. After a predetermined period of physical activity (say one semester), the children would be given a standardized test dealing with self-con-

cept. Finally, the data would be analyzed, and, using probability statistics, it would be determined whether physical activity affected the self-concept of each group differentially.

The preceding discussion indicates that there are many ways of conducting research in child

Table 1-3. Some methods of studying child development

Method	Brief description
Cross-sectional studies	Children of different ages studied to determine age differences in behavior
Longitudinal studies	*Same children* studied over a long period of time
Cross-cultural studies	Comparison of child behavior among different cultures
Survey	Series of questions developed to determine attitudes, opinions, and beliefs about an object or behavior
Interview	Similar to survey method except information obtained on a more personal basis
Case history	Detailed analysis of background information on individual children
Observation	Observation of child in a natural environment, generally without child being cognizant of observation
Clinical testing	Child's intelligence, interests, personality, motor skills, and so on tested primarily for diagnosis
Correlational	Statistical technique that describes relationship between two or more developmental variables
Experimental	Carefully designed procedures that call for *random selection* of subjects to groups and the *control* of important variables; most powerful method of determining causation of behavior

development. It would be incorrect to say that any one method is necessarily better than any other. All of the methods have distinct advantages and disadvantages; the methodological choice is dictated by the nature of the problem, time and resources available to the researchers, and the interest and expertise of the researchers. As we pointed out earlier, researchers differ considerably in their interests. Some are interested in theoretical research, others in applied research, and there are those who are interested in a specific age group or domain. Because of these diverse interests, there are a number of different methodologies (Table 1-3).

IMPORTANCE OF STUDYING CHILD DEVELOPMENT

If children are to be taught in the classroom, on the playground, or at home, it is important to have a basic understanding of the fundamental processes in child development. It is not sufficient to assume that teachers can work with children just because they were once children themselves (although it helps) and therefore know everything about their thoughts, feelings, and individual abilities. Researchers in child development have provided an enormous amount of valid information about the developing child. By using even a small amount of this information teachers and parents should become even better.

In order to be effective in dealings with children one should be cognizant of what they can and cannot do—cognitively, socially, and motorically—at different age levels. This understanding of and appreciation for overall readiness will better indicate *when* to teach certain cognitive, social, and motor skills. Understanding the way children develop will also provide better preparation to decide *what* kinds of cognitive, social, and motor experiences will enhance their development. It should no longer be necessary to base curriculum and program decisions on "wild hunches."

Besides understanding age-related behavior it is equally important to know whether boys and girls differ developmentally in the acquisition of cognitive, social, and motor skills. By being aware of possible sex differences or no sex differences one can be prepared for certain types of performance and structure appropriate learning experiences.

Understanding child development in its totality will also provide knowledge relating to personality—how it is acquired, how it may be modified, and how it relates to other aspects of child behavior, that is, cognitive and motor performance.

By understanding the psychomotor, cognitive, and social-psychological characteristics of boys and girls at various ages, one will not only benefit from knowing what to teach them, but will also better understand the importance and significance of knowing *how* to teach. It is hoped that teachers and parents have acquired a variety of teaching styles and are capable of adapting them so that they will allow a child to observe, explore, and discover, thus enhancing the developmental process. For movement educators this is most important because through movement and play children learn more than motor skills; they learn to employ cognitive strategies, to understand their psychological self, and how to interact with other children.

Above all one will learn that there are *individual differences* in child development, and as a result, teachers have to be flexible in what they teach, when, and how.

References

Ames, L. B. The sequential patterning of prone progression in the human infant. *Genetic Psychological Monograph*, 1937, *19*, 409-460.

Bandura, A. Social learning through imitation. In M. R. Jones (Ed.), *Nebraska symposium on motivation*. Lincoln: University of Nebraska Press, 1962.

Bayley, N. The development of motor abilities during the first three years. *Monographs on Child Development*, 1935, *1*, 1-26.

Bijou, S., & Baer, D. *Child development* (Vol. 1). New York: Appleton-Century-Crofts, 1961.

Bruner, J., Olver, R., & Greenfield, P. (Eds.). *Studies in cognitive growth*. New York: John Wiley & Sons, Inc., 1966.

Erikson, E. H. *Childhood and society* (2nd ed.). New York: W. W. Norton Co., Inc., 1963.

Gesell, A. *Infancy and human growth*. New York: Macmillan, Inc., 1928.

Hunsicker, P. A., & Reiff, G. G. A survey and comparison of youth fitness: 1958-1965. *Journal of Health, Physical Education, and Recreation*, 1966, *37*, 23-25.

Kohlberg, L. Development of moral character and moral ideology. In M. L. Hoffman & L. W. Hoffman (Eds.),

Review of child development research (Vol. 1). New York: Russell Sage Foundation, 1964.

Mandler, G., & Kessen, W. *The language of psychology.* New York: John Wiley & Sons, Inc., 1959.

Maslow, A. *Toward a psychology of being* (2nd ed.). New York: Van Nostrand Co., 1968.

Piaget, J. *The origins of intelligence in children.* New York: International Universities Press, 1952.

Rogers, C. R. *Client-centered therapy.* Boston: Houghton Mifflin Co., 1951.

Sears, R. R., Maccoby, E. E., & Levin, H. *Patterns of child rearing.* New York: Harper & Row, Publishers, 1957.

Shirley, M. M. Postural and locomotor development. *The first two years: a study of twenty-five babies* (Vol. 1). Minneapolis: University of Minnesota Press, 1931.

Singer, R. N., & Dick, W. *Teaching physical education: a systems approach.* Boston: Houghton Mifflin Co., 1974.

Student projects

1. The purpose of this exercise will be to introduce you to the techniques of observation, a method of studying child behavior. In learning the technique you will undoubtedly become aware of its shortcomings; however you will also learn a great deal about what children do in a short time period. Let us suggest some steps that will guide you in your observation.

   a. Find a child between the ages of 2 and 5 years.

   b. Obtain permission from the child's parents to observe and record the child's behavior. If the child is at a day-care center, obtain the permission of the director as well.

   c. Arrange to make your observations while the child is at play for 30 minutes to an hour. The key to observation is that you must be unobtrusive. That is, you should position yourself with a notebook and pen such that you can freely observe without being obvious. (Do not attempt this task while babysitting.) If the child asks what you are doing, indicate that you are writing some things down and cannot play at this time. In other words, gently avoid contact of any sort.

   d. For the 30-60 minutes record everything the child does, including conversations with other children. Be as thorough as possible in describing the child's movements and play behavior. Try to keep your descriptions free of personal evaluations such as "Jean went to the sandbox to play with the shovel and pails." Since you do not know why Jean went to the sandbox, it is initially sufficient to write, "Jean went to the sandbox."

   e. After you have completed your observation, attempt to organize the data in some meaningful way. Were you able to remain objective? Was there a trend or pattern in the behavior? Is there something you can say about this child's behavior? Do you think your presence affected the child's behavior? What changes in your observation patterns would you introduce to extract more meaningful information?

2. The major objective of this exercise is to introduce you to journals that publish research studies dealing with child development. We introduce this experience at the end of this chapter, but we see it as an exercise that could be conducted at the end of all chapters. Your task now is to visit your library and peruse as many journals as possible that publish developmental studies. Write a review of a study that interests you. The review should first include a documentation of the author(s), title, name of journal, year of publication, volume number, and page numbers. Second, you should describe the *purpose of the study* and the *methods* used for carrying it out. Next, summarize the *results* and *conclusions*. Finally, provide some of your own comments on the "goodness" of the study. You will find it useful to review a study after completing a chapter on a specific topic, for example, motor skill development or moral development. You may wish to review some of the studies listed in our reference list or other appropriate studies. Following is a list of selected journals that publish some developmental studies:

   Child Development
   Developmental Psychology
   Human Development
   Journal of Educational Psychology
   Journal of Educational Research
   Journal of Experimental Child Psychology
   Journal of Genetic Psychology
   Journal of Motor Behavior
   Merrill-Palmer Quarterly
   Perceptual and Motor Skills
   Research Quarterly

Part one

PSYCHOMOTOR DEVELOPMENT

Chapter 2

PHYSICAL GROWTH AND DEVELOPMENT

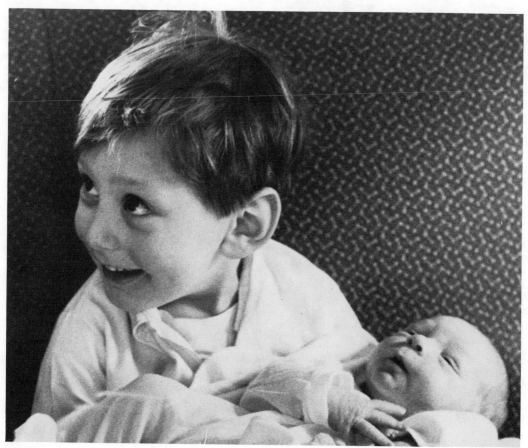

Stars and Stripes

Physical growth and development refers to changes in height and weight and changes in the muscular, skeletal, and nervous systems. In this chapter the age-related changes in physical development and the hereditary and environmental factors that influence growth and development will be described.

PRENATAL DEVELOPMENT

The *prenatal* period plays a significant role in the development of the child. This period from *conception* to *birth* lays the foundation for postnatal growth and development. Although other sections of this text do not discuss developmental changes during the prenatal period, an introduction to the events taking place during this period is necessary for a greater appreciation and understanding of the total developmental process.

The beginning of life (conception) is a complex process. Conception occurs when a single male sperm cell penetrates the wall of the female ovum or egg. At conception 23 chromosomes from the sperm cell nucleus combine with 23 chromosomes from the nucleus of the ovum to produce 46 chromosomes. These chromosomes then line up and split, yielding 46 pairs of chromosomes, which serve as the template in the development of the individual child.

A process of cell division called *mitosis* occurs at some time during the first 24 to 36 hours after conception. New cells are thus formed, each containing 23 pairs of chromosomes. Specialized cells later result from rapid mitosis and eventually group to assume the shape and function of the body (Fig. 2-1).

The developing child is technically referred to as an *embryo* until about 8 weeks after conception. Although the embryo is only 2.5 or 5.0 cm (1 or 2 in.) long after 8 weeks, it does have eyes, ears, a mouth, a nose, a liver (that secretes bile), a heart with rudimentary beat, arms with elbows, fingers and toes, a spinal cord, and bones.

The period from 8 weeks after conception to birth is known as the period of the *fetus*. The previously mentioned organs become further refined, and motor functions become differentiated. Some of the significant developments that occur during the fetal period are as follows:

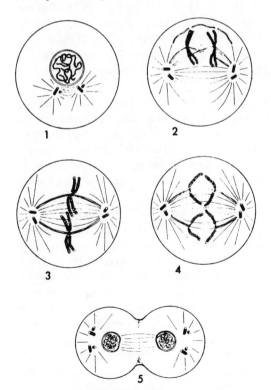

Fig. 2-1. Major stages of mitosis. **1,** Interphase. **2,** Prophase (late). **3,** Metaphase. **4,** Anaphase. **5,** Early telophase. (From L. J. A. DiDio. *Synopsis of anatomy.* St. Louis: The C. V. Mosby Co., 1970.)

1. By the end of 12 weeks the fetus weighs about ¾ ounce and is about 3 inches long. The muscles are increasingly developed, eyelids and nails begin to form and the sex organs are developed to the point where the sex of the child can be determined.
2. By the end of 16 weeks the fetus is about 4½ inches long, weighs nearly ½ pound, and begins movements that the mother can feel them.
3. By the end of 20 weeks the fetus is about 10 inches in length and weighs 8 or 9 ounces. Hair appears on the head and body, and the mouth is capable of opening and closing.
4. By 24 weeks the eyes are completely formed and taste buds appear on the tongue. The fetus is also capable of breathing, although survival is difficult and rare for an infant born this prematurely.
5. The fetal age of 28 weeks is a most important one for it generally represents the time of viability or nonviability (ability to live or not to live). Body length is about 16 inches and weight about 3 pounds. The nervous, respira-

tory, and circulatory systems are sufficiently developed to sustain life under special care. However, premature babies at this age have difficulty surviving.

6. From 28 weeks to 40 weeks (full term) the fetus increases muscle tone, develops the ability to cry, and develops a strong sucking reflex. In general there is a gradual improvement in the development of the circulatory, respiratory, and endocrine systems as well as an increase in functioning of the sensory and nervous systems. (Mussen et al., 1974)

FACTORS INFLUENCING PRENATAL DEVELOPMENT

Prenatal development is influenced by two interacting factors—*genetic* and *environmental.* Genes of the mother and father determine how the child develops, and the environment the fetus lives in for nine months determines, to a large extent, the developmental patterns of the child.

Hereditary influences

The 46 chromosomes of the fertilized ovum are made up of small particles called genes, the carriers of the child's heredity. A gene is largely composed of deoxyribonucleic acid (DNA). The DNA molecule contains the genetic code that determines what is to be transmitted from one generation to the next. The molecule is structured like a twisted ladder (called a double helix). The "rungs" of the ladder are composed of chemicals called bases, which are attached to sugar and phosphate molecules. The DNA molecule is capable of "unzipping" up the center and reproducing itself. It is this process, which occurs during mitosis, that enables the new cell to contain the complete genetic code. (Fig. 2-2).

Heredity determines many of our characteristics. For example, the sex of a child is determined by one of the 23 pairs of chromosomes, In the female both members of the pair are large and are referred to as X chromosomes. In the male one member of the pair is a large X chromosome and the other is a smaller Y chromosome. When an X male chromosome unites with an X female chromosome, a female is produced. When a Y male chromosome unites with an X female chromosome, a male is produced.

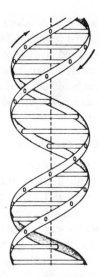

Fig. 2-2. Model of DNA molecule (double helix). (From S. M. Brooks. *Basic science and the human body.* St. Louis: The C. V. Mosby Co., 1975.)

Height or stature is essentially an inherited trait (Garn, 1966; Malina et al., 1970). Tall parents tend to have tall children and short parents tend to have short children. Heredity also influences the age of onset of menarche, time of tooth eruption, and the development of skeletal age.

Mental retardation can be caused by inheriting specific recessive genes, an event that occurs most often when the mother and father are close relatives. Down's syndrome or mongolism is a form of mental retardation caused by an abnormality in the structure of the chromosomes. Children with this disorder have 47 chromosomes instead of the normal 46. Phenylketonuria (PKU) is also an inherited syndrome. Children with this disease lack a specific enzyme for eliminating phenylketonuric acid; this acid, upon accumulation, damages the nervous system sufficiently to cause mental retardation.

Although other personal characteristics are also inherited, the exact contribution of heredity is difficult to determine. As a result scientists have ongoing controversies often referred to as *nature* versus *nurture,* or heredity versus environment. The more significant areas of controversy related to heritability are those of personality and intelligence (Chess and Thomas, 1973; Jensen, 1969; Telfer et al., 1968).

Prenatal environmental influences

Various prenatal environmental factors can influence child growth and development.

Diseases of the mother. Several mother-contracted diseases affect the unborn child. Perhaps the most significant is German measles, or rubella. If the mother has this disease during the first three months of pregnancy, the baby is likely to be aborted, stillborn, or born with handicaps such as deafness, blindness, and mental retardation. Other diseases known to pass through the placental membrane and affect the child include syphilis, diphtheria, influenza, and typhoid fever.

Drugs taken by the mother. Drugs taken by a pregnant woman may pass through the placenta and affect the fetus. The drug thalidomide, taken by pregnant women in the early 1960s as a sedative, is perhaps the most dramatic example. Babies born of mothers who had taken it had deformed or rudimentary arms, sometimes little more than flippers. Nicotine from cigarettes smoked by pregnant women affects the body weight of infants at birth, although most of them eventually catch up to other children after several months. Infants born to alcoholic mothers have demonstrated what is referred to as fetal alcoholism syndrome. In extreme alcoholism cases the infants can be retarded and have physical deformities, but more often they are underweight at birth and slow to develop (Hanson et al., 1976).

Use of addictive drugs such as heroin and barbiturates can lead to a child's being born with withdrawal symptoms. Scientists are not certain of the effect the drugs themselves have on the child, since often the mother has a poor diet; it is difficult to determine whether the mother's diet, the drug, or both contribute to the abnormal child.

Mother's diet. A mother's diet has a strong influence on the welfare of the developing child. Bee in summarizing the research concludes—

1. Malnutrition resulting from insufficient protein in particular and calories in general increases the likelihood of complications during pregnancy and birth.
2. Malnutrition can produce a 20% reduction in the total number of brain cells, besides retarding the growth of myelin. (Bee, 1975, p. 59)

X-rays. Large doses of x-rays such as those used in cancer therapy can result in increased risk of miscarriage as well as possible physical deformities in children.

Mother's psychological state. Although there are no direct connections between the mother's nervous system and that of the fetus, the mother's emotional state can still influence fetal reactions and development. Squier and Dunbar (1946) point out that secretions from the mother's adrenal glands during fear and anxiety alter the chemical substances that pass through the placenta sufficiently to affect fetal activity. In other words, fetal activity becomes high when the mother is under stress. According to Bee (1975) prolonged maternal stress may have detrimental effects, since children born of mothers who experienced considerable emotional stress are prone to various kinds of illnesses and physical problems throughout life.

Mother's age. Although recent advances in medical science have reduced birth difficulties and infant mortality, there is evidence that mortality rates are higher if the mother is under 20 years of age or over 35. Mothers in these age groups also tend to have a higher proportion of retarded children than do mothers between 20 and 35.

POSTNATAL DEVELOPMENT

Physical development is important in determining total development from infancy through adulthood. Perhaps the best description of the importance of physical growth and development is provided by the eminent English researcher and writer Tanner, who stated, "All the skills, aptitudes and emotions of the growing child are rooted in or conditioned by his bodily structure" (Tanner, 1970, p. 77). Tanner is to physical development what Piaget is to cognitive development. Both are giants in their respective areas of inquiry.

Overview of the growth curve

Observing and recording the growth of children is an exercise that most parents enthusiastically engage in. Generally parents are interested in how tall their child is at any given time. When these heights are recorded and plotted on a graph from one year to the next, the result is

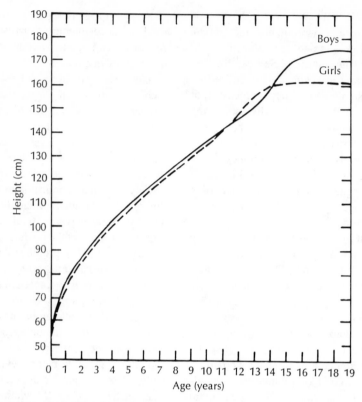

Fig. 2-3. Typical individual height-attained curves for boys and girls (supine length to the age of 2). (From J. Tanner, R. Whitehouse, and M. Takaishi. *Archives of Diseases in Childhood,* 1966, *41,* 454-471; 613-635.)

called a *distance* curve. In Fig. 2-3 the distance curve gradually increases and then levels off, an indication that growth in height has ceased. This graph represents typical individual height curves based on data from many individuals. The graph of one individual child would probably not show such a smooth curve.

Another method of revealing child growth is by measuring the *rate* or *velocity* of growth. According to Tanner (1978, p. 6), "The velocity, or rate of growth, naturally reflects the child's state at any particular time better than does the distance achieved, which depends largely on how much the child has grown in all the preceding year." The velocity of growth represented in Fig. 2-4 refers to increments in height from year to year. The rate of growth declines or decelerates rapidly from birth until age 4 or 5 years, then stays relatively constant until the growth spurt occurs at adolescence.

Until recently the most commonly used reference population for determining growth in children was that collected in Boston and Iowa during the 1930s and early 1940s by Stuart and Meredith. Since the data were old, gathered from a small sample, and represented only white, middle-class children, several expert groups in the United States recommended that new expanded data be collected. Consequently, the National Center for Health Statistics, the Fels Research Institute, and the Center for Disease Control have collaborated in developing the data that constitute the growth charts in Appendix A. There are four parts, one for boys and one for girls in two age groups, birth to 36 months and 2 to 18 years. Included are length or stature-for-age, weight-for-age, head circumference-for age, and weight-for-length from birth until puberty.

Height and weight in infancy

Great variation in birth weight and height occurs in children for a variety of reasons. Nonetheless, normative measures can give us a general picture of body size during early devel-

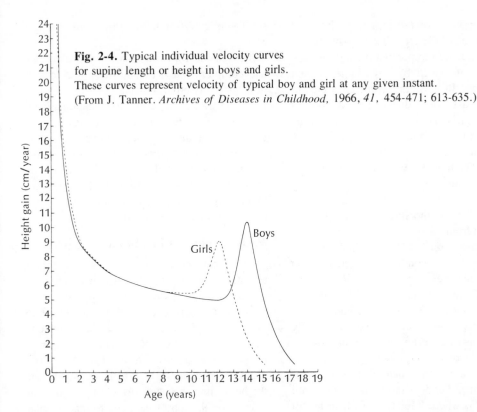

Fig. 2-4. Typical individual velocity curves for supine length or height in boys and girls. These curves represent velocity of typical boy and girl at any given instant. (From J. Tanner. *Archives of Diseases in Childhood,* 1966, *41,* 454-471; 613-635.)

opment. On the average males are about 51 cm (20 in.) tall and weigh 3.4 kg (7.5 lbs.) at birth. Females are slightly smaller (see Appendix A-1, fiftieth percentile*). The first year of a child's life brings rapid physical changes. Body length for boys increases to about 76 cm (30 in.) and weight to about 10 kg (22 lbs.). Similar dramatic changes occur for girls—74 cm (29.25 in.) and 9.5 kg (21 lbs.). The increase in height and weight from age 1 to 2 years is less dramatic than that from birth to 1 year. Boys are about 88 cm (34½ in.) tall and weigh about 12.75 kg (28 lbs.). Girls are about 86.5 cm (34 in.) tall and weigh 11.8 kg (26 lbs.) (refer to Appendices A-1 to A-6).

Height and weight in early and late childhood

The velocity curve (Fig. 2-4) shows that after age 2 years, height increases gradually

(about 5 cm [2 in.] per year [Tanner, 1970]) for boys and girls until puberty, which occurs during the adolescent period. By looking at Appendices A-7 to A-12, it is possible to determine what the height and weight would be for the "average" boy and girl during early childhood (2 to 5) and late childhood (5 to 10). According to Tanner (1970) weight velocity is almost constant from age 3 to puberty, rising from 2.0 kg per year (4.4 lbs.) to about 2.7 kg per year (5.9 lbs.).

Height and weight during adolescence

The beginning of adolescence usually results in a dramatic increase in both height and weight for both sexes, with the growth spurt occurring earlier for girls. Figs. 2-3 and 2-4 neatly portray the sudden change in growth. By the end of adolescence an individual's height approximates adult measurements; however, this is usually not the case for weight.

There is a great deal of variability in the onset of the growth spurt and the rate of growth during this period, but these two factors are not correlated. That is, children who start their growth spurt earlier (early maturers) do not

---

*Although average or mean scores are referred to here, the charts represent percentiles, with the fiftieth percentile being the median. Height and weight are assumed to be normally distributed; since large samples are used, the median and the mean should approximate the same point.

necessarily grow to be taller than the late ma-turers. The time of the growth spurt usually dif-fers from population to population and thus ap-pears to be influenced by environmental and genetic factors. In Western Europe peak growth for middle-class youth during puberty occurs at age 12 in girls and 14 in boys, while in the United States the mean age is reached about six months earlier (Tanner, 1970).

Over the last hundred years there has been a tendency for children to become progressively larger at all ages (Tanner, 1970), a phenom-enon referred to as the *secular trend*. On the basis of data from European and American pop-ulations Tanner concluded that children from average economic conditions increased in height between the ages of 5 and 7 years by about 1 to 2 cm each decade, and between 10 and 14 years by 2 to 3 cm each decade. It ap-pears that this secular trend starts immediately after birth; that is, children when measured short-ly after birth are found to be larger than their counterparts who were measured several de-cades ago. In earlier days individuals grew until about age 25, whereas today growth in height usually stops at about 18 years. Tanner (1970) reports that the age of onset of menarche has also accelerated by about four months per decade since 1850 in average Western European pop-ulations. Thus, individuals are not only growing taller, they reach maturity earlier. For an exten-sive treatment of the aspect of the secular trend, see Tanner (1970, pp. 144-148; 1978, pp. 150-153).

The reasons for the secular trend are multiple and complex, but better nutrition and less ill-ness are likely environmental factors, and there is probably a partial genetic explanation as well. Tanner (1978) believes that "tallness" genes may be dominant to "shortness' genes, a kind of human "hybrid vigor." This "hybrid vigor" becomes more developed as outbreeding oc-curs. Outbreeding, according to Tanner, refers to marriage to unrelated persons (rather than cousins or distant relatives).

Measurement of height and weight

The measurement of height and weight is essential in evaluating the health of children, with height perhaps the more important.

When measuring a child up to 24 or 36 months of age, height (or body length) should be measured with the child lying on his or her back. Two examiners are needed. One person should hold the child's head in alignment with the body, line of vision straight up, and gentle traction on the top of the head to make contact with a fixed headboard. The other holds the child's feet with toes straight up, pushes down on the knees, and brings a movable footboard to rest firmly against the heels (Fig. 2-5).

Children over 36 months should be measured standing. This measurement is referred to as *stature*. The child should be told to stand up

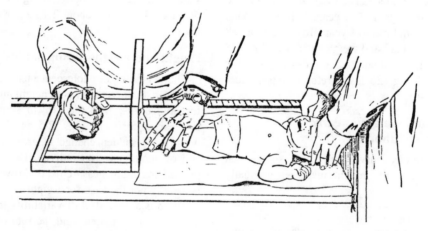

Fig. 2-5. Length measurement of the infant. (From U.S. Department of Health, Education and Welfare, Center for Disease Control.)

straight and tall and look straight ahead. Bare heels should be close together, back straight, heels, buttocks, and back of shoulders touching the wall or vertical surface of measuring device. A block, squared at right angles against the wall, should be brought to the crown of the head and the measurement taken (Fig. 2-6). Length or stature should be measured to the nearest 1 mm (⅛ in.). It is not recommended to use the metal rods attached to weighing scales to measure stature; usually they are bent and unreliable.

Weight should be measured on an *accurate* and recently calibrated scale. Infants should be nude, and older children clothed only in underpants or light gown. Precautions should be taken to protect children from possible embarrassment when taking these measurements. Body weight should be measured to the nearest 10 g (½ oz.) for infants and 100 g (¼ lb.) for children.

Skeletal development

The bones of the body originate as soft cartilage tissue but become ossified, or hardened. The ossification process begins during the prenatal period and continues until late adolescence for some bones. Because the bones of a developing child are not completely ossified, they are more pliable and hence less susceptible to breakage—a positive feature considering the constant strain playful children place on the skeletal system (Fig. 2-7). The onset and rate of ossification differs considerably among the various bones as well as among individuals.

A long bone, such as the radius, first contains a primary center of ossification (center of bone during fetal stage). Shortly after birth secondary centers of ossification, referred to as *epiphyses,* appear at the two ends of the bone (Fig. 2-8). Basically a long bone grows inward from its epiphyseal ends. An x-ray of a rapidly growing bone (Fig. 2-9) shows a fairly wide white band, representing large concentrations of calcium, next to the main shaft. With increased age and growth this band becomes narrower. When the bone of the main shaft finally

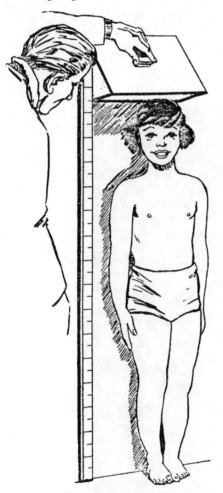

Fig. 2-6. Stature measurement of the child. (From U.S. Department of Health, Education and Welfare, Center for Disease Control.)

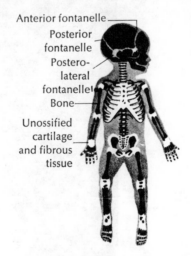

Anterior fontanelle
Posterior fontanelle
Postero-lateral fontanelle
Bone
Unossified cartilage and fibrous tissue

Fig. 2-7. Skeleton at birth. (From W. Osburn, Philadelphia: W. B. Saunders Co., 1966.)

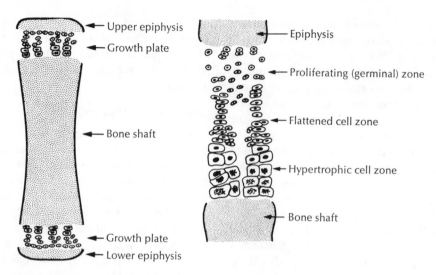

Fig. 2-8. *Left,* Diagram of limb bone with upper and lower epiphyses. *Right,* Magnification of epiphysis-shaft junction to show zones of cells. New cells are formed in proliferation zone and pass to hypertrophic zone to add to bone accumulating on top of bone shaft. (From J. Tanner. *Fetus into man.* Cambridge, Mass.: Harvard University Press, 1978.)

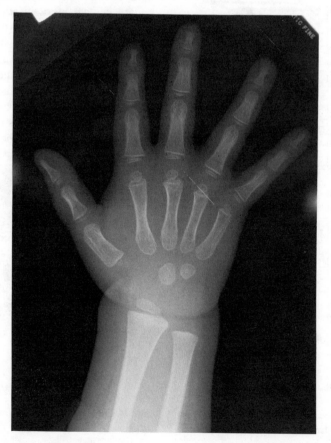

Fig. 2-9. X-ray film showing bone age of boy whose chronological age is 3 years.

reaches the bone of the epiphysis, growth is no longer possible. The epiphysis is said to be closed or fused (Tanner, 1978).

Although most limb bones have epiphyses at both ends, they vary in activity. For example, the forearm bones grow chiefly at the wrist. The round bones of the wrist and foot also have growth plates, but they surround the bone; hence, these bones grow in toward their center.

The growth in width of bone does not involve cartilage. Instead, new layers of bone are deposited on the outside of existing bone. The bones of the skull and face grow in this manner.

Generally, girls have a more developed skeleton than boys at birth, and this difference increases with age. There is also less variability in rate of ossification in girls. For some reason, skeletal development, as are many other traits, is much more stable in girls than in boys. As a result, prediction of final development can be more accurate with girls than boys.

Predicting body size

There are numerous situations in life where it would be desirable to predict final body size. For example, girls training for a career in ballet may be counseled away from the vocation because body size prediction during this training age (9 to 10 years) fails to match specified limits (Tanner, 1970). Other examples occur and generally exist when vocations have size restrictions (for example, jockeys). Because so many factors affect body size, prediction is rarely perfect.

The simplest and least accurate method involves the use of the *present chronological age of the child, present size of the child,* and a *calculated multiplier.* Garn (1966) has published a table of multipliers based on data collected at the Fels Research Center from children of parents with average stature. Some of these values are the following:

Age	Boy's height	Girl's height
1 year	Multiply by 2.46	Multiply by 2.30
2 years	Multiply by 2.06	Multiply by 2.01
5 years	Multiply by 1.62	Multiply by 1.51
10 years	Multiply by 1.29	Multiply by 1.17

A limitation of this technique is that a child's *chronological age* is imperfectly related to *physiological* or *developmental age.* Because

Table 2-1. Percentage of adult height reached at successive ages by boys and girls*

Age (Yr)	Boys		Girls	
	U.K.	U.S.A.	U.K.	U.S.A.
0.08	30.9	30.8	32.7	32.6
0.25	34.7		36.4	
0.50	39.0	38.5	40.4	40.3
0.75	41.6		43.3	
1.00	43.7	43.0	45.7	45.3
1.25	45.4		47.8	
1.50	47.0	46.7	49.7	49.3
1.75	48.4		51.3	
2.00	49.8	49.4	52.8	52.7
2.00	49.2	48.8	52.1	52.7
2.5	51.6		54.8	
3.0	53.9	53.8	57.3	57.4
3.5	56.1		59.7	
4.0	58.2	58.1	61.9	62.0
4.5	60.1		64.0	
5.0	62.0	62.0	66.1	66.4
5.5	63.8		68.0	
6.0	65.6	65.7	69.9	70.0
6.5	67.3		71.8	
7.0	69.0	68.9	73.6	73.6
7.5	70.6		75.3	
8.0	72.2	71.7	77.1	77.2
8.5	73.8		78.8	
9.0	75.4	74.6	80.5	80.6
9.5	76.9		82.2	
10.0	78.3	77.6	83.8	84.5
10.5	79.8		85.5	
11.0	81.3	81.1	87.3	88.4
11.5	82.7		89.5	
12.0	84.1	84.6	92.2	91.1
12.5	85.5		94.7	
13.0	87.1	88.1	96.7	96.1
13.5	89.1		98.0	
14.0	92.0	92.1	98.9	98.0
14.5	94.6		99.5	
15.0	96.6	95.4	99.8	99.1
15.5	97.9		99.9	
16.0	98.8	98.1	100.0	99.2
16.5	99.4		—	
17.0	99.8	99.7	—	99.5
17.5	99.9		—	
18.0	100.0	100.0	—	100.0

*From Tanner, J. M. *Fetus into man.* Cambridge, Mass.: Harvard University Press, © 1978.

some children mature early and others late, error readily enters into our prediction. What is needed then is a measure of *developmental* age, which could then be substituted for chronological age in Table 2-1.

The most commonly used measure of developmental age is *skeletal* or bone age; other indices include puberty standards (such as breast development in girls, stages of genital development and pubic hair development in boys and girls, and dental development). Skeletal age is a measure of how far given bones have progressed toward maturity, not in size, but with respect to shape and position to one another in a radiograph. Although any bone or bones can be used to estimate skeletal age, generally an x-ray of the left hand and wrist is used (Fig. 2-9). It is then compared to standard plates (separate for boys and girls) based upon the Tanner-Whitehouse or Greulich-Pyle system (Greulich and Pyle, 1959). A more recent technique (Acheson, 1966) assigns "maturity points" to the bones found in the x-ray. The accumulated points are then compared to a standard. If a child is 10 years of age chronologically but has a calculated developmental (bone) age of 12 years, this age (12) would be substituted for chronological age in a prediction table.

More recently Tanner (1978) has published a table that gives the percentage of adult height attained for a given age. Table 2-1 contains standards for both British and American children. By perusing the table you will note that a 2-year-old American boy has reached almost 49% of his final height. A 5-year-old American girl has reached about 66% of her final height. The values from Garn's publication are thus closely related to those in Table 2-1. The so-called old wives' tale that a child's adult height is double her or his height at about 2 years of age seems to have some merit.

Muscle development

During normal development muscles grow along with bones, and although it is generally conceded that we are born with all the muscle fibers we are going to have, there is a large increase in muscle length and breadth with age. Like bone growth, muscle development varies considerably between individuals as well as by

location within individuals. Muscles near the head and neck tend to develop before those of the extremities, a phenomenon called *cephalo-caudal* development. Boys generally have a greater proportion of muscle tissue than girls from infancy through adulthood. Muscle development is further discussed later in this chapter and also in Chapter 4.

Nervous system development

The development of the nervous system is perhaps the most important aspect of physical development in humans, although it is the one that we know the least about. It is difficult to conduct research on such a delicate complex system. The nervous system includes the brain, the spinal cord, and the peripheral nerves that innervate the muscles.

The basic unit of the nervous system is a specialized cell called a *neuron* (Fig. 2-10). The human brain contains an estimated 10 billion of these cells. It is presently thought that the full complement of brain cells is present at birth; however, changes in structure and function take place with increase in age. During these changes, referred to as increased integration and differentiation, cells become bigger, myelinated, and at the same time build up interconnections among themselves.

Athough the brain becomes more integrated and differentiated with age, in terms of total weight it is the organ nearest that of an adult value at birth (25%). By age 5 years weight of the brain is 90% of its final adult weight.

The part of the brain most fully developed at birth is the *midbrain* (Fig. 2-11), located in the lower part of the brain. It controls many of the necessary early reflexes in infants. These reflexes (discussed further in Chapter 3) disappear with increased development of the cerebral cortex.

Development of the *cerebral cortex* is about 5% complete by 6 months, 75% complete by age 2, and almost entirely complete by age 4. The brain cortex controls voluntary motor responses and is necessary for the development of language, abstract thinking, and essentially all cognitive processes. It does not develop all at once or at the same rate. By age 6 months the parts of the cortex controlling hearing and

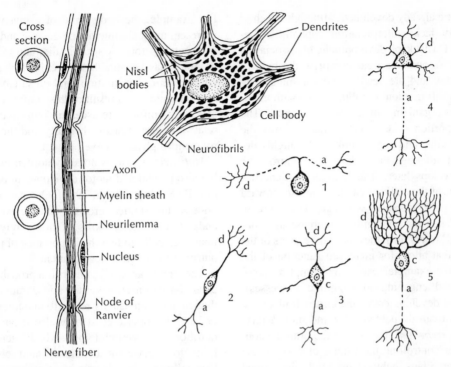

Fig. 2-10. Neuron. Basic types and microscopic details of cell body and nerve fiber. **1,** Unipolar cell. **2,** Bipolar cell. **3,** Cell of cerebral cortex. **4,** Motor cell. **5,** Purkinje cell of cerebellar cortex. *a,* Axon; *c,* cell body; *d,* dendrites. (From Brooks, S. M. *Basic Science and the Human Body.* St. Louis: The C. V. Mosby Co., 1975.)

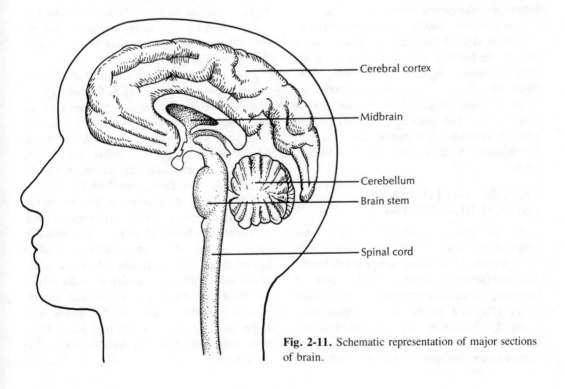

Fig. 2-11. Schematic representation of major sections of brain.

vision are already developed, although the child probably lacks interpretation capabilities because of a lack of development of association areas. (Association areas comprise the bulk of the cortex and are responsible for integrating sensory information, combining this with memory, and organizing muscular movements.) The motor portion of the cortex that controls the hands, arms, and upper trunk is also highly developed, although the portion that controls the legs develops later. The number of dendrites (the part of the cell that carries impulses toward the cell) also increases with age. This increase in dendrites and concomitant increase in "connecting" fibers form the associative areas of the cortex that allow for increased function of the brain (for example, executing complex motor skills and engaging in cognitive processes). Thus the development of the cortex limits what the child can do perceptually and motorically.

The *cerebellum,* the area of the brain responsible for controlling the timing of coordinated responses, lags behind the midbrain, spinal cord, and cerebral cortex in development.

An important process in nervous system development is *myelination,* or the development of myelin, a white, fatty tissue that forms a sheath around neurons, thereby allowing them to transmit nerve impulses (communicate) more effectively (Fig. 2-10). At birth many neurons lack myelin but with increased age myelination becomes more complete. For example, nerve fibers connecting the cerebellum and the cortex do not become completely myelinated until 4 years of age. The reticular formation responsible for attention and consciousness continues to myelinate at least until puberty (Tanner, 1970).

FACTORS THAT INFLUENCE PHYSICAL DEVELOPMENT

Prenatal environmental factors were discussed earlier; however, the specific postnatal environmental effectors are somewhat different. The environmental factors we will discuss are nutrition, socioeconomic status (SES), season of the year, and illness. No one factor independently influences physical development. Hereditary factors and the various environmental factors *interact* to exert their influence.

For example, the body build of a given child represent uniquely interacting genetic and environmental factors. A specific diet and exercise program may be suitable for a child with a specific genetic constitution and unsuitable for another child. As a result of this complex interaction it is difficult to ascertain objectively the relative contributions of heredity and the environment to physical development.

Malnutrition affects not only normal growth, but also mental and motor development (Cravioto, 1968; Monckeberg, 1968). One has only to observe the stunted growth, muscle wasting, and retarded motor skills of a severely malnourished child to feel the importance of proper nutrition in physical development.

The significance of malnutrition probably depends on its onset, severity, and duration. Although nutrition usually refers to undernutrition or lack of proper diet, it may also mean overnutrition or overindulging, which generally leads to overweight conditions and obesity. Generally, children have a great capacity to recuperate and catch up in growth if malnutrition is temporary. However, if it is chronic, a small-sized adult may result. Greulich (1957) suggests that diet causes Japanese children raised in California to be larger than those raised in Japan. Girls are able to withstand adverse nutritional conditions better than boys, because their growth is more stable.

Several studies clearly illustrate the impact of *socioeconomic status* (SES) factors on body size (Tanner, 1961). At all age levels children from upper SES families were taller—2.5 cm (1 in.) at 3 years and 4 to 5 cm (1½ to 2 in.) at adolescence. Children from upper SES families also reached menarche up to three months earlier than those from lower SES families.

It is difficult to pinpoint the exact cause of SES differences in growth, although nutrition is a likely candidate. Poorer families probably cannot provide the same nutritional food at critical times as those families with few financial worries. Along with nutrition go the related factors of regularity of eating, sleeping, and exercising. Generally lower SES parents have larger families, and this fact may affect nutrition, since there may very well be less food to go around.

There is evidence that *season of the year* also affects human growth, specifically the velocity of growth. According to Tanner (1970) growth in height is fastest in the spring, and growth in weight is fastest in autumn. This phenomenon exists for all ages after the first year, although there is considerable variability among individuals, and not all children exhibit these seasonal fluctuations. This seasonal effect is apparently due to subtle changes in endocrine and hypothalamic reactivity.

A short *illness* has little effect on the normal growth of the majority of well-nourished children. However, a chronic disease coupled with a poor diet and little exercise has a more permanent effect.

EFFECT OF PHYSICAL ACTIVITY ON PHYSICAL DEVELOPMENT AND ITS IMPLICATIONS
Exercise and bone growth

Generally speaking, bones, like other tissues, adapt to stress placed upon them. Thus according to Larson (1973) stress within limits is beneficial to the growing bones. Low stress (inactivity) has detrimental effects on bone growth, as does stress that is intense enough to cause inflammation and fracture. There are also individual differences in response to these levels of stress. For some children activities such as jumping, throwing, and lifting may be very stressful to bone tissue, and for others they may not be.

Exercise increases bone width and mineralization, whereas cast immobilization, space flights, and general recumbent inactivity decrease bone mineralization. The most severe imbalance is with calcium; however, when normal activity is restored, calcium levels also return to normal. Demineralized bones are weaker and more brittle than "normal" bones; hence it is safe to say that well-conditioned athletes have stronger bones and muscles, and as a result their bones are less likely to be broken when subjected to stress. As Bailey emphasizes:

. . . it takes extreme deficiency of calcium or Vitamin D in our diet, or a marked abnormality of the parathyroid glands to cause demineralization of bone. Yet only one week of inactivity often causes noticeable demineralization—loss of half the calcium from a bone. So the amount of activity we get is much more important than the amount of milk we drink. If we are active, our bones will be well mineralized and both bones and muscles will be strong. . . . It seems obvious that continued exercise is necessary for the maintenance of normal bone and muscle strength and normal health.*

The effects of exercise on bone growth are difficult to evaluate accurately because of a host of interactive modifying factors, including individual differences in stress (exercise) responsiveness. The principal mechanism controlling bone growth appears to be hormonal, and presently there is no knowledge that shows physical activity affecting hormonal mechanisms. Nevertheless, there is evidence that physical activity (undoubtedly in combination with other factors) is significant in the normal development of bone tissue.

Exercise and muscle growth

Increase in muscle size, whether from normal growth or induced by exercise, is called hypertrophy. Muscle tissue, like bone, responds and adapts to stress loads. Both skeletal muscle and cardiac muscle demonstrate this adaptation by increasing in size when subjected to work loads greater than normal. Muscle mass and strength increase when an individual uses a training regimen that calls for high resistance and few repetitions. In a weight training program muscle hypertrophy and strength would be best attained by lifting maximum weights with only two or three repetitions. If an individual's day-to-day physical work demanded this kind of stress on the muscular system, muscular hypertrophy would be greater than that which would occur under normal developmental conditions.

Systematic physical activity affects muscle composition as well as size. Physically active children have a higher proportion of lean body mass to body fat. In one study, "boys with higher levels of physical activity showed a greater increase in lean body mass as well as characteristic changes in body build; i.e. rela-

*From Bailey, D. A. The growing child and the need for physical activity. In J. G. Albinson & G. M. Andrew (Eds.), *Child in sport and physical activity*, p. 82. © 1976, University Park Press, Baltimore.

tively narrower pelvis" (Parizkova, 1973, p. 104).

Exercise and physique

A research topic that is closely related to bone and muscle development is that of *physique*. Physique refers to an individual's body form, build, or shape. Perhaps the most important classification of physique or body type (somatotyping) was that developed by Sheldon (1940), who attempted to relate physique to a variety of behavioral, occupational, disease, and performance variables. More recently Parnell (1958) and Heath and Carter (1967) have expanded upon Sheldon's work in developing their own classification systems.

Sheldon classified physiques as *endomorphic, mesomorphic,* and *ectomorphic;* this classification was based largely on the amount of fat, muscle, and bone length. An endomorph was "soft and round." A mesomorph was well muscled, thick chested, and broad shouldered. The ectomorph was "tall and thin." Sheldon recognized that everyone's body build contained all three components, so his rating method utilized a seven-point scale for each of the three categories. A "1" represented the least expression and a "7" the most expression of a given category. Thus, a 1-7-1 physique would represent low endomorphy and ectomorphy, but extreme mesomorphy. For a more thorough discussion of physique, see Malina and Rarick (1973).

Tanner doubted that exercise's effects on physical development were permanent. His (1952) four-month study of adults showed that after training, muscle size regressed to pretraining levels. Four months is a relatively short training period, and it seems reasonable that there would not be lasting effects. However, persons who undergo long periods of training do retain some training effects even after they have stopped active training (for example, many retired football players retain the rather large necks they developed during training in high school and college). These persons are usually in late adolescence or early adulthood. Another example of "training effects" is exhibited by world-class tennis performers, who have enlarged dominant or playing arms. This effect is usually permanent. Godin (1920) found that gymnasts observed from 14 through 18 years of age were slightly taller, heavier, and larger in thoracic and forearm measurements than nongymnasts. Godin attributed these differences to prolonged gymnastic participation.

Many laborers who must do much physical work over long periods of time also develop physiques that show a definite "training effect." The permanence of exercise effects appears to be directly related to the length of training. If training continues for a long period of time, the body shape will tend to persist for a long time.

An important unanswered question is that of exercise effects on the physique of young children. What positive or negative effects of exercise might there be for young children? Undoubtedly persistent highly stressful activity results in damage to bone and muscle tissue of an immature individual. A good example of this is the development of "Little League elbow" by young baseball pitchers. Physical activity does not always have a positive effect on the physical development of young children. It is important that there be proper conditioning techniques, appropriate and safe equipment, and proper supervision and coaching.

One recent development in athletics, the use of anabolic steroids, relates to our last statement regarding proper supervision and conditioning. Anabolic steroids are being promoted and used rather extensively by professional, college, and high school athletes for the purpose of increasing muscle size and strength. There are even anecdotal reports of this irresponsible and illegal use filtering down to the level of Little League. The consequences of anabolic steroid use are well documented for males and females at all age levels. Although steroid use may result in strength and performance gains for some athletes, the price they have to pay is quite large. This is particularly true for the prepubertal or pubertal boy. The most significant effect is accelerated epiphyseal development and possible early epiphyseal closure. The result would be diminished terminal height. For this reason alone anabolic steroids should not be used by growing children for the purpose of accelerating growth and strength. Additional steroid effects may include altered sex characteristics, liver damage, growth of hair, and a deepening of the voice (Frasier, 1973).

Well-supervised physical exercise can benefit young children. If they are inactive their musculature is poorly defined, and if they have a poorly balanced diet they will also be endomorphic (fat). So at the very least physical activity should reduce endomorphy—in itself a positive aspect of development in early childhood.

References

Acheson, R. M. Maturation of the skeleton. In P. Falkner (Ed.), *Human development*. Philadelphia: W. B. Saunders Co., 1966.

Bailey, D. A. The growing child and the need for physical activity. In J. G. Albinson & G. M. Andrew (Eds.), *Child in sport and physical activity*. Baltimore: University Park Press, 1976.

Bee, H. *The developing child*. New York: Harper & Row, Publishers, 1975.

Chess, S. & Thomas, A. Temperament in the normal infant. In I. C. Westman (Ed.), *Individuals differences in children*. New York: John Wiley & Sons, Inc., 1973.

Cravioto, J. Nutritional deficiencies and mental performance in childhood. In D. C. Glass (Ed.), *Environmental influences*. New York: The Rockefeller University Press and Russell Sage Foundation, 1963.

Frasier, S. D. Androgens and athletes. *American Journal of Diseases in Children*, 1973, *125*, 479-480.

Garn, S. M. Body size and its implications. In L. W. Hoffman & M. L. Hoffman (Eds.), *Review of child development research* (Vol. 2). New York: Russell Sage Foundation, 1966.

Godin, P. In S. L. Eby (Trans.), *Growth during school age*. Boston: Gorham Press, 1920.

Greulich, W. W. A comparison of the physical growth and development of American-born and native Japanese children. *American Journal of Physical Anthropology*, 1957, *15*, 489-515.

Greulich, W. W., & Pyle, S. I. *Radiographic atlas of skeletal development of the hand and wrist* (2nd ed.). Palo Alto, Calif.: Stanford University Press, 1959.

Hanson, J., Jones, K., & Smith, D. Fetal alcohol syndrome. *Journal of the American Medical Association*, 1976, *235*, 1453-1460.

Heath, B. H., & Carter, J. E. L. A modified somatotype method. *American Journal of Physical Anthropology*, 1967, *21*, 57-74.

Jensen, A. R. How much can we boost IQ and scholastic achievement? *Harvard Educational Review*, 1969, *39*, 1-123.

Larson, R. L. Physical activity and the growth and development of bone and joint structures. In G. L. Rarick (Ed.), *Physical activity: human growth and development*. New York: Academic Press, Inc., 1973.

Malina, R. M., Harper, A. B., & Holman, J. D. Growth status and performance relative to parental size. *Research Quarterly*, 1970, *41*, 503.

Malina, R. M., & Rarick, G. L. Growth, physique, and motor performance. In G. L. Rarick (Ed.), *Physical activity: human growth and development*. New York: Academic Press, Inc., 1973.

Monckenberg, F. Effect of early marasmic malnutrition on subsequent physical and psychological development. In N. S. Scrimshaw & J. E. Gordon (Eds.), *Malnutrition, learning, and behavior*. Cambridge, Mass.: The M.I.T. Press, 1968.

Mussen, P. H., Conger, J. J., & Kagan, J. *Child development and personality*. (4th ed.). New York: Harper & Row, Publishers, 1974.

Parizkova, J. Body composition and exercise during growth and development. In G. L. Rarick (Ed.), *Physical activity: human growth and development*. New York: Academic Press, Inc., 1973.

Parnell, R. W. *Behavior and physique: an introduction to practical and applied somatometry*. London: Edward Arnold Ltd., 1958.

Sheldon, W. H. *The varieties of human physique*. New York: Harper & Row, Publishers, 1940.

Squier, R., & Dunbar, F. Emotional factors in the course of pregnancy. *Psychosomatic Medicine*, 1946, *8*, 161-175.

Tanner, J. M. *Education and physical growth*. London: University of London Press, 1961.

Tanner, J. M. Physical growth. In P. H. Mussen (Ed.), *Carmichael's manual of child psychology* (Vol. 1). New York: John Wiley & Sons, Inc., 1970.

Tanner, J. M. *Fetus into man*. Cambridge, Mass.: Harvard University Press, 1978.

Telfer, M. A., Baker, D., Clark, G. R., & Richardson, C. E. Incidence of gross errors among tall criminal American males. *Science*, 1968, *159*, 1249-1250.

Student projects

1. Discuss with the parents of a boy or girl the possibility of using available records of height and weight from birth. If these records are available, plot their height and weight using the appropriate growth chart in Appendix A. Using the techniques described in this chapter, record the subject's present height and weight. At what percentile are the present scores? Have they remained at about the same percentile throughout development? Compare your findings with those of other classmates.

2. Let us see whether we can be successful in predicting height using Table 2-1. Try to obtain the growth records and see how accurate prediction would have been at various ages. Using data from Project 1, predict the adult height of the children. Discuss the factors that may contribute to error in prediction.

Chapter 3

DEVELOPMENT OF MOTOR SKILLS

Vancouver Sun

Chapter 2 focused exclusively on the development of physical characteristics, that is, growth of bone, muscle, and the nervous system. Now how a child develops basic motor skills will be investigated and performance characteristics of boys and girls as they move from infancy through adolescence will be described.

As a youngster's physique develops there is an increase in the development of basic motor responses such as crawling, creeping, walking, throwing, jumping, and so forth. Without question a youngster's state of maturation sets limits on what can be performed at any point in development. It is known, for instance, that a 6-month-old child will be able to sit and perhaps crawl, but one certainly would not expect the infant to be able to walk. The reason the child cannot walk is a lack of maturity. The child's bones, muscles, and nervous system have not developed sufficiently to sustain weight and coordinate leg movements.

Although it is unlikely in this example, an alternative explanation could be that the child has not yet *learned* to walk. Learning results in a change of behavior that is seen as performance. Thus, as a child acquires various motor skills he will probably learn them; however, his level of maturation will dictate whether certain skills can be learned. In some cases performance occurs independently of learning, but these are usually restricted to reflexes. The bulk of our behaviors are unquestionably learned, but since maturation sets limits on what can be learned, it must be said that maturation and learning are intricately interwoven and thus interact in the development of basic motor skills.

PHASES OF MOTOR DEVELOPMENT

The development of a child's motor behavior follows a sequential process, starting with very simple reflexes and terminating with very complex coordinated motor skills. Generally, motor behavior will move from reflexes, to the learning of postural movements, to transport or locomotor movements, and finally to manipulative movements. It should be pointed out that these behaviors increase simultaneously with the development of motor control, which develops in a *cephalocaudal* direction (from head to feet) and also in a *proximodistal* direction (from midline of the body to the extremities).

Using the four stages of development as a guideline, one could roughly say that during infancy children will move from *reflexive* responses to *rudimentary movement* abilities (Fig. 3-1). These rudimentary behaviors, which would include sitting, crawling, creeping, standing, and walking, essentially form the foundation for the development of other fundamental abilities.

During early childhood children develop, among others, the ability to run, jump, balance, catch, and throw. These skills are commonly labeled *general fundamental skills,* since they are characterized by being common to all children and are necessary for ordinary survival. There will, however, be large individual differences in a child's ability to perform these fundamental skills. With respect to individual differences it should be pointed out that the order in which rudimentary and fundamental skills normally develop will be the same for all children; only the rate at which these skills develop will vary.

During late childhood more *specific* movement skills will appear in the child's repertoire of movement abilities. The early general fundamental skills becomes further refined and hence will appear as more fluid and more automatic. More emphasis is placed on form, accuracy, and adaptability, and the child can now apply these skills to sports performance.

At adolescence specific abilities develop sufficiently to be called *specialized*. This process evolves slowly from late childhood through late adolescence and really depends on the amount of practice an individual has with specific skills. For example, pole vaulting is a skill that might readily be termed specialized. However, the abilities needed to execute it are made up of general and specific skills acquired at an earlier age. The ability to run and coordinate pole carrying and placement could be well learned and hence somewhat general. However, the actual vaulting technique is very specialized, and in order to execute it one needs adolescent strength and coordination and well-developed fundamental skills.

It could also be said that skills develop not only along a continuum from rudimentary to specialized, but also along the continuum from *gross* to *fine*. Gross motor skills incorporate large muscles, usually several muscle groups of the body. Examples of gross motor skills include running, jumping, balancing, and throwing. Fine motor skills involve small muscles and limited activities of the body extremities. Examples of fine motor skills are threading a needle, typing, and handwriting.

There is an abundance of empirical research support for the phases of motor skill development illustrated in Fig. 3-1. Most gross motor activities require basic components or "factors" such as strength, agility, balance, and flexibility in varying degrees. These factors are common to most motor skills but really vary with the type of skill or task. Studies such as those conducted by Cumbee (1954), Fleishman (1964), Fleishman and Hempel (1954), and Rarick and co-workers (1976) using factor analysis (a statistical technique) have demonstrated that simple gross tasks will be dominated by general factors. As the skills become more complex, they will contain specific factors as well as some general factors.

General factors are particularly operative during early fundamental skill acquisiton in children. Support for our contention that general factors dominate in young children comes from the study by Rarick and co-workers (1976). This extensive study, which looked at the factor structure of forty-seven variables in

normal and educable retarded children (ages 6 to 13 years), found that there was less specificity in the motor skills of these children than of those in the earlier factor analytic studies that had used older subjects. According to Rarick, "With increasing age the basic components tend to become more clearly defined and factors such as Strength-Power-Body Size factor will be split up into several strength components, as well as components of power and body size" (Rarick et al., 1976, p. 116).

FACTORS THAT INFLUENCE SKILL DEVELOPMENT

We have previously discussed the problem of determining to what extent physical development was mediated by hereditary and environmental factors. The same problem of "nature versus nurture" appears in determining whether certain skills are a result of genetic predisposition or are learned. We often hear such phrases as "just a natural athlete" or "a born shooter," implying that one is born with certain athletic skills and hence further practice will not add appreciably to one's "endowed" performance. By now, of course, we know that these statements are not true and that both heredity and environment are actually involved in determining our level of skill. This is true at all levels of skill development from the most rudimentary to specialized skills. We have all observed individuals practicing the same skill for the same period of time, and yet when the actual performance is observed, there are large differences in ability. Not everyone started at the same level of ability, and all did not derive equal benefits from practice. These dissimilar capabilities for performing certain motor skills can be due to heredity or environmental factors.

Several methodologies have been used by researchers to try to separate the effects of heredity and environment on the behavior of organisms. With animals the techniques most commonly used are inbreeding and selective breeding. Inbreeding, or the mating of related individuals (for example, brothers and sisters), often produces undesirable characteristics or traits. Although the effects of inbreeding on humans have been observed, few studies have systematically employed it as a technique for

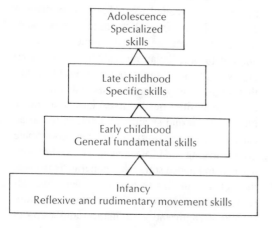

Fig. 3-1. Phases of motor skill development.

studying hereditary effects (because of obvious moral standards). One such study on intelligence was, however, conducted by Schull and Neel (1965) using a Japanese population of first and second cousins. The inbred children showed expected lower Wechsler intelligence scores than did a control group.

The technique of selective breeding with animals involves mating animals who exhibit extreme manifestations of a particular trait (for example, very small or very aggressive). The extreme offspring are then selected to be the parents of the succeeding generation, and so on. This technique is obviously not used with humans.

With humans the usual procedure is to select the variables or characteristics of interest (for example, IQ, age walking begins, balancing ability) and correlate these scores between various family and nonfamily members, particularly twins. Although correlations are task specific, studies typically find that there are low correlations between adults and adopted children. Correlations between parents and their natural children typically yield higher coefficients, as do children with other children in the same family. Still higher correlations are found between fraternal or dizygotic twins (DZ). The highest correlations are ordinarily found between identical or monozygotic twins (MZ). Identical twins (MZ) are individuals with identical *genotypes* having arisen from the same fertilized egg. Fraternal twins (DZ), on the other hand, are no more alike genetically than ordinary siblings.

Perhaps this correlational technique can be made clearer by using the example of intelligence, unquestionably the most controversial of the nature-nurture topics. The correlation between parents' intelligence and the intelligence of children chosen at random (not their own children) is typically zero. The correlation between parents and their adopted children is about .25, but that between parents and natural children is about .50. The correlation between fraternal twins reared together is about .55. The IQs of identical twins correlate at about .90; however, when these identical twins are reared in different environments, the correlation drops to about .55 (data from Mussen et al., 1974).

Thus, heredity and environment are both important factors in the determination of intelligence.

Role of heredity in motor skill development

Just how much does heredity contribute to our ability to perform motor skills? Certainly there are anecdotal reports testifying on behalf of heredity, such as: "I am a klutz," "a motor moron," "but why shouldn't I be, my mother and father were not athletic." Then we have the evidence from the very visible amateur and professional sporting world where members of the same family have competed. There is probably no better father-son(s) example than that of the Howe family in professional hockey. Father, Gordie (a hockey legend), has two sons not only playing professional hockey but playing with him when he is 50. The Wills (family (Maury and Bump) in professional baseball constitutes another father-son example. Numerous brother-brother examples can be found in professional sports. For example, hockey has had the Richard brothers, the Espositos, and the Hulls. Baseball has had the Dean brothers, the DiMaggio brothers, and more recently the Niekro brothers. There are even examples of brother-sister combinations who are world-class athletes. There is Billie Jean King in tennis and her brother Randy Moffit, who is a major league relief pitcher. We also have Dave Meyers, former UCLA basketball player now in the NBA and his sister Jean Meyers, a four-time All-American in women's basketball at UCLA. The famous Wallenda family who perform very sophisticated motor skills on a high wire could serve as another example of family predisposition for performing motor skills. These examples and many more would prompt many to claim that these specialized skills are genetically endowed.

But can we make this claim? Could we not as easily say that we would expect family members to have similar aptitudes for motor skill performance because their environment created it? For example, one might argue that the reason Marty and Mark Howe are successful professional hockey players is that they grew up in a hockey environment. They received early exposure to the sport and had plenty of opportunities to practice their skills under expert coaching. Let us take a look at what the research has to say about this question.

Bouchard (1977) presents an excellent review of the studies that have looked at genetic influences on motor behavior. All of these studies were twin studies, and generally the evidence points to a strong genetic contribution. The study of Wilson and Harpring (1972) found MZ correlations in motor development consistently higher than DZ correlations. In fine motor tasks MZ twins have been shown to be more alike DZ twins (Holzinger, 1929; Newman et al., 1937; McNemar, 1933). Similar findings have been reported for gross motor tasks (Klissouras, 1973; Vandenberg, 1962; Williams and Hearfield, 1973).

The recent comprehensive work of Sklad (1975) on 27 MZ twins and 23 DZ twins provides more interesting findings on genetics and motor performance by using various measures of motor performance. Sklad concluded that DZ twins differed more in motor learning capacity than did MZ twins, that level and rate of learning showed higher genetic control in boys than in girls, and that genetic influences in the learning of motor skills was task specific, something that we mentioned earlier.

One of the largest contributions regarding family predispositions to sports participation is provided by Gedda (1961). In his 1961 study Gedda reported little dissimilarity in sports participation between MZ twins; however, DZ twins differed considerably in their interest and participation in sports. Gedda and co-workers (1964) essentially verified these findings in a study conducted on athletes at the 1960 Olympic Games in Rome. One conclusion reached was that the athlete and his family practiced similar activities. Although the work of Gedda points toward a possible heredity-environment interaction, the earlier-reported studies strongly favor the conclusion that genes play a critical and influential role in the development, learning, and performance of motor skills.

Role of the environment in motor skill development

We have provided considerable research evidence suggesting that heredity plays an impor-

tant role in the development of motor skills. However, we can say without reservation that the *experiences* (learning and training) of a child during the critical formative years help to shape what will become "skilled behavior." Motor skills do not simply evolve as the child matures; they must be learned. Learning motor skills requires that two important conditions be present: (1) feedback regarding the adequacy of the movement behavior and (2) practice of the task. Although understanding motor learning theory is important, it is not our purpose to theorize about how children learn motor skills; rather we are concerned with how experience (learning) contributes (regardless of the process) to the development of motor skills. Those interested in reading about motor skill learning per se should see several outstanding texts such as Cratty (1973), Drowatzky (1975), Sage (1971), and Singer (1975).

Two general approaches are taken in studying the effects of early training on motor development. One approach is to deprive an organism of sensory and motor stimulation and observe the effects. Studies of this nature obviously lend themselves more to animal research, and there is in fact an abundance of these studies (for an excellent review, see Beach and Jaynes [1954]). There are human studies that have used this model, but we should point out that it is truly a rare event for a researcher purposely to deprive individuals of important sensory and motor stimulation for an extended period of time. This is particularly true today, since there are strong ethical standards on research using human subjects. Most studies of this nature are conducted on individuals or cultures after the fact; researchers refer to these as ex post facto studies. Two examples of these studies are classics reported by Dennis in 1940 and 1960. In the 1940 study Dennis observed the Hopi Indian cultural practice of strapping their infant children to a cradleboard, thereby restricting their movements for the first year of life. It is interesting that Dennis found these children no slower in learning to walk than children whose movements had not been restricted. The 1960 study was based on children who were raised in Iranian orphanages where infants had very little contact with adults and, further, had a nonstimulating physical environment. These children lagged behind normal children in motor development, among other deficiencies. Most notable was the fact that only 15% of the 4-year-old children could walk alone.

A second method of study is more experimental; that is, the researcher gives training or practice to one group of children and no training to a comparable group. It is generally assumed that if maturation is crucial to the development of a specific skill, the untrained children will perform as well as the trained ones or at least will catch up very quickly. However, if experience is the critical factor in the acquisition of skill, then the trained children's performance should be superior to that of the untrained.

As we pointed out in the section on heredity, identical twins serve as ideal subjects for studies of this nature, since we can readily control for hereditary effects. The study by McGraw (1935) on twins Johnny and Jimmy is without question a classic in the field of developmental psychology. This study has contributed immensely to our knowledge about the effects of early experience on motor development in children, and we would like to provide you with some details about it.

Development of Johnny and Jimmy

McGraw (1935) selected twin boys referred to as Johnny and Jimmy for the purpose of determining what effect early training had on motor development. She worked with them from the time they were 20 days old until shortly after their second birthday. The twins spent eight hours a day, five days a week in the laboratory and the rest of the time with their family in the home.

Johnny was chosen as the experimental twin because Jimmy appeared to be slightly stronger. The reasoning was that since Jimmy was developmentally advanced, if Johnny's training was effective, the gains over Jimmy would be more significant than if the stronger twin were trained.

During the initial phases of the study Johnny was given short training sessions every two hours, and Jimmy was left in a crib behind a screen. Periodically Jimmy would be tested on the skills in which Johnny had been trained. The early motor training consisted of stimulating Johnny's reflexes. On testing, no differences in performance were obtained between the two boys; however, this should not be unexpected since learning does not influence reflexes.

As the twins developed, Johnny was given practice on all of the fundamental motor tasks such as rolling over, sitting, standing, and so on. Practice in rolling over did not particularly enhance Johnny's performance, and with respect to sitting, Jimmy sat alone first. To this point, then, it appears as though early training does not have an appreciable effect on motor skill development.

At about 1 year of age Johnny was given training in more advanced motor skills, skills that are normally learned later in life, for example, riding a tricycle, swimming and diving, roller skating, jumping from heights, and sliding. Jimmy was provided with intensive practice in the same activities for 2½ months when he was 22 months old.

After Jimmy's training the performance of the two boys was compared. In swimming and diving Johnny demonstrated superiority because of his early practice. He likewise exhibited superiority in skating and had a more coordinated jump from heights. Some skills, however, were not facilitated by early practice. This effect occurred in walking, where both boys demonstrated similar patterns, and in tricycle riding, where Johnny had learned unskillful habits. McGraw does emphasize one major difference in the performance of Johnny and Jimmy: in all cases Johnny showed more interest, less fear, and more confidence in performing the complex skills.

After the two years of training and testing McGraw introduced both boys to novel complex tasks to see what effect Johnny's early training had on the performance of novel tasks. The result was that early training in specific skill did not transfer to novel skills, a finding we should not be very surprised about, since modern transfer theory would make this prediction.

The McGraw study allows us to make some

generalizations about the effect of early experience on motor development. One is the reaffirmation of the belief that behaviors not controlled by the cerebral cortex, such as reflexes (controlled by lower brain centers), are unaffected by specific training or practice. Another generalization is that rudimentary skills such as turning over, crawling, and walking are not enhanced by early practice; hence, we can say that maturation dictates this type of behavior. Other more complex behaviors can be enhanced, but the degree of success depends on the task. General coordination appears to be enhanced, as is the development of a more daring attitude. The long-term effects of early training on these complex skills are difficult to assess.

One further conclusion we can draw from the McGraw study is related to the idea of *critical periods of development* (Tanner [1978] refers to this as *sensitive* periods). The concept of critical periods has many connotations and brings up many important questions. In general a critical period is assumed to be a point in the development of a specific behavior during which experience or training has an optimal effect. Experience at an earlier or later time, according to some writers, has no effect on, or retards, later skill acquisition.

The idea of critical periods developed from early research on animals and birds, in whom it appears that there are indeed critical times for the acquisition of certain behaviors. In fact certain behaviors *must* be learned at this time, or else they will probably never be learned. For example the phenomenon of *imprinting* takes place with ducklings within a critical time frame in the first few days of life. In imprinting the duckling becomes attached to almost any object that is introduced to it at that time. The duckling will not respond normally to its mother if she is introduced at a point past this critical period. For a more extensive treatment of the critical period concept, refer to Magill (1978) and Singer (1975).

We can conclude from the McGraw study that with children there is no one critical period. The human system appears to be quite plastic and is most amenable to "playing catch-up ball." There does, however, seem to be an optimal time for skill learning. According to McGraw it is that time when the skill is changing most rapidly. If training is introduced at that point, when there is rapid skill development, it will be most effective. Unfortunately, it is not always easy to determine this period of rapid change.

In summary we can say, on the basis of twin studies, that heredity seems to play a major role in the development and performance of motor skills. It is also true that the environment makes a significant contribution to the development of motor skills. Klissouras (1976, p. 200) in writing about superior athletic performance stated, "Genetic factors are decisive in the attainment and prediction of outstanding athletic performance . . . yet the difference between athletes lies not entirely in physiological functions, histochemical quantities, biochemical activities and morphological dimensions." These other differences, according to Klissouras, are basically environmental.

DEVELOPMENT OF MOTOR SKILLS IN INFANTS

The first movements that can be elicited from newborn infants are involuntary responses that we term reflexes. Although reflexes are "primitive" motor responses, they are important for the early survival of the child. The most obvious of the "survival" reflexes are sucking and rooting. An infant automatically begins to suck when an object—such as nipple, finger, or pencil—is placed in her mouth. Closely related to this reflex is the rooting, which is elicited when an infant's cheek is touched lightly. The normal response by the infant is to turn in the direction of the stimulation and open her mouth in preparation for sucking. Other survival reflexes that occur in infancy and persist through life are coughing, sneezing, and blinking.

Reflexes are not only important for the survival of infants, but they also serve as an indicator of the maturity and soundness of the infant's nervous system. Since the full complement of reflexes in children is well documented in terms of the age of onset, persistence, and disappearance, it is possible to determine whether an infant's nervous system is developing normally. If a reflex is uneven in strength when both sides of the body are stimulated or is too strong or too weak, we have reason to suspect some kind of neurological dysfunction.

It is also true that if a specific reflex fails to appear or even persists longer than "normal," then we can suspect central nervous system impairment.

We would also like to point out that reflexes as we now know them tell us only whether there is normal or abnormal development. They have no useful predictive value for later motor and cognitive skills. "Super" elicitation of reflexes does not mean that the infant will have "super" reaction times in childhood, adolescence, or adulthood. These attibutes (reflexes and reaction time) are in fact independent in both definition and function.

The early "survival" reflexes reflect the relatively undeveloped nervous system. As the nervous system matures, reflexes change from those solely under spinal control to those under brainstem control and others under midbrain control. Finally, as the highest nervous system center matures, many of these "transient" reflexes become assimilated and are gradually inhibited. Voluntary responses then take over.

There are a tremendously large number of reflexes in a young child, far too many for us to discuss in detail in this chapter. Rather we will present you with a summary (Table 3-1) that includes a brief description of selected reflexes and their age of onset, persistence, and disappearance. For a more thorough description of reflexes, see Fiorentino (1970), McGraw (1969), and Sukiennicki (1971).

Development of voluntary movement

As the infant's nervous system matures, many of the reflexes give way to voluntary

Table 3-1. Appearance, persistence, and disappearance of selected reflexes

Reflex	Description	1	2	3	4	5	6	7	8	9	10	11	12
Moro	Strike pillow—infant spreads arms and fingers, and legs somewhat	+	+	+	+	+	+	+	+	+			
Sucking	Lightly touch lips, gums, or front—infant will suck	+	+	+									
Rooting	Lightly touch side of cheek near mouth—head should turn to direction of stimulation	+	+	+									
Grasp	Press rod or other object into palm—fingers should curl around object	+	+	+	+	+	+						
Tonic neck (asymmetrical)	Turn infant's head—will be an increase in limb tone on side facing head; opposite limbs flex	+	+	+	+	+	+	−					
Tonic neck (symmetrical)	Flex infant's head forward—arms flex, legs extend; reversal when head bent back	+	+	+	+	+	+						
Babinski	Scratch sole from toe to heel—toes spread	+	+	+									
Labyrinthine righting	Tip child forward—head remains upright or backward; tip child backward—head remains upright or forward		+	+	+	+	+						
Walking reflex	Hold infant in upright position—infant will execute stepping movements	+	+	+	+	+							
Swimming reflex	Hold infant in water, supporting head—infant will execute rhythmic swimming movements	+	+	+	+	+							

motor responses. These responses that we termed rudimentary and basic at the outset of the chapter are abilities such as rolling over, sitting, crawling, creeping, standing, and finally walking. A number of detailed studies have been conducted on the normal development of these early motor skills (Gesell, 1940; McGraw, 1969; and Shirley, 1931). From these studies and others we know that although there are individual differences and hence variation in the age at which these skills are acquired, they always proceed in a sequential manner and from this standpoint are predictable. For instance, we know that rolling over will always occur before sitting, and sitting will occur before crawling and creeping.

The following discussion will focus on the development of rolling, sitting, crawling, creeping, standing, and walking, as well as manipulative skills.

Rolling. It should be pointed out that prior to the development of rolling the child will first develop control over head and neck muscles (1 to 5 months); and rolling or trunk muscle development occurs afterward. Sometimes the newborn will involuntarily roll from his back to his side, perhaps 180 degrees, but this is in response to head-turning action. As the child matures, segmental rolling appears, namely when the hips and shoulders are turned, the other body segments will follow. The first voluntary rolling is from the abdominal-lying position to the back-lying position (about 3 months). Later the infant will roll from his back to his stomach.

Sitting. The ability to get into a sitting position follows the development of rolling behavior. Initially when an infant is pulled into a sitting position, the head will sag backward, then, after the vertical position is reached, will fall forward on the child's chest. No head sag will normally take place at about 5 months, but it will not be until 6½ months that the child will sit without support. Voluntarily getting into a sitting position will not occur until about 9 months.

Creeping and crawling. Crawling generally refers to dragging the body along a surface using arm and leg movements and creeping to movement in which the arms and legs propel the body, which has the abdomen clearly lifted

from the surface. We say generally because there are some authors (Cratty, 1970) who interchange these two terms; that is, they refer to crawling as being hands and knees (abdomen raised) and creeping the dragging response. Crawling occurs first in the progression, and this happens at about 7 months; as with the rest of these gross motor skills, there will be a lot of individual differences between children. Creeping will develop from crawling, with the first phase one of developing a stationary-knee, extended-arm posture. Then one limb is moved at a time. For example, the right arm will move forward, followed by the left knee, then the left arm and right knee. As the child matures, these movements will become smooth and efficient.

Standing and walking. Most children will be able to pull themselves up to a standing posture at about 9 months of age; however, it may take several more months before they are able to stand without any type of support. The child, upon getting to an upright posture, will begin moving laterally around her playpen or perhaps a coffee table.

Although there are instances when children actually walk without support at 8 months, this is a rare event. Most children do not start to walk until they are about 13 to 14 months. The ability to walk backward does not develop until about 19 months, and walking up steps will not occur until about 21 months. Even at this age these responses will not be free of awkwardness.

Development of manipulative skills

Although an infant sees an object at a very young age, reaching movements toward that object do not take place until about 4 months. Initially these movements are slow and awkward; by the sixth month the infant is capable of accurate hand movements and can grasp objects. This is not to say that an infant will not grasp an object before age 4 months. We noted earlier that the grasp reflex occurred very early in infants, but this was an involuntary response. Halverson (1931) in an early study of prehension in infants described the development of grasping in this sequence—

4 months: no contact
5 months: contact and primitive squeeze

6 months: squeeze grasp
7 months: hand and palm grasp
8 months: superior palm grip
9 months: inferior forefinger
13 months: superior forefinger grip

It is interesting to note that grasping moves from crude palm "grabbing" to "pincer-type" grasps utilizing the thumb and forefinger; this illustrates the proximodistal development that we noted earlier (see page 31).

Since grasping appears to be such a difficult skill to develop, it seems that releasing should be easy. However, this is not the case. Most of us have undoubtedly observed a frustrated infant attempt to release a toy without success. This occurs because the child is not maturationally able to consciously relax the musculature of the hand so that the object will be released. By the age of 18 months most children have mastered the skill of voluntary release.

EARLY CHILDHOOD AND THE DEVELOPMENT OF GENERAL FUNDAMENTAL SKILLS

After 2 years of age the child begins to gain proficiency in locomotion such that running, jumping, hopping, galloping, and skipping become part of her locomotor repertoire. The following section will describe the locomotor changes that take place between the ages of 2 and 5 years. Further, we will describe the development of other essential fundamental skills such as climbing, balancing, and throwing and catching.

Running. Some time after a child becomes proficient in walking, running develops. The initial pattern resembles a hurried walk and is readily seen when a child of about 18 months attempts to "run" when playfully pursued. This is not a genuine run, since the child does not have sufficient balance or leg strength to allow both feet to leave the ground momentarily. Sometime between the age of 2 and 3 years the child will demonstrate "true" running. By age 4 or 5 years a smooth coordinated running pattern will be exhibited. For this age level researchers are typically not so much concerned with performance time in running as they are with the pattern of running.

Jumping. A child will generally not begin to jump until some skill has been achieved in walking and running. The first pattern of jumping will essentially be an exaggerated step with one foot from an elevated level. As greater strength develops in the lower extremities, the child will move to a two-foot takeoff from elevated levels (2 to 2½ years), to long jumping, to jumping over barriers. Bayley's (1935) extensive description of motor skill development in children places two-foot jumping at about 28 months and long jumping for a distance of 36 to 60 cm at about 40 months. Gutteridge (1939) reported that 42% of preschool children will jump well by the age of 3 years, and by 4½ years 72% are deemed to be skillful jumpers.

Hopping. Hopping requires more strength and balance than does jumping, since the child must be able to take off and land on the same foot. Since static balance is not achieved until about 29 months (Bayley, 1935) and lower-leg strength is still minimal, hopping will not develop until about the age of 4 years and even then only for a short distance. Skillful hopping ability will not be achieved until about age 6. As with many motor skills there are large individual differences in hopping ability. Girls are generally more proficient at hopping than boys, presumably because of their slightly advanced physical maturity and social environment, which provides them with more opportunities to practice hopping than does the boys' social environment.

Galloping and skipping. Galloping is a variation of locomotion that draws on walking, running, and leaping and appears to be sex linked to some extent; that is, boys appear to prefer galloping at about age 4 and 5, whereas girls seem to prefer skipping. The ability to skip develops slightly later than galloping, but in both cases skillful execution does not occur until age 6½ (Cratty, 1970).

Climbing. Climbing, although requiring a degree of bravery in children, is essentially an outgrowth of creeping. Many children who have the opportunity will learn to ascend and descend stairs before they are able to walk. Although the initial intent of the child is to descend head first, a few falls and experimentation will result in backward descending. After learning to walk the child will climb up and down stairs in an upright position but will usually lead with the same foot, thereby "marking time" for a moment on each step (about 3 years of age). Eventually a foot-alternating pattern will develop, first for ascending then for descending (about 4 years of age).

Ladder climbing shows a similar progression to stair climbing. The child first places both feet on a single rung before ascending to the next, then with maturity and experience alternates feet on the ladder rung.

Balance. Several researchers have attempted to describe the balancing ability of children up to 5 years of age using both static (stationary) balance and dynamic (moving) balance. In general it can be said that up until 2 years of age a child will not be able to demonstrate much in the way of one-foot static balance or dynamic beam-walking balance. At this age they have enough trouble maintaining an upright posture. At about 3 years of age most children can maintain balance on one foot (static) for three to four seconds. Also at about this age the child is able to walk a distance of 300 cm (10 ft) on a 2.5 cm (1 in.) wide line successfully (Bayley, 1935). The initial pattern for beam walking in children has them leading with the same foot (similar to stair climbing). At approximately 3 years the child feels comfortable in alternating feet on a balance beam.

Interesting sex differences have been reported for balancing ability in 5-year-old children. Studies by Cratty and Martin (1969) and Holbrook (1953) showed that girls were superior to boys in tests of static balance. This difference may be attributed to girls' slightly advanced neurological development.

Ball skills—throwing and catching. Before the age of 2 years a child may be seen throwing an object (such as food when frustrated or angry); however, the action will be a jerky, side-armed movement. Occasionally a ball will be thrown, but it will be with two hands or so crude as to seem accidental. An early cinematographic study by Wild (1938) revealed four distinct patterns in the development of throwing—

1. Children of 2 and 3 throw primarily using forearm extension and little or no footwork or body rotation.

2. Children of 3½ throw with more body rotation and arm range.
3. Children of 5 and 6 introduce a forward step with the foot that is on the same side as the throwing arm (often erroneously referred to as "throwing like a girl").
4. Children 6½ and older exhibit the so-called mature throwing action. For a right-handed thrower weight is transferred to the right foot during the preparatory phase of throwing, followed by a forward step with the left foot, hip rotations, and forearm extension.

Throwing is most interesting to observe, since there is wide variation within and between ages, sexes, and cultures. It seems that environmental factors play a significant role in determining one's throwing pattern. It is no secret that girls generally do not throw as well as boys. One might be able to explain this phenomenon by implicating the slightly different physical structure of the female, but more likely the explanation is one of practice and learning. Girls who have the opportunity to play ball and achieve a high level of skill throw as well as boys. Likewise, men who live in countries where ball throwing is not emphasized demonstrate an "immature" throwing form. These two points suggest that throwing is by and large a learned skill, at least beyond early childhood.

Catching is a very difficult skill for children simply because the response must be to a moving rather than a stationary object. Above all, this requires good hand-eye coordination, something that is minimally present during early childhood. At about 3½ years children attempt to catch a ball by holding their arms straight out in front of the body. Later they place their arms in a more favorable "receiving" position. According to Cratty (1970) an average 5-year-old child can catch a 20 cm (8 in.) diameter ball 60 to 80% of the time when it is bounced from 4.5 m (15 ft.) and arrives chest high. Interestingly, Cratty reported that in his study girls were more successful than boys in ball catching.

LATE CHILDHOOD AND THE DEVELOPMENT OF MORE SPECIFIC MOTOR SKILLS

One noticeable feature of children as they move from early to late childhood is the decrease in the rate of physical growth. Although growth still occurs, it is not quite so dramatic as it was during the first five years. Motor skills, however, continue to improve, particularly the fundamental running, jumping, and ball skills. Also during the period of late childhood children begin to experience and perform different motor activities because they are exposed to different social interactions and environmental demands. Motor skills thus become more specialized in children, something that has been demonstrated in numerous studies. The acquisition of these specialized skills and the further development of fundamental skills allow the child to participate in games and sports that call for the utilization and hence development of unique motor skills. For example, children now convert their running and jumping skills to basketball playing; strength and flexibility, to gymnastics; throwing and catching skills, to baseball; and balance, strength, and coordination, to skating and hockey. All of these sports require specific motor abilities.

Studies on children during late childhood also take a different focus. Rather than only describing performance changes and viewing developmental patterns, researchers begin to focus on performance changes in other skills such as flexibility, agility, and strength as well as laboratory-tested skills. These more specific laboratory tasks include tests of balance, reaction time, and pursuit rotor performance. These tasks are only a sample of the numerous motor tasks that have been utilized in developmental research. Examples of two large-scale studies that used a multitude of motor tests are those of Clarke (1971) and Rarick and co-workers (1976).

Almost without exception one observes that mean scores on motor tasks improve as the child grows older. It should be pointed out, however, that these mean scores represent group, not individual performance, and because there is variability between individuals we should expect some individual children to perform as well as children who are one or two years older. To get a better idea of some of these age-related changes let us look as some of the more commonly researched tasks.

Running. Because it is possible to measure

running ability in so many different ways using time and distance, it is difficult to make meaningful comparisons across studies. By and large, however, running speed increases as the child gets older, and generally sex differences are in favor of the boys. A recent study by Milne and co-workers (1976) that investigated running in children grades kindergarten through second found significant grade differences on both the 30-yard dash and 400-foot run. Significant sex differences favoring the boys were also reported. In addition Di Nucci (1976) reported age and sex differences favoring boys on a number of running tasks with 6-, 7-, and 8-year-old children.

Jumping. Numerous jumping tasks have been administered to children during this age period; the most popular are the vertical jump and the standing broad jump. A study by Johnson (1962) using the vertical jump showed that performance increased linearly between the ages of 7 and 11 years. Boys also exceeded girls in performance after the age of 7. At age 7 boys and girls can jump about 17.5 cm (7 in.) beyond their standing reach, but by age 11 girls can jump 26 cm (10.5 in.) and boys 29 cm (11.7 in.).

Keogh (1973), in his presentation of standing broad jump performance, reported that boys and girls increased in performance by 7.5 to 12.5 cm (3 to 5 in.) per year. Fig. 3-2 clearly

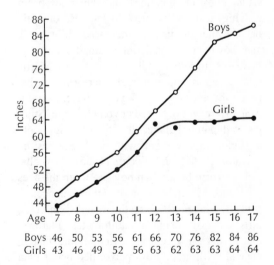

Age	7	8	9	10	11	12	13	14	15	16	17
Boys	46	50	53	56	61	66	70	76	82	84	86
Girls	43	46	49	52	56	63	62	63	63	64	64

Fig. 3-2. Standing broad jump performance of boys and girls. (Courtesy J. Keogh.)

illustrates the developmental changes in this task as well as sex differences. Data from Espenschade (1960) and Clarke (1971) also closely resemble the pattern depicted in Fig. 3-2.

Throwing. During early childhood, studies on throwing generally focus on form, but during late childhood more attention is paid to distance and accuracy, particularly during the latter years of this period. Roberton (1977, 1978) provides an excellent recent cinematographic analysis of the development of throwing in first-grade children. Robertson filmed the same children over a three-year period and concluded that stage categories in throwing appear to be universal and intransitive over time.

With respect to distance and accuracy Keogh (1973) points out that boys and girls improve more than 100% between the ages of 7 and 11, a rather large increase compared to the 20% to 39% found in other skills. In North American children boys consistently outperform girls. This is not necessarily the case when European children are tested. This indicates that cultural factors are most influential in the development of throwing skills. Other ball skills such as catching, kicking, and batting have also been investigated. For a more extensive review of ball skill development, we recommend a text by Whiting (1969).

Balancing. As was the case in studies with younger children, most studies of balance use static (one-foot standing) and dynamic (beam walking) tests of balance. In the case of static balance there is usually increased ability with age; however, the amount is small relative to increases in other skills. Cratty and Martin (1969) report superior male performance between the ages of 6 and 7 years, but no significant differences occurred beyond this age. Studies of dynamic balance also tend to show only a slight improvement with age. Studies by Govatos (1966) and Keogh (1965) show that girls perform better than boys between the ages of 7 and 11 on tests of dynamic balance. A study by Singer (1969) on third- and sixth-grade girls and boys using a stabilometer (platform that pivots on a central device) found that in general sixth-grade boys performed better than sixth-grade girls, who in turn performed better than third-grade boys and girls.

A study by Bachman (1961) points out very well the uniqueness of balancing performance. When tested on a stabilometer children scored progressively more poorly between the ages of 7 and 17. In contrast, scores on a ladder climb–balancing task became progressively better between these ages. Balancing then can be said to be very task specific; further, it differs from many other motor skills in that performance does not markedly improve as the child matures.

Body coordination. In recent years researchers in North America and Europe have used a West German test of body coordination to test the motor development of children (Schilling, 1974; Schilling and Kiphard, 1976). This test battery consists of backward balancing, a lateral jump, movement ability, and a one-foot controlled hop for height. Fig. 3-3 illustrates the four test items. A cross-sectional study by Martinek and co-workers (1977) using this test showed that first through fifth-grade children had increasingly higher performance scores. No sex differences were noted in this study. This linear improvement in body coordination is demonstrated in Fig. 3-4.

ADOLESCENCE AND THE DEVELOPMENT OF SPECIALIZED MOTOR SKILLS

Adolescence is a very trying period physically, psychologically, and socially for most girls and boys. Sometime between the ages of 10 and 18 (earlier for girls) significant changes take place within their bodies, and they perceive themselves as neither children nor adults. Motor skills learned during childhood continue to improve for most boys through adolescence, but this is not the case for most girls. For some reason, which we will discuss later, girls peak at about age 14 then either level off or decline in their performance of motor skills. Sex differences therefore become more apparent during adolescence.

Adolescence also marks the learning of more specialized motor skills because of a variety of increased novel experiences, many of them in games and sports. Those children "turned on" by these experiences continue to improve in these skills, be they gymnastics, track and field, baseball, basketball, volleyball, football, tennis, or hockey. Other children do not enjoy

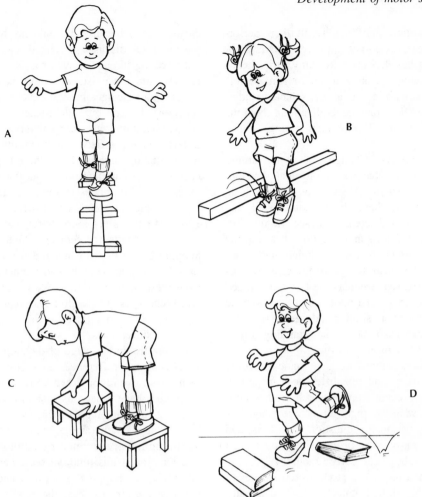

Fig. 3-3. Body coordination test items. **A,** Backward balancing. **B,** Lateral jump. **C,** Lateral movement. **D,** One-foot hopping.

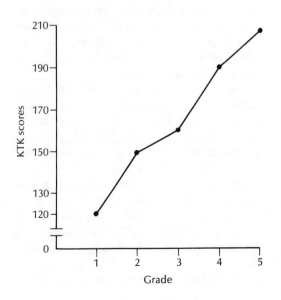

Fig. 3-4. Performance of boys and girls on KTK (body coordination) test. (Data from Martinek, T., et al. *Research Quarterly,* 1977, *48,* 349-357.)

these activities, and as a result their performance measures do not improve. This is probably what has happened to many girls, hence their premature peaking in motor skill performance. Let us briefly examine selected studies that can provide some generalizations about the pattern of motor development during adolescence.

Motor ability. Changes in motor ability closely parallel changes in physical development and strength. A study by Espenschade (1947) portrays these changes quite well. Espenschade administered the Brace Motor Ability Test to 325 girls and 285 boys between the ages of 10½ and 16 years. Included in the findings were that prior to age 14 the girls' performance decreased, whereas the boys' continued to increase. In another publication Espenschade (1960) reports very similar findings for running, a jump-and-reach task, the standing broad jump, and the distance throw.

The generalizations we have made regarding age differences and sex differences in performance have come from research studies conducted on what we might term "everyday children." A reasonable question to ask is, Do these patterns of linear progression and late teen peaking for boys and early (about 14) peaking for girls and increasing sex differences prevail when highly skilled athletes are used as subjects? Unfortunately, very few studies have been conducted on this population, both on laboratory-type tasks and competitive sports skills. The present evidence suggests, however, that the pattern is different. Although we still have the linear improvement in performance, age of peak performance is extended. This is particularly true for girls. What is happening is that we have highly motivated boys and girls who are constantly striving to improve their performance. Ages 14 and 17 are therefore not walls that automatically cause girls and boys to go "downhill" in performance. Continued practice will allow performance to improve to a much later time.

SEX DIFFERENCES IN MOTOR SKILL DEVELOPMENT

Throughout the preceding sections on age differences in motor development and performance we concurrently discussed sex differ-

ences, simply because it would not have been meaningful to discuss age-related changes without referring to either boys or girls. If sex differences did not exist, we could have simply talked about changes in skill development as a function of age, but our earlier discussions pointed out numerous studies that portrayed sex differences in a variety of motor skills. In addition to our research evidence there is plenty of observational data that points out that there are in fact sex differences in motor performance. For example, the present world record for the 100-yard dash is 9.1 seconds for males and an even 10 seconds for females. Men are high jumping 2.2 m (7 ft. 8 in.) and women 2.0 m (6 ft. 8 in.). Can we make some generalizations from these data? Questions we might first ask are, What types of tasks do boys excel in? What types of tasks do girls excel in and why are there sex differences?

During the infant stage of development few significant sex differences in motor development exist, even though we know that in most cases girls have a nervous system that is more mature than that of boys. During early childhood it appears that the socialization process has begun to have an impact on motor skill acquistion, for at this time we see emerging sex differences in hopping, skipping, and galloping. Because girls (at least historically) hop and skip in their play more than boys, they are more proficient. Boys, on the other hand, excel in galloping, a task that they practice more than girls. It also appears that girls perform better than boys in tests of static balance, although studies are somewhat equivocal here. Boys also tend to perform more skillfully in tests of throwing, in both form and distance.

The late childhood years show larger sex differences in a variety of tasks. The performance of boys exceeds that of girls in numerous tests of running speed, jumping ability, throwing, and some tests of balance. Tests of strength consistently show boys doing better than girls, but the differences are slight compared to what they will be during adolescence. When it comes to flexibility girls appear to have an edge on numerous measures. Girls also appear to do better on tasks requiring fine motor coordination.

Adolescence sees even greater sex differences than those observed during the childhood years. A consistent pattern that emerges in the research literature shows boys improving in performance on most motor skills through adolescence, whereas girls peak at about age 14 then either level off or decrease in performance. A common generalization made at this point is that boys do better on strength-type gross motor tasks and girls do better at tasks that require flexibility and fine motor coordination. Table 3-2 provides a summary of many of the studies on sex differences to which we have referred throughout this chapter. Let us now try to explain why we have sex differences in motor performance.

Table 3-2. Selected studies examining sex differences in motor performance*

Motor task	Age	Sex superiority	Authors
Agility	5-9	Females	Keogh (1965)
Balance	7-9	Females	Keogh (1965)
Dynamic	7-11	Females	Govatos (1966)
Static	5	Females	Cratty and Martin (1969)
	6-7	Males	Cratty and Martin (1969)
Ball skills			
Batting	6-12	Males	Cratty (1970)
Catching	6-12	None	Williams (1967)
Kicking	8-10	Males	Carpenter (1940)
	9-11	Males	Latchaw (1954)
Rolling	7-9	Males	Witte (1962)
Throwing	6-11	Males	Keogh (1965)
Accuracy	6-11	Males	Keogh (1965)
Distance	5-7	Males	Jenkins (1930)
	5-17	Males	Espenschade (1960)
	6-11	Males	Cron and Pronko (1957)
	10-17	Males	Hunsicker and Reiff (1966)
Fine hand movement	6-10	Females	Connolly et al. (1968)
Hopping	6-9	Females	Keogh (1965)
Jumping			
Vertical	8-11	Males	Johnson (1962)
	5-17	Males	Espenschade (1960)
Standing broad	6-11	Males	Keogh (1965)
	7-17	Males	Keogh (1973)
	5-17	Males	Espenschade (1960)
Pursuit rotor	5-8	None	Davol et al. (1961)
	8	Males	Ammons et al. (1955)
Running speed	6-8	Males	DiNucci (1976)
	6-11	Males	Keogh (1965)
	5-7	Males	Jenkins (1930)
	9-11	Males	Latchaw (1954)
	5-17	Males	Espenschade (1960)
	5-7	Males	Milne et al. (1976)
Serial motor	5-9	None	Zaichkowsky (1974)

*From "What psychological variables are important in an individual's movement?" by Leonard Zaichkowsky/Lois Smith in *Introduction to physical education: concepts of human movement,* edited by John Cheffers and Tom Evaul © 1978, p. 112. Adapted by permission of Prentice-Hall, Inc., Englewood Cliffs, New Jersey.

The literature on sex differences generally speaks to four different reasons for the differences in boys and girls performance. These include the variables of *body size, anatomical structure, physiological functioning,* and *social* and *cultural factors.* How valid are these explanatory candidates?

Eckert, in discussing age and sex differences in motor skills, stated, "Performance differences may be, in part, a reflection of the greater height and weight of boys from birth to maturity with the exception of early adolescence when the earlier sexual maturity and concomitant accelerated growth of girls tend to make them slightly taller and heavier than boys" (Eckert, 1973, p. 168). In our opinion body size up to the adolescent years does not seem to be a good explanatory variable. One reason is that if we analyze the tasks where there have been documented sex differences during the childhood years (for example, hopping, balancing, galloping), it is difficult to see logically how body size can effect a difference in performance between boys and girls. A second reason pertains to the fact that if one considered the median height and weight (see growth charts in Appendix A) through age 10, one would see very slight or nonexistent sex differences in these measures. Admittedly, in individual cases body size may explain performance differences in childhood, but in general we do not think this is the case. During adolescence, however, we do see initial growth measures favoring the female (through age 13) then increasingly large height and weight differences favoring boys. In motor skills that require strength it stands to reason, then, that boys will exceed girls in performance during adolescence.

Anatomical structure may account for sex differences in performance, particularly during adolescence. For instance, there are observable sex differences in the general structure of the pelvis that may contribute to sex differences in running and jumping (Eckert, 1973). Eckert further adds that after 11 years of age boys have a proportionally greater limb length, which may give them a mechanical advantage in certain motor skills. During adolescence boys increase in shoulder width and girls experience a reduction in shoulder growth. This anatomical difference may affect the arc of the shoulder-arm action and thereby limit the throwing ability of girls.

Like body size and anatomical structure, physiological functioning does not seem like a likely explanation for childhood sex differences. Åstrand (1976) points out maximum oxygen uptake when corrected for body weight shows little in the way of sex differences until adolescence. Pulmonary ventilation (lung function) is also similar for boys and girls through age 13. Beyond the age of 12, however, males have about a 30% higher oxygen-uptake capability than females. In endurance-type events, then, it seems reasonable that boys will perform better than girls. It is interesting to note, however, that when adolescent girls are trained, this 30% difference drops to about 12%; this suggests that societal factors play a prominent role in motor performance.

On the basis of this rather "thin support" for body size, anatomical structure, and physiological functioning, we believe that the broad category of societal and cultural factors provides the best single explanation for existing sex differences in motor performance. For instance, the reason girls perform better in hopping and boys in galloping tests is that they are socialized into practicing these respective tasks more. Girls are also expected to perform more fine motor skills and as a result build up skill in those tasks. Boys, on the other hand, spend more time practicing gross motor skills. We believe that if these roles were reversed, we would find a concomitant reversal in skill.

Societal values, although slowly changing, have had a strong historical tradition. Girls were not expected to perform well in sports and certainly not in competition with boys. Many myths about female sports participation have thereby evolved over the years. For example, some thought girls would grow mustaches or that they might not be able to bear children if they underwent rigorous physical training. It is our belief that society, until recently, has managed to discourage girls from performing well in motor skills.

We do have evidence clearly indicating that there need not be an early "plateauing effect" in female performance. For instance, Eckert

(1973) shows that Bulgarian girls continue to improve through 16 and 18 years in throwing and running skills, respectively, whereas American girls level off at 15 and 13 years of age, an indication that cultural values have an effect on performance. Jack Wilmore has spent many years researching adolescent sex differences, particularly with respect to strength, endurance, and body composition. Wilmore maintains that female athletes are capable of improving strength equivalent to males when subjected to weight training. The fact is that during adolescence girls have been conditioned to think that it is better to have a nice hairdo than to be able to run fast or jump high. Because of this lack of participation the muscle tissue in girls fails to develop maximally.

We firmly believe that if girls and boys received similar opportunities for participating and training as well as the same social approval, there would be no group differences in

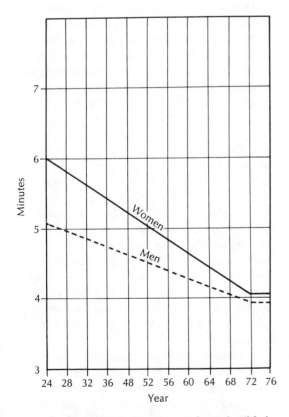

Fig. 3-5. Swim time for 400-meter freestyle. (Modified from Wilmore, J. *Women Sports,* 1974, *I,* 40.)

performance through childhood and, in fact, through the early adolescent years. During adolescence there will be sex differences favoring the males on strength tasks because of hormonal differences and on endurance tasks because of maximum oxygen-uptake capabilities. However, these differences need not be as great as they presently are. The cross-cultural data from Eckert as well as Wilmore's work point this out. Wilmore (1974) provides some interesting support for our thesis, depicted in Fig. 3-5. Since 1924 females have gradually been closing the gap in swim time for the 400-meter freestyle. With relatively recent changes in attitudes regarding child-rearing practices, as well as with provisions and encouragement made for female participation in a variety of activities, it is conceivable that this decrease in male-female differences will be present in other activities.

PHYSICAL ACTIVITY, SPORT, AND THE DEVELOPMENT OF MOTOR SKILLS—IMPLICATIONS

Our present family-rearing practices and educational practices tend to give the impression that motor skills if left alone will somehow develop by themselves. By this we mean that many parents fail to provide early sensory motor stimulation to infants and early encouragment to explore motorically. Many times these parents honestly believe they are serving the best interests of the child by being protective and restrictive. Schools likewise have been guilty of failing to provide children with optimal opportunities to develop motor skills. Many administrators and teachers perceive physical education as a "frill" subject and feel that it is not the role of the school to educate the child from the standpoint of motor skill enhancement. We take exception to the views and practices of many parents and educators. Motor skill learning and development should not be left to chance. We certainly do not leave cognitive skills to chance learning (undoubtedly some will say that we do). Parents are usually much more eager to encourage language skills, counting, alphabet learning, and so on than they are to encourage running, hopping, and throwing. Schools likewise continue this socialization process.

Motor skill learning is essential for all children for a variety of reasons. As we pointed out in the introductory section of this text, motor skill development is intricately related to cognitive development and affective or social-psychological development. Certainly these domains of behavior do not develop in a vacuum independent of each other. The work of Piaget gives us powerful evidence supporting the need for motor exploration in cognitive development (this will be discussed in Chapter 7). Positive childhood experiences with a variety of motor activities will also serve to enhance self-concept. Feeling good about one's abilities in motor skills will do a lot to encourage further participation in physical activity and sport, thereby increasing the chances of developing an individual who is physically and psychologically fit.

Motor skill development is essential in its own right, for simply surviving. If fundamental motor skills such as walking, running, and balancing were not adequately developed, we would have a great deal of trouble avoiding being hit by cars while crossing a street, and we would have to be extremely cautious in performing routine tasks such as stair climbing and walking on a narrow sidewalk. Although we tend to think of fundamental motor skills as essential for survival of early man (hunting, avoiding enemies), they are still very much needed for survival in today's fast-moving society.

Are there guidelines that can be suggested for teaching motor skills to children? If we accept Bruner's (1963) hypothesis that any subject can be taught effectively to any child at any state of development, then it seems reasonable that we should be able to introduce complex skills to children at a relatively young age. Although Bruner was referring to cognitive tasks, this does have implications for motor skill learning. Boys and girls can be taught fairly complex skills enabling them to participate in a variety of games and sports. But it is also true that children should not be rushed into sports participation if they are not physically and psychologically *ready*.

Unfortunately, research gives us few guidelines as to what skills should be taught when.

Although we tend to side with Bruner's statement, we feel that it is necessary to provide some qualifications. During infancy motor skill development is heavily dependent upon maturation. However, an environment that encourages motor exploration will certainly be beneficial for the early acquisition of certain motor skills (as evidenced in the McGraw study). During early childhood, in addition to encouraging the practice of fundamental skills, we can assist the development of more complex skills such as catching and striking. After *analyzing the components* of these more advanced skills and assessing the *previous experience* of each individual child in these tasks, we can indeed structure the environment to allow learning to take place. For example, catching skills can be progressively introduced by using slow-moving balloons, then larger balls. Striking skills, which are necessary in racket sports and baseball, can be introduced using a stationary as opposed to a thrown ball.

During late childhood the same basic principles apply. We must analyze the task that is to be learned, determine the amount of experience the child has had in the task, and then break the skill into meaningful components for learning by each individual child. Because of increased maturity and experience in a variety of motor skills, most children at this age are ready to learn skills that are necessary for participation in competitive individual and team sports. Children in this age group can learn to perform skills that are quite complex (following Bruner's hypothesis). However, there may be a need to modify the skills or the learning environment. For example, let us lower the basket and allow children the opportunity to practice shooting a smaller basketball. Let us introduce a lighter hockey puck. To our knowledge there is no research evidence that even slightly suggests detrimental learning and performance effects from modifying the learning medium or environment.

We would like to add that there is no place in the teaching of motor skills for sex-role stereotyping, either informally at home or formally at school. Girls and boys can and should learn the same type of motor skills and, if they are in school, at the same time.

Generally, fundamental skills should continue to be practiced during the adolescent period; however, increasingly more time should be devoted to the practice of the specific skills that are necessary in more specialized activities. For example, the child now has the strength and fundamental skills to execute moves on the parallel bars in gymnastics, difficult moves in figure skating, and the specialized skills that are indigenous to track and field events such as high jumping, pole vaulting, discus throwing, and javelin throwing.

Another guideline we can provide closely parallels the principle of general to specific skill learning. This principle is that of teaching styles or method of teaching general and specific skills. Our research as well as that of others suggests that during the early periods of fundamental skill learning *indirect* styles of teaching are preferred. The teacher should not make all of the decisions for the children; they should be allowed to explore and learn by doing as well as asking for assistance when it is needed. As more specialized skills are being learned, a more *direct* style of teaching appears to be more efficient and beneficial. Here the teacher controls more of the conditions related to learning. This is, in fact, what occurs in most coaching environments.

References

Ammons, R., Alprin, S., & Ammons, C. Rotary pursuit performance as related to sex and age of pre-adult subjects. *Journal of Experimental Psychology*, 1955, *49*, 127-133.

Åstrand, P. The child in sport and physical activity—physiology. In J. G. Albinson & G. M. Andrew (Eds.), *Child in sport and physical activity*. Baltimore: University Park Press, 1976.

Bachman, J. C. Motor learning and performance as related to age and sex in two measures of balance coordination. *Research Quarterly*, 1961, *32*, 123-137.

Bayley, N. A. The development of motor abilities during the first three years. *Monographs of the Society for Research in Child Development*, 1935, *1* (Serial No. 1).

Beach, F. A., & Jaynes, J. Effects of early experience upon the behavior of animals. *Psychological Bulletin*, 1954, *51*, 239-263.

Bouchard, C. Genetics and motor behavior. In D. M. Landers & R. W. Christina (Eds.), *Psychology of motor behavior and sport* (Vol. 2). Champaign, Ill.: Human Kinetics Publishers, 1977.

Bruner, J. *The process of education*. Cambridge, Mass.: Harvard University Press, 1963.

Carpenter, A. Tests of motor educability for the first three grades. *Child Development*, 1940, *11*, 293-299.

Clarke, H. H. *Physical and motor tests in the Medford Boys' growth study*. Englewood Cliffs, N.J.: Prentice-Hall, Inc., 1971.

Connolly, K., Brown, K., & Bassett, E. Developmental changes in some components of a motor skill. *British Journal of Psychology*, 1968, *59*, 305-314.

Cratty, B. J. *Perceptual and motor development in infants and children*. New York: Macmillan, Inc., 1970.

Cratty, B. J. *Movement behavior and motor learning*. Philadelphia: Lea & Febiger, 1973.

Cratty, B. J., & Martin, M. M. *Perceptual-motor efficiency in children*. Philadelphia: Lea & Febiger, 1969.

Cron, G. W., & Pronko, N. H. Development of the sense of balance in school children. *Journal of Educational Research*, 1957, *51*, 33-37.

Cumbee, F. Z. A factorial analysis of motor coordination. *Research Quarterly*, 1954, *25*, 412-428.

Davol, S., Hastings, M., & Klein, D. The effect of age, sex, and speed of rotary pursuit performance by young children. *Perceptual and Motor Skills*, 1961, *21*, 351-357.

Dennis, W. W. The effect of cradling practices upon the onset of walking in Hopi children. *Journal of Genetic Psychology*, 1940, *56*, 77-86.

Dennis, W. W. Causes of retardation among institutional children: Iran. *Journal of Genetic Psychology*, 1960, *96*, 47-59.

Di Nucci, J. M. Gross motor performance: a comprehensive analysis of age and sex differences between boys and girls ages six to nine years. In J. Broekhoff (Ed.), *Physical education, sports and the sciences*. Eugene: Microform Publications, University of Oregon, 1976.

Drowatzky, J. N. *Motor learning: principles and practices*. Minneapolis: Burgess Publishing Co., 1975.

Eckert, H. M. Age changes in motor skills. In G. L. Rarick (Ed.), *Physical activity: human growth and development*. New York: Academic Press, Inc., 1973.

Espenschade, A. Development of motor coordination in boys and girls. *Research Quarterly*, 1947, *18*, 30-43.

Espenschade, A. Motor development. In W. R. Johnson (Ed.), *Science and medicine of exercise and sports*. New York: Harper & Row, Publishers, 1960.

Fiorentino, M. R. *Reflex testing methods for evaluating CNS development*. Springfield, Ill.: Charles C Thomas, Publisher, 1970.

Fleishman, E. A., & Hempel, W. E. Changes in factor structure of a complex psychomotor test as a function of practice. *Psychometrika*, 1954, *19*, 239-252.

Fleishman, E. A. *The structure and measurement of physical fitness*. Englewood Cliffs, N.J.: Prentice-Hall, Inc., 1964.

Gedda, L. Sports and genetics, a study on twins (351 pairs). In *Health and fitness in the modern world*. Chicago: The Athletic Institute, 1961.

Gedda, L., Milani-Comparetti, M., & Brenci, G. A preliminary report on research made during the games of the Seventeenth Olympiad, Rome, 1960. In E. Jokl & E. Simon (Eds.), *International research in sport and physi-*

cal education. Springfield, Ill.: Charles C Thomas, Publisher, 1964.

Gesell, A. *The first five years of life*. New York: Harper & Row, Publishers, 1940.

Govatos, L. A. Sex differences in children's motor performance. In *Collected papers of the eleventh interinstitutional seminar in child development*. Dearborn, Mich.: Michigan Education Department of the Henry Ford Museum and Greenfield Village, 1966.

Gutteridge, M. V. A study of motor achievement of young children. *Archives of Psychology*, 1939, *244*.

Halverson, H. M. An experimental study of prehension in infants by means of systematic cinema records. *Genetic Psychology Monographs*, 1931, *10*, 107-286.

Holbrook, S. F. A study of the development of motor abilities between the ages of four and twelve, using a modification of the Oseretsky scale (Doctoral dissertation, University of Michigan, 1953) (University Microfilms No. 5537).

Holzinger, K. J. The relative effect of nature and nurture influence on twin differences. *Journal of Educational Psychology*, 1929, *20*, 241-248.

Hunsicker, P. A., & Reiff, G. G. A survey and comparison of youth fitness 1958-1965. *Journal of Health, Physical Education and Recreation*, 1966, *37*, 20-24.

Jenkins, L. M. *A comparative study of motor achievements of children five, six and seven years of age*. New York: Teachers College, Columbia University, 1930.

Johnson, R. D. Measurements of achievement in fundamental skills of elementary school children. *Research Quarterly*, 1962, *33*, 94-103.

Keogh, J. *Motor performance of elementary school children*. Los Angeles: University of California, Department of Physical Education, 1965.

Keogh, J. Fundamental motor tasks. In C. B. Corbin (Ed.), *A textbook of motor development*. Dubuque, Iowa: William C. Brown Co., 1973.

Klissouras, V. Genetic aspects of physical fitness. *Journal of Sports Medicine and Physical Fitness*, 1973, *13*, 164-170.

Klissouras, V. Prediction of athletic performance: genetic considerations. *Canadian Journal of Applied Sport Sciences*, 1976, *1*, 195-200.

Latchaw, M. Measuring selected motor skills in fourth, fifth, and sixth grades. *Research Quarterly*, 1954, *25*, 439-449.

Magill, R. A. Critical periods: relation to youth sports. In R. A. Magill, M. J. Ash, & F. L. Smoll (Eds.), *Children in sport: a contemporary anthology*. Champaign, Ill.: Human Kinetics Publishers, 1978.

Martinek, T. J., Zaichkowsky, L. D., & Cheffers, J. T. Decision-making in elementary age children: effects on motor skills and self-concept. *Research Quarterly*, 1977, *48*, 349-357.

McGraw, M. B. *Growth: a study of Johnny and Jimmy*. New York: Appleton-Century-Crofts, 1935.

McGraw, M. B. *The neuromuscular maturation of the human infant*. New York: Hafner Publishing Co., 1969.

McNemar, Q. Twin resemblances in motor skills and the effect of practice thereon. *Journal of Genetic Psychology*, 1933, *42*, 70-97.

Milne, C., Seefeldt, V., & Reuschlein, P. Relationship between grade, sex, race and motor performance in young children. *Research Quarterly*, 1976, *47*, 726-730.

Mussen, P. H., Conger, J. J., and Kagan, J. *Child development and personality* (4th ed.). New York: Harper & Row, Publishers, 1974.

Newman, H. H., Freeman, F. N., & Holzinger, K. J. *Twins: a study of heredity and environment*. Chicago: University of Chicago Press, 1937.

Rarick, G. L., Dobbins, D. A., & Broadhead, G. D. *The motor domain and its correlates in educationally handicapped children*. Englewood Cliffs, N.J.: Prentice-Hall, Inc., 1976.

Roberton, M. A. Stability of stage categorizations across trials: implications for the "stage theory" of overarm throw development. *Journal of Human Movement Studies*, 1977, *3*, 49-59.

Robertson, M. A. Stages in motor development. In M. V. Ridenour (Ed.), *Motor development: issues and applications*. Princeton, N.J.: Princeton Book Co., 1978.

Sage, G. H. *Introduction to motor behavior: a neuropsychological approach*. Reading, Mass.: Addison-Wesley Publishing Co., 1971.

Schilling, F. *Körper-koordination-test für Kinder KTK*. Weinheim: Beltz Test Gmbh., 1974.

Schilling, F., & Kiphard, E. The body coordination test. *Journal of Physical Education and Recreation*, 1976, *47*, 37.

Schull, W. J., & Neel, J. V. The effects of inbreeding on Japanese children. New York: Harper & Row, Publishers, 1965.

Shirley, M. M. Postural and locomotor development. In *The first two years: a study of twenty-five babies* (Vol. 1). Minneapolis: University of Minnesota Press, 1931.

Singer, R. N. Physical characteristics, perceptual-motor, and intelligence differences between third- and sixth-grade children. *Research Quarterly* 1969, *40*, 803-811.

Singer, R. N. *Motor learning and human performance*. New York: Macmillan, Inc., 1975.

Sklad, M. The genetic determination of the rate of learning of motor skills. *Study in Physical Anthropology*, 1975, *1*, 3-19.

Sukiennicki, D. A. Neuromotor development. In B. S. Banus (Ed.), *The developmental therapist*. Thorofare, N.J.: Charles B. Slack, Inc., 1971.

Tanner, J. M. *Fetus into man*. Cambridge, Mass.: Harvard University Press, 1978.

Vandenberg, S. G. The hereditary abilities study: hereditary components in a psychological test battery. *American Journal of Human Genetics*, 1962, *14*, 220-273.

Whiting, H. T. A. *Acquiring ball skill: a psychological interpretation*. London: G. Bell & Sons, Ltd., 1969.

Wild, M. R. The behavior pattern of throwing and some observations concerning its course of development in children. *Research Quarterly*, 1938, *9*, 20-24.

Williams, H. G. The perception of moving objects by children. Unpublished paper, University of Toledo, 1967.

Williams, L. R. T., & Hearfield, V. Heritability of a gross motor balance task. *Research Quarterly,* 1973, *44,* 109-112.

Wilmore, J. They told you you couldn't compete with men and you, like a fool, believed them. *Women Sports,* 1974, *1,* 40.

Wilson, R. S., & Harpring, E. G. Mental and motor de-velopment in infant twins. *Developmental Psychology,* 1972, *7,* 277-287.

Witte, F. Relation of kinesthetic perception to a selected motor skill for elementary children. *Research Quarterly,* 1962, *33,* 476-484.

Zaichkowsky, L. D. The development of perceptual-motor sequencing ability. *Journal of Motor Behavior,* 1974, *6,* 255-261.

Student projects

1. Observe an infant of 2 to 5 months. While work-ing with a parent and using the information from Table 3-1, attempt to elicit the listed reflexes.
2. Make an appointment to talk with a pediatrician directly, or call one on the telephone to discuss his or her use of reflex testing in infants. You may wish to ask what reflexes are evaluated and for what reason.
3. Do a process and product evaluation of children at different ages performing a variety of motor tasks. The following table may be used as a guide for this exercise. Use a separate table for girls and

boys. Your first task will be to find several boys and girls who represent the listed ages (cross-sectional data). Second, observe the children exe-cute each skill and pay particular attention to form (process). Record how the child focuses at-tention to the task, positions the body, utilizes preparatory movements, achieves smoothness of effort, and so forth. After form has been ob-served and recorded, record the distance, time, or number of successful catches (product). Plot these performance scores on a graph (separately for boys and girls).

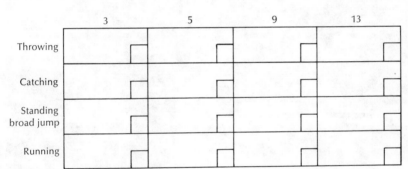

Record your process of evaluation in the large space and product measure in the lower right-hand box.

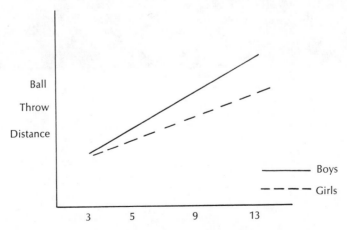

Example of graph plotting hypothetical throwing scores for boys and girls.

Chapter 4

DEVELOPMENT OF PHYSICAL FITNESS

Starts and Stripes

Survival of the human species has been due to man's ability to withstand a physically demanding and ever changing environment. Long before the days of civilized man the probability of survival was contingent on the physical fitness of each woman and man to perform rigorous tasks necessary for protection and shelter. Today physical fitness is no less a concern than it was hundreds of years ago.

Unfortunately, these concerns have not necessarily improved the fitness levels of today's society. In a recent report by the President's Council on Physical Fitness and Sport concern was expressed about the low fitness levels of American boys and girls. It was found that the majority of school children failed to meet minimum standards on a number of fitness tasks. This situation has been further compounded by a general decline in both elementary and secondary physical education programs. School physical education requirements are lowering at an alarming rate, with the result that only one out of three students is enrolled in a daily program. Worst of all, many schools with adequate personnel, facilities, and time allotment provide little emphasis on physical development. It is hoped that this trend will reverse itself.

Because modern technology has caused an increase in automation there is less opportunity for activity. We have consequently evolved into an "arm chair" society. Research clearly indicates that both physical and psychological diseases affecting adults arise from lifelong inactivity. Such conditions as high blood pressure, obesity, ulcers, and poor cardiorespiratory function can be partially attributed to a lack of physical activity.

Society's attitude toward fitness can become more positive by instilling in each child through formal and informal physical activity programs an understanding of the need for physical fitness. Even with the present humanistic focus on social-psychological development the concern for fitness still remains a central issue in program planning. In order to plan effectively it is important that the physical educator understand the basic principles of fitness development, as well as developmental factors influencing the well-being of the child and young adult.

The term "physical fitness" encompasses a number of different connotations: psychological well-being, cardiovascular endurance, restoration of physical capabilities, and performing well in various athletic events. The definition of fitness is multidimensional. The absence of a clear-cut definition may present problems for those practitioners who actively strive to develop programs for the promotion of physical fitness in children.

However, the Association for Research, Administration, Professional Councils, and Societies (ARAPCS), a division of the American Alliance for Health, Physical Education, and Recreation (AAHPER), has made an attempt to provide an operational definition of physical fitness. "Physical fitness was considered a multifaceted continuum which measured the quality of health ranging from death and diseases that severely limit activity to the optimal functional abilities of various aspects of life" (Plowman and Falls, 1978, p. 22). The committee differentiated physical fitness as it relates to "functional health from physical performance related primarily to athletic ability" (Plowman and Falls, 1978, p. 22). Some will recognize the differentiation between "functional health" and "physical performance" as the division of physical fitness into organic and motor fitness.

The committee further divided physical fitness relating to functional health into—

1. Cardiorespiratory function
2. Body composition
3. Abdominal and low back musculoskeletal function.

This chapter will be concerned mainly with the functional health aspect of physical fitness, as the physical performance aspect was covered in the chapter on motor skill development (Chapter 3).

CARDIORESPIRATORY FUNCTION

This is a specialized form of muscular endurance that involves the heart, lungs, blood, and vessels. Cardiorespiratory endurance is developed by continuous action of the large muscle groups in such activities as jogging, climbing, and bike riding. These activities require the heart to be strong enough to pump oxygen-rich blood through the blood vessels of the body to the working muscle groups. Frequently the ability of the body to sustain exercise is discussed in terms of *aerobic* and *anaerobic power*. Aerobic power refers to the amount of work possible for a period of 15 to 30 minutes through optimal activity resulting in the maximum delivery of oxygen to the working muscles. The aerobic capacity of the individual relies on the ability of the heart and lungs to resupply oxygen to the bloodstream and muscles during exercise. Anaerobic power refers to the amount of exercise possible in an all-out effort for a period of approximately 45 seconds. This is dependent on the natural oxygen supply capabilities of the blood (Larson, 1974).

BODY COMPOSITION

The major concern of this area is, of course, obesity. Many of you reading this chapter have concerned yourselves at one time or another with being overweight. Generally speaking it can be assumed that the worry over obesity exists mainly in adult populations. However, the incidence of obesity in young children has been found to be increasing in most industrialized countries. It used to be believed that "baby fat is a sign of good health." Consequently, many parents have been resistant to helping an obese child because they believe that the child will simply "grow out of it." The present-day attitude toward the baby fat myth has fortunately changed (Corbin, 1973). More and more parents and teachers have become sensitized to the fact that obesity is a problem that prevails in young children as well as adults. In fact there is convincing evidence to show that childhood obesity will continue into and throughout adult life (Corbin, 1973; Heald, 1966).

There are a number of causes of obesity in children. Abnormal levels of caloric intake, inactivity, poor habits, emotional discomfort, and hormonal disorders are only a few of the many reasons why children become overweight. In many instances the ego state of parents causes a child to overeat because the child is taught not to waste food. Statements such as, "To waste food is sinful," "Think of all the starving people in China," or "There will be no dessert unless you finish everything on your plate"

further reinforce overeating habits. Although all of these factors have a significant influence on childhood obesity, studies have further indicated that physical activity plays an even more important role (Corbin and Pletcher, 1968; Rarick, 1973) in the reduction and maintenance of body weight. It has been demonstrated that even when participating in some activity, the obese child proves less active than the normal one (Rarick, 1973). The importance of physical activity to weight control will be discussed in more detail later in this chapter.

MUSCULOSKELETAL FUNCTION

This component of physical fitness deals with the "maintenance of minimal levels of trunk and hip strength/endurance and flexibility" (Plowman and Falls, 1978, p. 23). We will therefore discuss these three components separately.

Strength

Strength refers to the ability to exert force, such as lifting or pulling weight or lifting your own body. Strength is influenced by the size of the muscle and tonal quality. In most instances maturation, exercise, heredity, and good nutritional habits affect the quality and size of the various muscle groups. The majority of exercises require several muscle groups to be involved. This is true particularly with more complex activities. However, in all types of exercise the strength of the muscle is directly related to the amount of work during the exercise.

Strength is displayed in a number of ways. Arnheim and Pestolesi (1978) list three separate strength attributes. The first is *explosive strength,* which is used when one is performing an activity that requires immediate and spontaneous use of muscular energy. Examples would be jumping or running short distances. The second type is *static strength.* This refers to exerting force on an immovable object, thereby causing little change in muscle length. All the isometric exercises employ the use of static strength. Third, *dynamic strength* refers to the muscles' ability to exert repeated contractions. This is muscular endurance, which will be discussed next.

Muscular endurance

This is the ability of a muscle or groups of muscles to sustain repetitive contractions over a long period of time against a moderate resistance. Muscular endurance is generally related to strength. The main difference is that strength requires fewer contractions and is specific to the muscles exercised, whereas muscular endurance involves a greater number of contractions with moderate resistance. Examples of muscular endurance are represented in exercises such as sit-ups and push-ups.

Flexibility

The ability of various body segments to move through normal ranges of motion is called flexibility. Efficient movement is contingent on the flexibility of joints specific to various types of activities. Arnheim and Pestolesi (1978) describe two distinct types of flexibility unique to specific movements: *extent flexibility,* the ability to flex the torso of the body in various directions, and *dynamic flexibility,* the ability to perform spontaneous stretching muscular contractions.

ASSESSING PHYSICAL FITNESS

Many tests have been developed to test some or all of the components of fitness. Because fitness is multidimensional and physical education classes large, it is more tenable to assess fitness in terms of a selected number of fitness components than to try to develop a test that measures *everything.* The selection of items to include is dependent rather on personal decision and should reflect the philosophical intentions of the physical education program. We encourage the use of those tests that have been developed and established for use with specific age populations. The majority of tests provide some normative data for the purposes of comparing group and individual performance scores. The use of normative comparisons provides teachers with feedback on the fitness status of their students and helps identify those who may need special attention. It is not recommended that young children go through formal physical fitness testing. Since many of the fitness components in tests would not be apparent at the ages 5 to 7, it would be more beneficial for the teach-

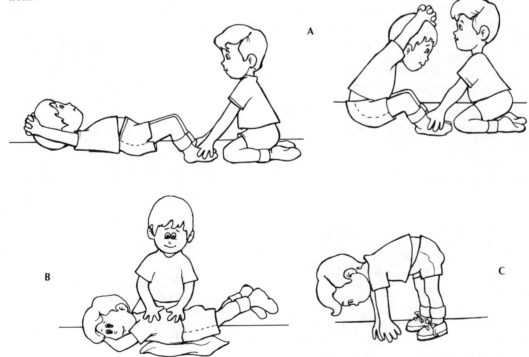

Fig. 4-1. Three examples of items from the Kraus-Weber Test. **A,** Bent-knee sit-up. **B,** Leg lift. **C,** Flexibility.

er to look at specific items in the development of basic motor skills.

Among the most commonly used tests to assess physical fitness of children are the Kraus-Weber Fitness Test and the Revised AAHPER Fitness Test. The Kraus-Weber (Kraus and Hirschland, 1954) test is a six-item test that measures *minimum muscular strength* and *flexibility*. Fig. 4-1 illustrates some of the six subtests of the Kraus-Weber test. This test has historical significance in that it was found that 57.9% of American children failed one or more items in contrast to only 8.7% of European children. It is interesting that the one item that American children had the most difficulty with was the item that measured the flexibility of hamstrings. One reason for this might have been that the national sport of European countries is soccer. Since the physical demands of soccer focus more on leg action than on upper body movements found in American basketball

and baseball, these differences may have been due to cultural factors.

One of the most widely used fitness tests was developed by the President's Youth Fitness Council and it is called the AAHPER Youth Fitness Test. The test (norms have been established for the fifth-grade through college populations) has been revised once and is undergoing a second revision. This second refinement will include four functional health items. These proposed tests are distance run test, skinfold measure of body fat composition, flexed-knee sit-up, and a sit-and-reach test (Plowman and Falls, 1978). Illustrations of the proposed items are shown in Fig. 4-2.

Recently Bailey and co-workers (1976) reported on the validation of a self-administered home test of cardiovascular fitness. The test was devised to initiate and sustain personal interest in the cardiorespiratory fitness of Canadian youths and adults. Unfortunately, the test

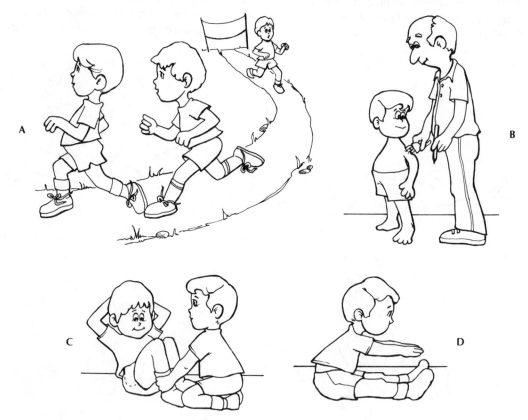

Fig. 4-2. Examples of proposed test items from newly revised AAHPER Youth Fitness Test. **A,** Distance run. **B,** Skinfold measure for body fat. **C,** Flexed-knee sit-up. **D,** Sit-and-reach test.

was not validated for children below 15 years of age.

AGE AND SEX DIFFERENCES IN PHYSICAL FITNESS

In order to optimize the chances for a child's total fitness development it is important for the teacher and parent to be aware that improvement in physical fitness will not be the same at every age. Corbin (1973) refers to "critical development stages" as focal points of concern when developing physical activity programs for a wide range of ages. If these were considered, children could concentrate on those areas of fitness that are developmentally appropriate for their specific ages. Therefore it is essential for the teacher to know the various fitness potentials characterized within different developmental stages of a child's life.

Infancy and early childhood

Most of us view physical fitness as the ability to lift heavy objects (strength), to run without tiring (endurance), or to play a good game of tennis. It is apparent, however, that the concepts of fitness for the infant and toddler take on different meanings. During this developmental period children are more capable of developing fitness skills that are necessary for basic movements such as crawling, walking, and running. Therefore it is important that the parent and teacher encourage activities that help to develop fitness qualities of agility, coordination, and balance that enable the child to perform these basic movements. Once these qualities are mastered, they can be used later in life to perform activities that will develop other areas of fitness. Nevertheless, we should not neglect the development of strength and flexibility. Providing an environment that will encourage the toddler to develop basic fitness skills is essential. In the home rolled-up socks or newspapers crunched into balls for kicking and manipulating are common pieces of "equipment" that an infant or toddler will choose to play with. Outside, fitness components are developed by "jumping down," "climbing up," and "hanging from upside-down" places. Chairs, stairs, spoons, balls, the backyard tree, or even parents' shoulders are everyday things that can be provided for children to play with and thereby discover various physical capabilities. Many nursery schools now provide unique and challenging pieces of playground equipment, which provide children with large movement opportunities that enhance strength, flexibility, and endurance (Riley et al., 1979).

During this period there should be no reason to provide formal periods of exercise, since the child, under "normal" conditions, will acquire the necessary skills through everyday activity. However, in special situations with the handicapped child more structured experiences need to be provided so that the child can acquire these skills. It is recommended that the parent of the handicapped youngster consult with the school physical educator, recreation specialist, or family physician for suggestions of activities to include in the child's program (Riley et al., 1979).

Late childhood and adolescence

Up to this point studying characteristics of fitness of various developmental stages has shown that there are very few differences between boys and girls. It is not until about first or second grade that sex differences begin to occur. Fig. 4-3 illustrates a comparison of fitness scores between girls and boys across an age range of 7 to 18 years. As one can see there is a linear increase for both sexes from 7 to about 12 years, with boys showing slightly higher degrees of fitness than girls. After 12 years there is a dramatic increase for boys, while girls show a decline or leveling off.

Although Fig. 4-3 represents an overall fitness difference between girls and boys, it is equally important to look at these age and sex differences in relation to various fitness components.

Cardiorespiratory function. As defined earlier, cardiorespiratory endurance refers to the heart's ability to supply oxygen to working muscles. In the developing child this ability depends on the size of the heart and large blood vessels in the body. It was believed many years ago that too much exercise was dangerous to the working heart of the young child (Corbin, 1973). Young (1923) thought that there was a

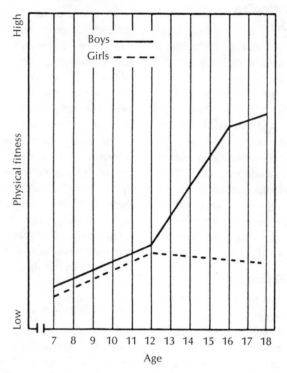

Fig. 4-3. Comparison of males and females for various ages on overall fitness. (From C. Corbin. The physical fitness of children: a discussion and point of view. In C. Corbin (Ed.), *A textbook of motor development*. Dubuque, Iowa: William C. Brown Co., 1973.)

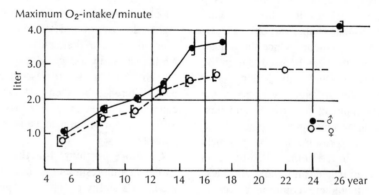

Fig. 4-4. Average values for maximal oxygen intake in relation to age. (From P.-O. Åstrand. *Experimental studies of physical working capacity in relation to sex and age.* Copenhagen: Munksgaard, 1952.)

discrepancy between the development of the size of the heart muscle and the size of large blood vessels. He thought that because the vessels developed at a relatively slower rate than the heart, the vessels would not be able to handle the blood flow created by a faster-growing heart. This was especially noticeable by the age of 7 and continued to get worse as the child grew older.

However, this belief was found to be untrue due to a simple but obvious error in Young's assumptions. Although the size of the vessels was smaller in proportion to the heart of younger children compared to older children, the blood-carrying capacity remained proportionate to heart development. Therefore what appears to be a vessel growing slower than the heart is one that is still capable of carrying blood in proportion to a growing heart's ability to supply it (Corbin, 1973; Karpovich, 1937).

There are several ways in which cardiovascular endurance can be measured. Åstrand (1976) suggested that maximum oxygen intake is the most valid method of assessing cardiorespiratory fitness in children. In a comprehensive study by Åstrand developmental comparisons were made using measures of maximum oxygen uptake with children and adults. Fig. 4-4 illustrates the results of this study from 141 subjects 4 to 18 years of age running on a treadmill. It can be seen that there is a gradual increase with age in oxygen uptake from the age of 13, with boys increasing their uptake at a higher rate than girls. This difference between boys and girls was more obvious when taking body weight into account. It was noted that the increase in weight has a more negative effect on oxygen intake with girls than with boys. Ås-

trand points out that in nonobese children the body weight gives a rough estimate of maximum oxygen intake; that is, improvement with age is mainly due to the increase in body size. This size is reflected in an increase in muscle mass. During the onset of puberty girls have an increase in fat tissue, rather than muscle size; this may account for the dramatic discrepancy between the two sexes at age 13.

Other studies have also looked at age differences in relation to heart-rate responses. Many of these studies were the result of early concerns about high heart rates in children during exercise. However, Corbin (1973) reported that this concern was unnecessary, and recent literature has proven that children are capable of having much higher heart rates than was originally believed. Table 4-1 shows that maximal heart rates exceed those of adults. We can also see that children are quite capable of achieving high heart rates in maximum work periods. Furthermore, there is a decrease in heart rate with age as well as a decrease in resting rate. This may be largely due to the increased size of the heart and subsequent increase in the blood volume pumped during ventricular contractions. Lastly, there is little sex difference in maximal heart rate for children, although adult women tend to show higher rates than men (Corbin, 1973).

Another area of research closely related to oxygen-intake and heart-rate indices is work capacity of children (Adams et al., 1961; Corbin, 1973). In general, studies have found that physical work capacity increased with age. In fact Corbin (1973) contends that age is a better predictor of work capacity than most fitness tests. It was also found that girls have a lower

Table 4-1. Maximal heart rates by age and sex*

Sex	Age					
	4-6	**7-9**	**10-11**	**12-13**	**14-15**	**16-18**
Male	203 ± 2.2† 7.0	208 ± 2.4 8.4	211 ± 2.3 8.1	205 ± 4.1 17.7	203 ± 4.1 12.8	202 ± 3.1 9.2
Female	204 ± 5.0 13.2	211 ± 2.0 7.5	209 ± 2.5 8.8	207 ± 2.8 10.0	202 ± 2.2 6.6	206 ± 2.5 7.7

*Modified from Åstrand, P. *Experimental studies of working capacity in relation to sex and age.* Copenhagen: Munksgaard, 1952.

†Numbers represent mean, standard error of the mean, and standard deviation.

work capacity than boys across all age groups. This may be due to cultural as well as physiological reasons. Girls may not be expected to do as much work as boys and therefore perform according to their perceived expectations. It is interesting to note that in one study comparing Swedish and American children it was found that although there was little cultural difference, boys continued to perform better than girls in both cultural groups (Adams, et al., 1961).

Body composition. During the onset of the school years we find a linear increase in fat tissue along with an increase in age. Table 4-2 shows the lower limits of obesity for male and

Table 4-2. Obesity standards for caucasian Americans

| Age (years) | Minimum triceps skinfold thickness indicating obesity (millimeters) | |
	Male	Female
5	12	14
6	12	15
7	13	16
8	14	17
9	15	18
10	16	20
11	17	21
12	18	22
13	18	23
14	17	23
15	16	24
16	15	25
17	14	26
18	15	27
19	15	27
20	16	28
21	17	28
22	18	28
23	18	28
24	19	28
25	20	29
26	20	29
27	21	29
28	22	29
29	22	29
30-50	23	30

*From Seltzer, C. C., & Mayer, J. A simple criterion of obesity. *Postgraduate Medicine,* 1965, *38,* 101. © McGraw-Hill Book Co. By permission.

female white Americans based on skinfold measurements of the triceps area. Since the triceps skinfold measure is considered representative of body fatness, these estimates are assumed to to be valid measures of obesity (Corbin, 1973).

Girls across all ages generally have a higher disposition of fat than boys. It is important to note that this difference is especially significant during puberty, when girls' fat deposits continue to increase while boys' show a slight decrease. Most girls will stay slightly plump during the two years of puberty and then slim down as they get further into adolescence. For example many girls will trim down around age 15 without great difficulty. This is important for the teacher and parent to know so that this weight incease does not become a central issue (Spock, 1969).

As we look further at the "fat child syndrome" across various ages, the problems of obesity also assume linear proportions. Obesity is a serious problem for the child during the school years. The majority of plump children entering school become acutely aware of how others feel about their fatness. This especially true for children at the age of 7. They perceive that parents, teachers, and peers feel sorry for them and find that their fatness interferes with their capacity to be involved with active play (Hurlock, 1964). Consequently, they become lonely and isolated. It is also during this age that the child begins to draw away from the parents and relies heavily on social relationships in the school environment. Unable to make friends easily, the child becomes depressed and subsequently overeats in order to satisfy his frustration. The problem becomes a vicious circle where, no matter how hard the child tries, social rejection continues and overeating is subsequently reinforced.

During puberty obesity becomes an even greater physical and social problem. This is especially true for the adolescent girl, since it is during this period that society places special emphasis on the feminine figure and views it as a prime qualitative feature for social acceptance. It is during this time that children begin to totally withdraw from social involvement such as dates, dances, and athletic events and accept their obesity as a permanent character-

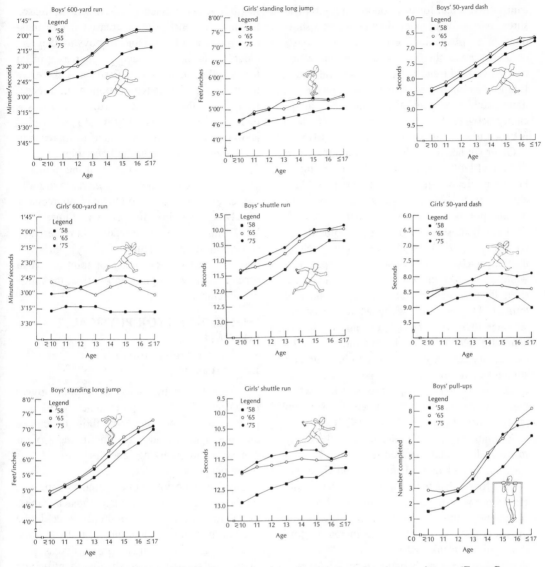

Fig. 4-5. Age and sex differences on a number of strength and endurance items. (From P. Hunsicker and G. Reiff. Youth fitness report: 1958-1965-1975. *Journal of Physical Education and Recreation,* 1977, *48,* 32.)

istic to be with them through life. As a result of their rejection and isolation they are prevented from learning how to get along in social situations. As they grow older, this will have damaging consequences in their ability to cope with the demands of society.

Musculoskeletal function. Development studies in physical fitness have looked at a number of different parameters of the child's strength and muscular endurance capabilities. Hunsicker and Reiff (1977) provided one of the

more comprehensive studies by administering the AAHPER Physical Fitness Test to a national sample of girls and boys in 1958, 1965, and 1975. Fig. 4-5 graphically illustrates the AAHPER test, which purports to measure strength and muscular endurance.

The performance for boys appears to increase with age, especially around the pubescent period. This is due to increased muscle size and consequent working capacity of the muscle groups. For girls the performance is significantly lower than for boys on all strength measures. It was found that unlike boys, girls show more of a "plateauing" effect during the onset of adolescence. In fact there is an indication of a downward trend for girls on several items. It is interesting to note that for most of the test items both boys and girls improved significantly between 1958 and 1965; however, there is very little change between 1965 and 1975.

Other studies have also looked at ethnic and racial and influences on strength performances. For example Malina (1968) found that black children, 6 to 12 years, had greater grip pushing and pulling strength values than white children for both sexes. However, Montpetit and co-workers (1967) found greater grip strength in black girls, 9 to 17 years, as compared to white girls. On the other hand, greater grip strength was demonstrated in black boys 9 through 11 years old, while white boys were stronger thereafter through the age of 14. In general it is said that black boys and girls in the elementary school years appear to have greater strength than whites. During adolescence both black and white boys appear to be equal, while black girls continue to show greater strength gains than white girls (Malina, 1973).

Available research indicates that flexibility of musculoskeletal function is very much joint specific. For example Hupprich and Sigerseth (1950) found that with 6-, 9-, and 12-year-old girls there was decreasing (with age) flexibility in the knees, thighs, and shoulder joints. As the girls increased in age there was increased flexibility in the trunk and wrist and with leg abduction. A recent study by Di Nucci (1976) confirms this specificity, since in some measures of flexibility there was increased performance and in other cases decreased performance with age. Females appear to maintain greater flexibility than males. Early studies by Phillips et al. (1955) and Kirchner and Glines (1957) showed that at every age level from 6 to 12 girls were superior to boys in hamstring flexibility (toe touching) on the Kraus-Weber Fitness Test. Although sex differences on the other test items were minor, girls appeared to be more muscularly fit because of the unique differences in flexibility of the two sexes.

Di Nucci (1976) recently reported that girls performed better than boys on all five tests of flexibility. As previously discussed the reason for this difference is the increased size of muscle groups and tone found in boys as they get older. Girls, however, acquire increases in fat tissue rather than muscle tissue and therefore maintain a greater range of motion. In a recent study by Krahenbuhl and Martin (1977) it was demonstrated that flexibility in adolescent girls and boys was negatively related to increase in body size, especially in the knee joint.

It is also important to note that the influence of Title IX legislation and the increase in girls' participation in active sports may appreciably affect the flexibility difference in future findings. Although we do not expect a remarkable change in the musculature of today's girls, we may find that the specificity of joint action in certain sports will significantly affect the range of movement.

IMPLICATIONS FOR PHYSICAL EDUCATION
Cardiorespiratory function and physical activity

Numerous programs for developing fitness have been offered to the practitioner. These programs cover a spectrum from those developed and based on sound research finding, to ill-conceived programs designed to "rip off" as many people as possible.

Physical educators and researchers appear to be the logical ones to evaluate physical fitness programs. At least two approaches could be used to make this evaluation: (1) to look at the longitudinal effects of proposed fitness programs and (2) to systematically identify and study factors that influence the improvement of fitness, such as the type of activity, frequency of practice, and the intensity of the physical activity. It would seem that the second alternative is a better approach, and there have been some encouraging first steps taken in that direction (Franks, 1975).

It is generally assumed that physical activity and fitness go hand in hand. A study by Stewart and Gutin (1976) examined the effects of an eight-week physical training program on the cardiorespiratory fitness of fifth- and sixth-grade boys. The training program was conducted within regular physical education classes four times per week for eight weeks. Interval running was the method used, with varied periods of work-recovery bouts. A control group that did not participate in the program was also used in order to make baseline comparisons. The results of the study demonstrated that an intense program of short-term physical training did not increase aerobic efficiency. However, it was interesting to note that although aerobic efficiency did not change, decreases in heart rate were evident. This is unique, since the well-trained individual is characterized by high aerobic efficiency and a slow heart rate during exercise. It was apparent that outside activity of the experimental and control children was significantly influencing the responses to short-term physical training. It was further suggested that most children of this age group are naturally active and can operate at maximal cardiorespiratory potential without short-term training (Stewart and Gutin, 1976). Therefore it would appear that a longer and more intense program would be required for the elementary school child if cardiorespiratory improvement is to be found.

Other factors that might interact with cardiorespiratory endurance during training programs were studied by Cureton and Sterling (1964). They factor analyzed 101 test items associated with cardiorespiratory endurance and found the following eight factors most influential:

1. Blood ejection rate
2. Oxygen requirement
3. Pulse pressure after work
4. Body weight
5. Pulse recovery time after easy work
6. Endurance in all-out treadmill run
7. Heart rate
8. Aerobic capacity

The relationships between these factors were not significant; this finding indicates the need for a broader approach to evaluating the effects of exercise programs for endurance than using a single test. Gutin and co-workers (1978) demonstrated the dominance of body composition and size in accounting for the variability of endurance performance in adolescent girls. The weight factor was very important in activity that requires the transport of the body over long distances. It was also noted that the variability in body fat during adolescence was a function of growth rates and that in girls increase of fat tissue is a natural secondary sexual characteristic.

Body composition and physical activity

As mentioned earlier in this chapter an often neglected condition of our youth is obesity. Certainly the concerns for the obese child should be no less than those for other special children. According to Pargman (1968, p. 115) the "disability of obesity in childhood, recognized by physicians, psychologists, and parents of obese children as a significant liability in social and physical experiences, might also be profitably scrutinized by elementary, junior high, and senior high school teachers." Recognizing the potential effects of physical activity programs on weight reduction, Rohrbacher (1972) investigated the effects of a developmental camp program based on success-type activities on weight change, body image, and self-concept. Two hundred and four obese boys underwent an eight-week special camp program. The boys ranged in age from 8 to 18 years and were drawn from all 50 states and 3 foreign countries. The results of the program showed significant weight losses, with all subjects losing an average of 15 kg (33 lbs.). It is interesting that it was also found that the special camp had a positive influence on body image but not self-concept. This finding added credence to the theory that self-concept is a rather stable construct for this particular age group. Furthermore it appears that weight loss has little effect on the variability of the construct.

Rohrbacher also looked at long-range effects of the camp experience and found that a trend toward weight gain continued after the camp but at a slow rate. It was therefore suggested that obesity has a tendency to persist and that the continuance of special assistance in regular physical education and camp programs is essential for longevity of weight control.

Musculoskeletal function and physical activity

Studies have looked at programmatic conditions affecting muscle strength and endurance. For example, Hellebrandt and Houtz (1956) found that strength and endurance increase when repetitive exercise is performed against heavy resistance. It was found that the amount of work done per unit of time is a critical variable upon the limits of performance.

Williams (1969) found that junior high school girls participating in a rope-climbing conditioning program improved significantly in arm and shoulder strength. It was also found that a group training with the bent-arm hang did nearly as well as those in the rope-climbing group, while a push-up training group scored the lowest on arm and shoulder strength. All three groups showed significant gains over a control group receiving no training program.

There has been considerable debate regarding femininity and the development of strength in girls. It is generally assumed that girls who work to strengthen muscles are actually more concerned with improvement of their figures than muscle development. Indeed, we have all seen examples of the girl athlete who is "muscular" and therefore have quickly labeled her as masculine. Corbin and co-workers (1974) maintain that this association probably stems from the fact that muscular girls are apt to be more successful in such sports as track and field. Consequently the boundaries for such generalizations are quite restricted. In fact it has been shown that properly designed programs actually enhance femininity, and because of the physiological makeup of girls there is very little likelihood that the average girl will develop oversize muscles.

Instructional strategies and physical fitness

While concerns for program implementation have always remained a central issue, physical educators and coaches have also begun to look at the appropriateness of instructional strategies in the development of fitness. Studies by Dougherty (1970), Keller (1963), and Scott (1967) provide recent information dealing with the effect of teaching styles on fitness development. In Keller's study formal and informal styles of teaching were compared. He defined formal and informal methods in terms of a program consisting of one instructional class and two laboratory periods. During the laboratory periods the students were expected to achieve specific goals with no opportunity to interact with the teacher. It was found that there was no significant difference between the two styles in the development of fitness or sports skills. Scott also found no significant difference in the area of physical fitness, but he did find that the informal method was more effective than the formal method in developing creative ability.

Dougherty looked at three specific styles of teaching proposed by Mosston (1966): the command, the task, and the individual. The styles of teaching used in this study were not significantly different from one another in terms of overall fitness improvement between pretreatment and posttreatment tests. However, an interesting occurrence was noted. The command group achieved significantly greater gains between pretreatment and midtreatment testing than either the task or individual program group. Between the midtreatment and posttreatment tests this trend reversed itself, with the effect of the three treatments being equivalent. According to Dougherty (1970) the reason for this variation in the rate of improvement was that calisthenic-type activities involve discomfort when done vigorously. Therefore it was necessary for the individual and task groups to "learn" to push themselves in order to achieve optimal improvement. This was not present in the command style, where the instructor set goals and was able to command the students beyond their initial levels of physical discomfort. In other words, if there is to be only a brief training period for the development of physical fitness, then it appears that the command style would be the most efficient method of instruction. On the other hand, if time is not a concern, then any of the three styles appears to be equally effective.

In our opinion the most important factor in total fitness development is being physically active. In order to be fully involved in reasonable periods of activity it is essential that one explore different ways of enjoying physical activity. Over the spectrum of physical activity (aquatics to Zen) it is likely that some will be enjoyable. As a result we may get rid of the persistent negative attitudes toward participation in physical activity. Perhaps one explanation for negative attitudes is that physical activity is often used as a punishment. Another may be overemphasis on competition at higher skill levels rather than emphasis on equal competition at all levels of skill. Mosston (1970) maintains that many of the prevailing negative attitudes are the result of poor methodologies that exclude children from activities rather than including them. Perhaps even the actions of parents and other adults make the purpose of physical activity seem unimportant. Whatever the case, the extent to which we make physical activity fun will determine whether fitness is for the majority or for just a few.

References

Adams, F. H., Linde, L. M., & Hisazumi, M. The physical working capacity of normal children (Pt. 1). *Pediatrics,* 1961, *28,* 55.

Arnheim, D. D., & Pestolesi, R. A. Elementary physical education: a developmental approach (2nd ed.). St. Louis: The C. V. Mosby Co., 1978.

Åstrand, P. *Experimental studies of working capacity in relation to sex and age.* Copenhagen: Munksgaard, 1952.

Åstrand, P. The child in sport and physical activity—physiology, In J. G. Albinson & G. M. Andrews (Eds.), *Child in sport and physical activity.* Baltimore: University Park Press, 1976.

Bailey, D. A., Shephard, R. J., & Mirwald, R. L. Validation of a self-administered Home Test of Cardiorespiratory Fitness. *Canadian Journal of Applied Sport Sciences,* 1976, *1,* 67-78.

Corbin, C. *A textbook of motor development.* Dubuque, Iowa: William C. Brown Co., Publishers, 1973.

Corbin, C., Dowell, L., Lindsey, R., & Tolson, H. *Concepts of physical education.* Dubuque, Iowa: William C. Brown Co., Publishers, 1974.

Corbin, C., & Pletcher, P. Diet and physical activity patterns of obese and nonobese elementary school children. *Research Quarterly,* 1968, *39,* 922-926.

Cureton, T. K., & Sterling, L. F. Factor analysis of cardiovascular test variables. *Journal of Sports Medicine and Physical Fitness,* 1964, *4,* 1-4.

Di Nucci, J. M. Gross motor performance: a comprehensive analysis of age and sex differences between boys and girls ages six to nine years. In J. Broekhoff (Ed.), *Physical education, sport and the sciences.* Eugene: Microform Publications, University of Oregon, 1976.

Dougherty, N. J. *A comparison of the effects of command, task, and individual program styles of teaching in the development of physical fitness and motor skills.* Unpublished doctoral dissertation, Temple University, 1970.

Franks, D. *Review of the effects of regular, vigorous physical activity with implications for exercise prescription.* Paper presented to Institute of Physical Fitness, Boston University, 1975.

Gutin, B., Trinidad, A., Norton, C., Giles, E., Stewart, K., & Giles, A. Morphological and physiological factors related to endurance performance of 11 to 12 year old girls. *Research Quarterly,* 1978, *49,* 44-52.

Heald, F. P. Natural history and physiological basis of adolescent obesity. *Federation Proceedings,* 1966, *25,* 4-7.

Hellebrandt, F. A., & Houtz, S. J. Mechanisms of muscle training in man: experimental demonstration of the overload principle. *Physical Therapy Review,* 1956, *36,* 371-383.

Hunsicker, P. A., & Reiff, G. G. Youth fitness report: 1958-1965-1975. *Journal of Physical Education and Recreation,* 1977, *48* (1), 31-33.

Hupprich, F. L., & Sigerseth, P. D. The specificity of flexibility in girls. *Research Quarterly,* 1950, *21,* 25-33.

Hurlock, E. B. *Child development.* New York: McGraw-Hill Book Co., 1964.

Karpovich, P. V. Textbook fallacies regarding the development of a child's heart. *Research Quarterly,* 1937, *8,* 33-36.

Keller, R. J. *A comparison of two methods of teaching physical education to secondary school boys.* Unpublished doctoral dissertation, University of Illinois, 1963.

Kirchner, G., & Glines, D. Comparative analysis of Eugene, Oregon elementary school children using the Kraus-Weber Test of Minimum Muscular Endurance. *Research Quarterly,* 1957, *28,* 16-25.

Krahenbuhl, G. S., & Martin, S. L. Adolescent body size and flexibility. *Research Quarterly,* 1977, *48,* 797-799.

Kraus, H., and Hirschland, R. Minimum muscular fitness tests in school children. *Research Quarterly,* 1954, *25,* 178-182.

Larson, L. A. (Ed.). *Fitness, health, and work capacity: international standards for assessment.* New York: Macmillan, Inc., 1974.

Malina, R. M. *Growth, maturation, and performance of Philadelphia Negro and white elementary school children.* Unpublished doctoral dissertation, University of Pennsylvania, 1968.

Malina, R. M. Ethnic and cultural factors in the development of motor abilities and strength in American children. In L. Rarick (Ed.), *Human growth and development.* New York: Academic Press, Inc., 1973.

Montpetit, R. R., Laeding, L., & Montoye, H. J. Grip strength of school children, Saginaw, Michigan: 1899-1964. *Research Quarterly,* 1967, *38,* 231.

Mosston, M. *Teaching physical education.* Columbus, Ohio: Charles E. Merrill Pub. Co., 1966.

Mosston, M. *Inclusion and exclusion in education.* Somerville, N.J.: INEDCO Press, 1970.

Pargman, D. The obese child, the teacher's responsibility. *Educational Horizons,* 1968, *46,* 115-117.

Phillips, M., Bookwalter, C., Denman, C., et al. Analysis of results of Kraus-Weber test of minimum muscular fitness in children. *Research Quarterly,* 1955, *26,* 314-318.

Plowman, S. A., & Falls, H. B. AAHPER Youth Fitness Test revision. *Journal of Physical Education and Recreation,* 1978, *49* (9), 22-24.

Rarick, G. L. (Ed.). *Human growth and development.* New York: Academic Press, Inc., 1973.

Riley, M., Barrett, K. R., Roberton, M., & Martinek, T. J. *Physical activity and your child's well-being.* Washington, D.C.: Health, Education and Welfare Printing Office, 1979.

Rohrbacher, R. Influence of a special camp program for obese boys on weight loss, self-concept, and body image. *Research Quarterly,* 1972, *44,* 150-157.

Scott, R. S. A comparison of teaching two methods of physical education with grade one pupils. *Research Quarterly,* 1967, *38,* 151-154.

Seltzer, C. C., & Mayer, J. A simple criterion of obesity. *Postgraduate Medicine,* 1965, *38,* 101.

Spock, B. *Baby and child care.* New York: Pocket Books, 1969.

Stewart, K. J., & Gutin, B. Effects of physical training on cardiorespiratory fitness in children. *Research Quarterly,* 1976, *47,* 110-120.

Williams, B. J. *Three exercise programs' effectiveness in developing junior high school girls' arm and shoulder and ability to perform a pull up.* Unpublished master's thesis, University of Washington, 1969.

Young, E. *Hygiene of the school age.* Philadelphia: W. B. Saunders Co., 1923.

Student projects

1. Examine several fitness tests that have been consistently used by schools, for example, AAHPER, Kraus-Weber, and so forth. Describe the items in terms of their ability to measure functional health or motor fitness attributes. List the items that correspond to the two fitness attributes. From your examination do you see the tests as biased toward one specific area of measurement?

2. Observe a first-, fourth-, and eighth-grade physical education class. Identify the obese child in each of the three classes and describe some of the difficulties in skill performance that are influenced by the child's obesity. Also describe some of the unique social and behavioral characteristics of the three children that can be attributed to their age as well as obesity.

3. Youth sports make many physical demands on children who participate. Sometimes these demands are inconsistent with the developmental and physical readiness of the child. Observe a youth football, soccer, and baseball practice and identify some of these inconsistencies prevalent during the practice drills and games. Describe how these inconsistencies appear to affect the overall performance and motivation of the children.

Chapter 5

PERCEPTUAL-MOTOR DEVELOPMENT

Over the years the hyphenated term perceptual-motor has taken on a variety of meanings for different people. As a result a certain amount of confusion exists regarding the topic. To some perceptual-motor refers to all overt motor skills; the hyphen merely serves to express the interdependence of perceptual and motor responses. To others perceptual-motor has erroneously come to be associated with so-called perceptual-motor programs, which have sprung up all over North America to deal with children who have cognitive, emotional, and motor problems. For these people perceptual-motor means a remedial program designed to overcome learning deficits.

It is our hope that this chapter will clarify some of the issues surrounding the broad topic of perceptual-motor development. First there will be a theoretical overview that tackles definition. Second, the development of the various perceptual modalities, including the perception of body awareness, will be discussed. Last, the implications of perceptual-motor development for physical education will be examined. This chapter will differ from many of the others in that the development of the various perceptual modalities across all four developmental stages will generally not be discussed. Since the bulk of perceptual development occurs during infancy and the early childhood years, the discussion will, by and large, be confined to these two developmental stages.

WHAT IS PERCEPTUAL-MOTOR DEVELOPMENT?

As you read this page your eyes are focused on the printed words, your ears pick up the noise of a fan in the room, and you may even be writing down some notes. All that is occurring in the above example could appropriately be termed perceptual-motor. The first two events, namely, vision and hearing, start off being received by specialized receptors (eyes and ears). We term this reception *sensations*. However, sensations must then be organized and interpreted in the brain to be meaningful. It is this organization and interpretation that we term *perception*. The writing down of notes is primarily an overt motor event, but it should be noted that we do actually receive sensory infor-

mation during the execution of motor responses. Thus, it is not difficult to understand why we have coined the term perceptual-motor, for indeed all of our overt motor behaviors require a strong perceptual component. Fig. 5-1 illustrates the perceptual-motor system. In summary it can be said that the perceptual-motor system contains the following components: (1) a sensory (afferent), (2) a central processing (perception), and (3) an overt motor (efferent) response.

Since Chapter 3 dealt essentially with the motor component of the perceptual-motor system, this chapter will describe the development of the perceptual component. When the word "perception" is used, most of us think of visual perception. This is somewhat understandable in that vision is the dominant sense in most people; however, as Fig. 5-1 illustrates, it is not the only source of sensory input. We can have auditory (hearing), tactile (touch), kinesthetic (awareness or feeling), olfactory (smell), and gustatory (taste) perception.

In complex motor performance we rely on all of our senses to perform efficiently in an *integrated* manner. Although perceptual processes may develop somewhat independently of motor responses, we cannot perform motor skills without perception (Cratty, 1970a). For a more extensive discussion of this point consider an example that illustrates the integration of various perceptual modalities. A baseball player uses vision to perceive the velocity, location, and spin of the ball; the player's ears detect subtle movements of the catcher, perhaps by cuing location of the pitch; the hands squeeze the bat, thereby providing pressure; the player is aware of the location of the arms and bat (kinesthesis), and possibly the player tastes the bubble gum or chewing tobacco and smells the hot dogs in the stands (it is hoped that the batter will not be focusing attention on the latter two events).

On the basis of the preceding discussion, which spelled out what perception referred to as well as its documented relationship to motor activity, it can be said that perceptual-motor development refers primarily to changes in a child's sensoriperceptual processes as a function of age. With increasing age a child is better

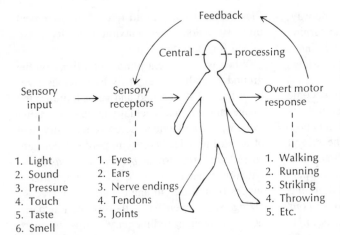

Feedback

Central — processing

Sensory input → Sensory receptors →

Overt motor response

1. Light
2. Sound
3. Pressure
4. Touch
5. Taste
6. Smell

1. Eyes
2. Ears
3. Nerve endings
4. Tendons
5. Joints

1. Walking
2. Running
3. Striking
4. Throwing
5. Etc.

Fig. 5-1. Perceptual-motor system (From "What Psychological Variables Are Important in an Individual's Movement?" by Leonard Zaichkowsky/Lois Smith in *Introduction to Physical Education: Concepts of Human Movement* edited by John Cheffers, Tom Evaul, © 1978, p. 107. Adapted by permission of Prentice-Hall, Inc., Englewood Cliffs, New Jersey.)

able to process complex sensory information. Since this is intricately related to motor responses, the child also has better control over motor acts such as running, catching, throwing, and hitting.

Williams (1973) points out that as children grow older the changes in the sensoriperceptual components are of three major forms: (1) a shift in the hierarchy of the dominant sensory systems; (2) an increase in intersensory communication; and (3) an accompanying improvement in intrasensory discrimination. The shift in dominance of the sensory system is characterized by a shift from early tactile-kinesthetic dominance in children to a primary reliance on visual information. More specifically, during the early years (infancy) a child relies heavily on information gained from fondling objects and perhaps tasting them. However, in later years the more sophisticated visual system begins to take over as the dominant source of information for regulating motor acts.

The second developmental change in sensoriperceptual processes is that of improved intersensory communication. With increasing age the child is able to rely effectively on numerous modalities for useful information in regulating motor behavior. Rather than relying exclusively on one modality, the child is able to utilize multimodal information efficiently.

The third change that reflects a more mature sensoriperceptual process is the development of increased discrimination capabilities by the various modalities. In essence the child is able to see better, hear better, and respond to other

stimuli with greater facilitation; finer discriminations are being made. As a result of this increased sensory control greater motor control is also developed.

MEASURING PERCEPTUAL ABILITIES

Measuring the development of perceptual abilities in young children is a difficult task methodologically. By and large infants are not cooperative subjects when it comes to experimentation. Nevertheless, several ingenious methods have been developed to measure the various parameters of visual perception. The most general technique involves simple experimenter *observation*. The observer notes behavioral changes such as attention, motor behavior, excitement, and so forth when various stimuli are presented. The work of Gibson and Walk (1960) exemplifies the observational technique (see p. 71) (Fig. 5-2). A second technique that attempts to determine whether infants can perceive various stimuli involves the monitoring of physiological responses such as heartbeat and respiration. This technique assumes that perception of a novel stimulus (visual or auditory) stimulates the infant's physiological processes. As the infant becomes habituated to the stimulus, there is generally a deceleration in responses such as heartbeat. An example of such a study is Bridges' (1961). A third technique employs principles of conditioning and is perhaps best exemplified by the experimentation of Bower (1966). Basically researchers such as Bower teach the infant to make a response such as head turning to a stimulus; then the stimulus is changed in some way, and the researcher notes whether head turning occurs. If the response does occur, it is interpreted as an indication that the infant considers the two stimuli similar.

Experimentation with children does become easier as they increase in age and become verbal. We can then simply ask them what and how much they can see, what they can hear, and where the sound is coming from. Although the earlier-described experimental techniques, particularly the physiological and conditioning ones, are ingenious, we must be cautious in our interpretation of the results, since our assumptions regarding infant responses to stimuli may not be correct.

COMPONENTS OF THE PERCEPTUAL-MOTOR SYSTEM: PERCEPTUAL MODALITIES
Visual perception

The topic of visual perception is so broad and extensive that whole books have been written on specialized aspects of it. Instead of dealing with all the concerns surrounding visual perception, the topics of perceptual acuity, perceptual constancies, depth perception, and the perception of moving objects will be covered. Those wishing a more extensive treatment of visual perception are referred to the references.

Visual acuity (clearness of vision) will introduce the topic of visual perception, since it pertains to the basic question, How well can a child see? Up until the time of Fantz's (1961) pioneering work in infant perception it was thought that neonates could see very little, if anything. Fantz, using the technique of presenting paired stimuli, demonstrated that neonates preferred to look at patterns rather than gray fields. Based upon this observational technique Fantz (1965) reported, in a later publication, that infants can see stripes of 1 mm (⅛ in.) at a distance of 22.5 cm (9 in.) from the eyes; at 3 months of age the infant can see 0.4 mm (¹⁄₆₄ in.) stripes at a distance of 67.5 cm (15 in.). Pick and Pick (1970) in reviewing the literature on visual acuity in infants reported that infants 0 to 1 month have Snellen vision in the range of 20/150 and 20/400. Beyond this age Pick and

Pick report a fairly rapid rate of improvement until 10 years, when maximum acuity is attained for most children.

When we observe a jumbo jet airliner on the ground, we all marvel at its tremendous size. As it lifts off the ground and gains altitude, the image on the retina is actually quite small; however, we are still able to perceive the initial size of the airliner. This ability to perceive constant size is referred to as *perceptual constancy.* Other constancies include shape (recognizing shapes from different angles) and color (recognizing colors even when there is partial darkness). Although rudimentary forms of these constancies are present during the first months of life, most have a developmental course that extends through early childhood.

Related to the constancy phenomenon is *object permanence,* the ability to perceive the existence of an object that has been removed from visual contact. If you present a 2-month-old infant with a toy, then put a screen between the child and toy, remove the toy and then the screen, the 2-month-old will show some surprise, indicating that the infant expected the toy to still be there. Although the child will not search for the toy, there is some evidence of early object permanence (Bee, 1978). By about 6 months the infant exhibits greater signs of object permanence. If a toy is dropped over the edge of a crib, the infant will look for it. Also at about this age a child will search for an object that is partially hidden. However, if the object is completely covered, the infant will not bother to search for it even if he viewed the covering. Between the ages of 8 and 12 months the infant begins to search for covered objects, indicating that at about 1 year most infants have grasped the fact that objects continue to exist even though they cannot see them.

Depth perception is a necessary skill for size constancy. Its developmental course, however, is not certain. Theorists and researchers cannot agree on whether depth perception is present at birth, develops as the nervous system matures, or is dependent on learning. The classic study by Gibson and Walk (1960) on an apparatus called the "visual cliff" provides some hard evidence that infants are capable of perceiving depth at least as early as 6 months.

Fig. 5-2. Visual cliff experiment; infant is capable of perceiving depth at very young age.

Gibson and Walk designed an apparatus that resembled a table covered with a clear glass (Fig. 5-2). Under the glass was a checkerboard pattern; however, part of the table had this pattern considerably below the table top, thus bringing about an illusion of depth. Mothers would station themselves at the "cliff side" of the table and coax the infants to crawl toward them. Most children perceived the depth of the "cliff" and did not crawl toward their mothers.

Bower (1966) has also provided some evidence showing that infants are capable of perceiving depth as early as 2 to 3 months. In the Bower study children were trained to respond (head turning) to cubes placed in front of their eyes. By moving the cubes away from the child in a systematic manner Bower was able to determine that infants did in fact respond to depth cues. This was interpreted as meaning that infants did have depth perception, but the mechanism they used to perceive depth was motion parallax rather than binocular parallax. Motion parallax means that the view of a three-dimensional object changes when you move your head. These changes do not occur when you move your head while viewing two-dimensional objects. The cues obtained from binocular parallax are a result of the fact that the two

eyes are several centimeters apart in the head and consequently receive a slightly different image.

We also have more crude observational data on infants around 3 to 4 months suggesting that they possess some form of depth perception. When objects are placed within grasping range, the infant will invariably attempt to grasp the object. When the object is out of grasping reach, the infant will rarely grab for it.

The now-classic study by Held and Hein (1963) strongly points to the fact that movement, particularly self-induced, is necessary for the adequate development of depth perception. Held and Hein raised kittens in the dark until the age of 8 to 12 weeks, thus incorporating a research technique generally referred to as deprivation. The kittens were then exposed to visual stimulation three hours per day in a unique manner. One, called the experimental kitten, was paired with another (the control kitten) at opposite ends of a pivoted bar. The bar was set inside a vertically striped cylinder, and the kittens were harnessed in such a manner that the experiemental animal walked the control animal around the cylinder (Fig. 5-3). Both kittens were deprived of seeing their limbs and other body parts. The control kitten was raised off the floor and hence did not move itself; it received a free ride. When tested for depth perception on a "visual cliff," the experimental kittens made appropriate depth responses, whereas the control kittens displayed random responses when presented with illusions of depth. This very clever experiment demonstrated not only that movement was important for the development of certain perceptual abilities, but also that visual perception is dependent upon experience. One is not born with endowed perceptual abilities.

Perception of moving stimuli. Despite the increased concern for perceptual development in the last several decades few experimental studies have investigated the perception of movement, either of objects in space or children's own bodies. Pick and Pick (1970) point out that many more studies have looked at children's responses to apparent movement (sequencing lights that adults perceive as moving) than to true movement. Nevertheless, a few

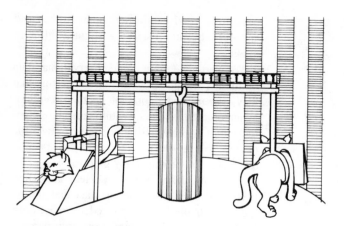

Fig. 5-3. Experiment demonstrating effect of movement on development of perception in kittens.

significant studies have made some interesting revelations about the perception of movement.

Most of us have undoubtedly observed that infants are extremely captivated by objects moving in their visual field. It is not difficult to get a very young infant to track a large slowly moving object. Haith (1966) has reported that infants as young as 3 to 5 days old will respond to the intermittent movement of a visual stimulus. The novelty of the stimulus does not appear to wear off, since the infant continues to track the object even after repeated presentations. At 1 month the infant is capable of following an object through an arc of 90 degrees. During the next several months the ability to track objects through a greater range of motion increases. In addition the child can track faster-moving objects and can even follow the object as it reverses its field. It is also at this time that the infant begins to notice movements of its own arms and legs and becomes fascinated by them. As the infant matures, she continues to be impressed with the movement of balls, cars, and other inanimate and animate objects; at the same time she increases her ability to track the object accurately from the center to the periphery of her visual field.

One of the best studies to investigate the development of the perception of moving objects during the childhood years was that conducted by Williams (1967). In a cleverly designed study Williams had children ages 6 to 11 years old judge the speed and direction of a projected ball. The children were asked to move as quickly as possible to a spot where they thought the ball would land. The children never received feedback regarding the actual landing of the ball past its initial projection because a canvas ceiling interrupted the flight of the ball. As would be expected, the older children were significantly more accurate than the younger children in estimating the flight of the ball. Williams noted some interesting sequential changes in the development of this particular perceptual skill. Children in the age range 6 to 8 years did not seem capable of monitoring their motor behavior with visual information. When the ball was projected, these children would run as fast and as far as they could, thereby consistently overshooting the true landing point. Nine-year-old children, however, began making accurate but slow judgments; this suggests that at this age children are capable of using visual information to control their motor behavior, but slowly. The 10-year-old children displayed even different characteristics. They responded more quickly than the 9-year-olds to the moving stimulus but were less accurate in their judgments; in essence they sacrificed accuracy for speed. The 11-year-old children demonstrated a more fully developed interphase between the perceptual and motor components since they responded both quickly and accurately.

The research evidence just presented on visual perception points out that in contrast to motor abilities some visual abilities are highly developed at a very young age. For example, it was pointed out that the newborn is capable of seeing objects quite clearly, particularly if the objects are presented within a restricted range. Further, evidence was presented showing that development of object permanence is nearly complete by 1 year and that infants are capable of perceiving depth by at least 6 months and quite probably as early as 3 months.

Infants are likewise sensitive and responsive to moving objects; however, the perception of motion, particularly when it pertains to controlling locomotor activity, continues to improve through the childhood years.

Auditory perception

Auditory, like visual, perception is a complex process that contains many identifiable subskills. Some of these subskills include: awareness (ability to indicate that there is sound or no sound), discrimination (ability to recognize differences in sounds), localization (the awareness of source or direction of sound), figure-ground differentiation (ability to select relevant from irrelevant stimuli), and memory (ability to store and recall what one has heard).

Although the experimental research in auditory development is sparse, there are data regarding the development of the first three subskills in infants. The other auditory subskills have been investigated and described more in clinical settings where children, because of diagnosed deficits in auditory perception, have impaired language development, motor development, and basic intellectual functioning.

Numerous research studies using indicators such as changes in cardiac response, direction of gaze, and motor activity level have demonstrated that infants are sensitive to sound from birth onward. Wertheimer (1961), for example, showed that infants only 2 minutes old moved their eyes in the direction of a series of sounds. This would seem to indicate that infants are not only sensitive to sound but are also aware of the directional source, something we call auditory localization. Kessen and co-workers (1970) present an excellent review of numerous other studies that demonstrate early competence in auditory perception.

Attempts have also been made to quantify infants' sensitivity to other properties of sound, such as intensity and frequency or pitch. Some of the early attempts were futile because of the use of crude instruments for emitting these sound properties, for example, squeak of a

rubber rat, the crinkling of paper, and other assorted sound-makers. There does, however, seem to be a consensus among researchers that infants display differential responses to sounds of high and low frequency (Pick and Pick, 1970). It is generally found that low-pitched sounds tend to quiet a distressed infant, while high-pitched sounds tend to cause "freezing" behavior followed by agitation. Perhaps this is why parents almost universally coo to their fussy infants in low-pitched voices.

Auditory acuity in older children has not been studied as extensively as it has been in infants. There is, however, one study that provides at least some descriptive data on the auditory skills of school-age children. Eagles and co-workers (1963), using a large sample of children between the ages of 5 and 14, reported increased sensitivity to sound until age 13. At the age of 14 there was a slight decrease in sensitivity. It should be pointed out, however, that the difference between the 5- and 13-year-olds was very slight (6 to 7 db). Because a large number of subjects were used the differences were statistically significant. Whether this difference is functionally significant is open to question.

Touch, taste, and smell

The perceptual modalities of vision and audition were described as complex yet rather advanced, even in the infant. The following three modalities, sometimes referred to as the "lower senses," are not considered advanced in infants. It is also true that considerably less research has been conducted on these "lower senses." It is commonly believed that infants are relatively insensitive to pain stimuli, even those born free from effects of the mother's medication. Sensitivity appears to be greater in the region of the head than of the extremities. This is, of course, consistent with the principle of cephalocaudal and proximodistal development. An interesting sex difference has been reported by Lipsitt and Levy (1959). Using shock as a pain stimulus the researchers concluded that girls were more sensitive to pain than boys.

Very few studies have been conducted on the development of taste and smell. We do know that children have a larger distribution of taste buds in their mouth than adults, but it is not known whether this means children have greater sensitivity to taste. Many parents testify unequivocally that their children are sensitive to taste even during infancy. Cake and ice cream seem to taste better than vegetables. It is also known that the newborn is capable of responding to odors by turning away from unpleasant ones such as ammonia or acetic acid (Mussen et al., 1974).

In general it seems that infants show some early sensitivity with the lower senses and that this sensitivity increases up to early childhood, at which time children are capable of mature responses.

SEX DIFFERENCES IN PERCEPTION

There is relatively little definitive information available regarding possible sex difference in perceptual skills. The limited literature does, however, conclude that girls have a lower tolerance for pain and are more responsive to taste differences than boys. No one has speculated on the practical significance of these small differences. Maccoby and Jacklin (1974) have gathered a tremendous amount of data on possible sex differences in perception and basically conclude that boys and girls are remarkably similar in responsiveness to visual and auditory cues.

PERCEPTION OF THE BODY, OR BODY AWARENESS

At the outset of this chapter it was indicated that the thrust of the chapter would be to describe developmental changes in the perceptual component of the perceptual-motor system. By this we meant that we would deal with perception of such modalities as sight, sound, touch, taste, and smell. It would be remiss in the discussion of perceptual-motor development not to deal with the development of perception about one's own body, something we term *body awareness*. One could logically argue (and rightly so) that the development of body awareness characteristics should be discussed with the development of fine and gross motor skills, cognition, or, for that matter, language. Body awareness does indeed have implications for the development of all these skills, but since a great number of perceptual-motor theorists (partic-

ularly those who have developed remedial programs) pay a great deal of attention to the development of body awareness characteristics, we have chosen to discuss body awareness in this section of the text.

Body awareness characteristics are numerous, poorly understood, and often provide as much confusion to readers as they do to the children who are in the process of developing these characteristics. In the literature are such terms as laterality, lateral dominance, lateral awareness, body part identification, right-left awareness, directionality, and so forth. An attempt will be made to provide some structure, definition, and a description of the developmental course of these body awareness characteristics.

The newborn infant is not capable of perceiving much about its body; however, during the first month there appears to be at least a crude awareness that his body is distinct from the surroundings. Although this may not be a "true conscious" awareness, it may be what Piaget calls a prereflective awareness. As the child grows, he becomes cognizant of his capabilities in moving arms, legs, head, and trunk. Later on as the child learns to recognize verbal cues (or labels), he is capable of identifying a body part with a particular word. The ability to *label body parts* is therefore one of the first body awareness characteristics a child develops. Although there is little normative data in the literature, our interactions with infants indicate that children as young as 12 to 15 months are capable of accurately identifying body parts such as nose, ears, eyes, hands, and feet, first on their own bodies and then later on other people. As these children get older and are exposed to experiences that increase their body part vocabulary, they are capable of accurately identifying most body parts. Data from Ilg and Ames (1966) indicate that by the age of 5 years, 80 percent of the children were able to name their eyes, and about 50 percent were able to identify eyebrows. For some children, then, eyebrows are not an early part of the vocabulary. Williams (1973) indicates that at age 5 years, 55% of the children accurately describe their body parts, and this ability increases in a linear manner until age 12 years, at which time there is 100% accuracy. Williams also points out the importance of vocabulary development and environmental interaction (adult influences) for the mature development of this ability.

The development of *laterality,* the ability to distinguish between the two sides of the body, is developed quite early in most children. Although the child may not have the verbal labels left and right, he does in fact have the conscious notion that there are two hands, two feet, two eyes, and so on, and that they are on two different sides of the body. It is thought that the development of laterality is really the foundation for the development of other body awareness characteristics. After children develop what we have called laterality (3 to 4 years), they begin to attach the verbal labels left and right to these distinctly different sides of the body. Although left and right are in the child's repertoire of words, he is not capable of correctly labeling the two sides of the body. The correct labeling of the two sides of the body is termed *lateral awareness,* a process that is usually not fully developed until about 7 years. Although most researchers are interested in the development of left-right characteristics, other body spatial descriptions such as front-back and up-down are also developed. In fact these relationships (front-back, up-down) are developed before left-right awareness (about 3 to 4 years).

A term that is often confused with laterality is *lateral dominance.* Lateral dominance is merely a preference for use of the left or right hand, left or right foot, and left or right eye. If no dominance is reflected, an individual is referred to as *mixed dominant.* Dominance is usually assessed (informally) by observing the hand and noting which hand is preferred in throwing, cutting, and writing tasks. With the foot one likewise observes which foot is preferred for hopping and kicking. The dominant eye is usually designated as the preferred eye in aiming at an object or some similar task.

The development of preferential handedness, eyedness, and footedness is a most interesting process, one in which there is still incomplete understanding and some myths. Areas of controversy include the following: whether the preferred use of one of the hands, eyes, or feet is something we are genetically endowed with or is something we learn; whether incomplete or mixed dominance results in cognitive, emotional, and psychomotor disorders; and how hand, eye, and foot dominance are related to cerebral dominance (one side of the cerebral cortex is physiologically dominant in interpretive functions).

Handedness has been investigated more than all the other dominance characteristics put together. It appears that during infancy children employ the use of both hands in playing with toys and "shoveling" food into their mouths. At 1 year of age the infant does not appear to have a preferred hand. Some parents consciously encourage the infant to develop a preferred hand by placing toys and other objects in the infant's right hand. As the child approaches late infancy (2 years), she begins to prefer the use of one hand. According to the data of McCarthy (1972), at the age of 2½ about 58% of the children have established a dominant hand. Table 5-1 shows that by age 3, 70% have established hand dominance. It is interesting to note that this figure does not change much until age 8½; this suggests that there is a certain amount of ambivalence between the ages of 3 and 7 regarding the development of a dominant hand. An interesting cross-cultural study by Motegi (1977) showed that hand dominance is not nearly so complete in Japanese children. Although the percentage was nearly the same for 2½-year-olds as that reported by McCarthy, children between the ages of 3 and 4½ are markedly lower in the development of hand dominance. At ages 4 and 4½ less than 50% of the Japanese children had established hand dominance. This is a significant contrast to the 70% figure reported by McCarthy on American children. Data from Belmont and Birch (1963) also add that by age 11, 94% of the children have established hand dominance; the remaining 6% are mixed dominant.

The development of footedness, according to Belmont and Birch (1963), is different from handedness and eyedness in that children establish an early clear-cut preference for a particular foot (Table 5-2). By age 5, 94% of the children in the Belmont and Birch study had estab-

Table 5-1. Hand dominance by age*

Age group	N	Right-handed	Left-handed	Total	Percent with dominance not established	Percent not scorable
		Percent with dominance established†				
2½	102	53.9	3.9	57.8	33.3	8.8
3	104	66.3	3.9	70.2	24.0	5.8
3½	100	70.0	2.0	72.0	26.0	2.0
4	102	67.7	3.0	70.7	27.5	2.0
4½	104	64.4	5.7	70.1	27.9	1.9
5	102	66.6	3.9	70.5	29.4	0.0
5½	104	66.4	5.8	72.2	27.9	0.0
6½	104	67.3	3.8	71.1	28.8	0.0
7½	104	71.2	3.8	75.0	23.1	1.9
8½	106	80.2	4.7	84.9	15.1	0.0

*Reproduced from the McCarthy Scales of Children's Abilities by permission. Copyright © 1970, 1972 by the Psychological Corporation. All rights reserved.

†To be categorized as dominance established a child had to be observed and rated on at least three of the four items on hand dominance, and all of his ratings (whether three or four) had to be consistently right-handed or consistently left-handed. All children who were rated on at least three of the four handedness items, but who did not respond with the same hand each time, were categorized as dominance not established. Children who were rated on two or fewer items (due to items not administered because of the limits of testing, items refused by the child, or the examiner's failure to record hand preference) were categorized as not scorable. However, a few children who were rated on only two items and responded inconsistently to them were categorized as dominance not established.

Table 5-2. Laterality preferences for children (5 to 11 years)*

	Handedness (%)	Eyedness (%)	Footedness (%)
Right	76	53	85
Left	10	21	12
Mixed	14	26	4

*Data from Belmont, L., & Birch, H. G. Lateral dominance and right-left awareness in normal children. *Child Development,* 1963, *34,* 257-270.

lished foot dominance. It has been our experience that children as early as 15 months prefer to use only one foot in kicking a ball.

Eye preference does not exhibit the same degree of lateralization as foot and hand preference. Twenty-six percent of the 5 to 11-year-old children in the Belmont and Birch study failed to exhibit a clear-cut preference for the use of one eye.

An interesting finding from the laterality research is that there are low correlations between preferences for a specific hand, foot, or eye. Many people incorrectly believe that if an individual is right-handed she will also be right-eyed and right-footed. This is not necessarily the case. The reported low correlations indicate that if one is left-handed, there is a good chance that this individual will not be left-eyed or left-footed. Further, if there fails to be consistency across handedness, eyedness, and footedness, there will not necessarily be learning problems or psychomotor problems—a common misconception. Although there is considerable controversy regarding incomplete dominance, left-handedness, and learning disabilities, there are some theoreticians who strongly believe that lateral dominance is a necessary condition for avoiding learning problems.

Before concluding the discussion on handedness a brief comment will be made on the interesting ongoing debate regarding the genesis of handedness, namely, whether handedness is learned or inherited. Most of the available cross-cultural data on incidence of handedness point out that about 90% of the adult human population uses the right hand for skilled activities. You will note that the McCarthy data for children through 8½ years show an 80% incidence of right-handedness, suggesting that handedness is not yet complete at this age. Numerous studies have been carried out during the past hundred years in an attempt to determine the genesis of the 90% right-handed phenomenon. A recent comprehensive review by Hicks and Kinsbourne (1976) shows that Wilson reported on a topic called "palaeolithic dexterity" as early as 1885.

Collins (1970) is probably the most avid supporter today of a learning/cultural influence on the development of a preferred hand. He provides some very interesting human and animal studies to support his claim. Hicks and Kinsbourne claim, however, that the overwhelming evidence supports a genetic explanation of handedness. A more recent study by Coren and Porac (1977) using a most unusual "historic" technique also lends some support for a genetic predisposition for left- and right-handedness. Coren and Porac sampled over 1100 pieces of art work from a period spanning 500 years and demonstrated that the incidence of right-handedness before 3,000 B.C. was about 90%, and that this figure has not changed significantly to the present. It is indeed remarkable that this research technique demonstrated similarity in incidence of right- and left-handedness over a period of 50 centuries. Our thoughts on the controversy of the origin of handedness are similar to those of Cratty who stated, "Eye, hand, and foot preference seem initially to be determined by heredity and are later molded by subtle social and cultural pressures" (Cratty, 1970a, p. 42).

Directionality refers to the ability to identify and relate objects or people other than self to each other in terms of left and right (Chancy and Kephart, 1968). In other words, a child has mature directionality capabilities when it is no longer necessary to refer to his own body to conceptualize about positions and directions of objects in external space. It is speculated that this conceptualization is an outgrowth of the development of awareness of one's own body first. That is, it is first necessary for a child to develop an adequate reference system within himself before it is possible to relate objects to each other in external space in terms of right and left. There does seem to be some support for this developmental notion, since lateral awareness is mastered by most children by the

age of 7, but directionality skills are not mastered until about 9 years. Perhaps an example will more clearly illustrate the difference between directionality and its hypothesized precursor, lateral awareness.

If one were in a room looking at two chairs with each chair in a different half of the room, the observer (if mature) should conclude that one chair is in the right half of the room and the other object is in the left half. The terms right and left half are totally dependent upon the location of the person who is viewing them. If another individual was located in the same room but facing a different direction, the labels right and left would be incorrect. In this case where the terms left-right are dependent upon the position of the observer, we are employing the use of lateral awareness.

Suppose the concern is not with where the chairs are in relationship to the observer but with where they are in relationship to each other. The observer must then state which chair is to the right or left of the other, without consciously referring to her own body. The observer in essence must place herself in the position of one of chairs and relate this to the position of the other chair. This skill is termed directionality.

It is speculated that incomplete development of lateral awareness and directionality leads to a variety of learning disorders such as having difficulty in distinguishing between *b*'s and *d*'s, inability to read maps, and difficulty in performing certain mathematical computations. Although this hypothesis seems entirely logical, there are presently few empirical data to support or refute it.

The measurement of these body awareness characteristics, namely, laterality, lateral awareness, and directionality, has been confined to a few instruments that require subject-examiner interaction (Belmont and Birch, 1963; Benton, 1959; Elkind, 1961; Harris, 1957). For example, a child might be told, "Raise your right hand, touch your left ear" (lateral awareness) or asked, "Is the pencil to the right or to the left of the penny" (directionality). It is our opinion that some of the inconsistencies regarding the development of body awareness characteristics and its implications can be attributed to a lack of adequately standardized measuring instruments. A recent instrument developed by Lockavitch (1977) seems to hold promise for improved research findings in this controversial area.

SEX DIFFERENCES IN BODY AWARENESS

Although there have been suggestions made that more boys tend to be left-handed than girls and further that they exhibit more confusion in lateralization (Brain, 1945; Hildreth, 1949), the studies of Belmont and Birch (1963) and Harris (1957) failed to verify this. Belmont and Birch concluded from their study that boys and girls do not differ on right-left awareness. The "hard data" therefore indicate that no significant sex differences exist in the development of body awareness characteristics.

IMPLICATIONS FOR PHYSICAL EDUCATION
Relationship between perceptual, motor, and cognitive abilities

At the beginning of this chapter it was pointed out that the hyphenated term perceptual-motor referred to the fact that perceptual and motor processes are interdependent components of a moving, growing, and learning individual. It could also be said cognitive processes interact with the perceptual-motor system. The interaction of perceptual, motor, and cognitive processes can perhaps best be depicted by Fig. 5-4.

There are some experimental data that support the position that perceptual, motor, and cognitive processes are interrelated in some ways. For example, evidence was presented earlier from the Held and Hein (1963) experiment showing that movement was necessary in kittens for adequate perceptual development. On the whole it is safe to say that the existence of this relationship is based more on observation and intuition than "hard" experimental data (for example, observations that children with learning disabilities have perceptual problems, motor problems, and often emotional problems). Nevertheless, several psychologists, educators, and other professionals have such a strong conviction regarding the relationship between cognitive, perceptual, and motor abilities that they have proposed so-called percep-

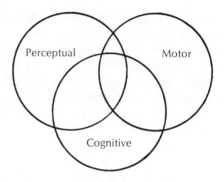

Fig. 5-4. Interrelationship between perceptual, motor, and cognitive processes.

tul-motor theories that attempt to show causal connections between these three processes. In other words these theorists maintain that movement is essential for the development of perceptual skills and that both of these skills are essential for cognitive development. According to some theorists (Frostig, 1966) perceptual deficits are responsible for learning disabilities in children. This discussion of the relationship between movement and cognitive development is continued and further elaborated on in Chapters 6 and 7. At this time, however, an overview of selected theories that postulate a causal relationship among perception, movement, and cognition is provided.

Perhaps the most controversial theory is that proposed by Doman and Delacato (1959). Doman and Delacato believe that many perceptual, motor, and cognitive disabilities stem from inadequate *neurological organization*. Doman-Delacato's central concept is based on the assumption that as the human organism grows, there is successive development of the brain and spinal cord. Doman and Delacato believe that perceptual-motor and cognitive disabilities can be remediated through a process called "patterning." Their treatment, among other prescriptions, calls for passive and active responses relating to crawling, creeping, and walking. In essence they attempt to restructure the organization of the developing nervous system so that the child can reach full development. It should be pointed out that the Doman-Delacato theory has been heavily criticized by both educators and medical specialists. Although positive case studies have been reported in the literature, no experimental studies support the efficacy of the theory.

Kephart (1960) has advanced a perceptual-motor theory that involves educating the peripheral functions, rather than central nervous system functions. It is Kephart's belief that the inadequate development of certain motor skills may tend to inhibit the child's development in later, more sophisticated skills. Kephart argues that today's complex society no longer offers the child the opportunity to explore his environment, and thus he develops the improper perceptual-motor match. If children do not learn to match sensory data to motor data, difficulties in reading, writing, and movement activities result. Therefore, perceptual inefficiency is suggested as a major cause of initial failure in school. While research results on the effectiveness of this program are contradictory, Kephart's theory and program have received widespread support among special educators, psychologists, and physical educators.

Barsch (1968) has supported Kephart's hypothesis by claiming that perceptual processes (visual, auditory, tactual, kinesthetic, gustatory, and olfactory) are antecedents to intellectual development. The quality of perceptions, as suggested by Barsch, is derived from the maturation of skills of movement efficiency.

From earlier efforts by Barsch (1965) came the development of his Movigenic Theory. This theory relates learning to efficient movement patterns. It suggests that movement efficiency is a prime requisite to the total architecture of the human organism. According to the Movigenic Theory the organism matures as it moves. The increased use of symbols begins to replace motoric ways of learning, although symbolic fluency is initially dependent on efficient movement patterns.

Frostig's training programs have specifically emphasized visual perception as it relates to motor ability (Frostig, 1966). It is her belief that it is important to develop several basic visual skills. These are visual and motor coordination, figure-ground perception, perceptual constancy, perception of positions in space, and perception of spatial relationships. The motor aspects of Frostig's program are agility, coordination (eye-hand), flexibility, strength, balance, and endurance (Frostig, 1970).

Getman (1962), an optometrist, has advanced the theory that a child's growth, intellectual development, and behavior are related to movement experiences and visual development. Getman contends that the majority of learning experiences depend on visual perceptions. His perceptual-motor program is organized around six stages—

1. General motor patterns (creeping, walking, hopping)
2. Special movement patterns (eye-hand coordination)
3. Eye movement patterns (matched movement for both eyes)
4. Visual language patterns (effective communication patterns)
5. Visualization patterns (visual memory skills)
6. Visual perception organization

Summary of perceptual-motor theories and programs

We have reviewed the basic philosophies of a number of theoreticians who have speculated on the relationship between perceptual, motor, and cognitive abilities. These theories all contain programs that are specifically designed to enhance perceptual, motor, and cognitive development. Interestingly enough, these theories have much in common. The common denominators appear to be—

1. Training to improve basic sensory skills (visual, auditory, tactile)
2. Fine and gross motor activities to improve basic motor skills and facilitate perceptual-motor integration
3. Emphasis on transfer of perceptual-motor abilities to cognitive functioning
4. Primarily designed for children who have learning disabilities

Role of perceptual-motor programs in the elementary school

Although the bulk of available research fails to support the contention that perceptual-motor programs improve cognitive functioning, it is our belief that this does not constitute a rationale for eliminating perceptual-motor programs or failing to introduce perceptual-motor programs into the elementary school curriculum. Cratty (1970b, p. 18), for example, has stated:

"Many experimental findings may have no immediate use, while some teaching practices do not require 'scientific' verification. They may just make good sense.'' We believe this is the case with perceptual-motor programs. Some aspects of these perceptual-motor programs just make good sense. One could criticize research design for failing to demonstrate academic increase through perceptual-motor programs; however, in reality we might not be able, and should not expect, to find *direct* contributions to academic functioning. We firmly believe—and there is some support for our position—that perceptual-motor experiences make *indirect* contributions to academic success. By indirect contributions we mean that perceptual-motor experiences may contribute to increased perceptual abilities, motor skills, self confidence, attention, to better student-teacher relations, and so on, all of which may ultimately affect academic achievement. As a result perceptual-motor programs should not be measured solely by IQ score gains and reading scores, but also by changes in perceptual and motor ability, self-concept, and other important variables (Zaichkowsky, 1975).

Perceptual-motor programs do have a place in our elementary school physical education curriculum, but not at the expense of other important developmental activities. In developing our curriculum we must take into consideration the age and the specific needs of the child. As we see it, perceptual-motor programs can and should serve one of two purposes. They can function as *remedial* as they historically have, or they may function as *preparatory* or *developmental*. A remedial program should be individually structured to deal with the particular disability, such as sensory motor training for the deaf and blind, through the medium of movement (specialized emphasis). The physical education teacher can function as a therapist in a team with other specialists in the school, that is, psychologist, speech therapist, and reading teacher, in structuring meaningful learning experiences for the child.

We see the preparatory-developmental program functioning in the form of readying the child for learning in a variety of situations. As a matter of fact movement experiences in regular elementary physical education classes should by nature be perceptual-motor activities, stressing gross locomotor movements and manipulative, balancing, and body awareness skills. Activities that are seen as perceptual-motor should, in our opinion, provide the solid backbone for early physical education programs. As the children get older, more specific motor skills should be taught (see Chapter 3). We need trained professionals as well as adequate time allotment for programs. Physical education graduates should, if they are deemed experts in movement, all be given thorough exposure to providing perceptual-motor experiences for normal and atypical children. Classroom teachers in areas other than physical education should learn the fundamentals of perceptual-motor theory through workshops, independent readings, and consultation with specialists.

References

Barsch, R. *A movigenic curriculum.* Madison, Wis.: State Department of Public Instruction, 1965.

Barsch, R. *Achieving perceptual motor efficiency.* Seattle: Special Child Publications, 1968.

Bee, H. *The developing child* (2nd ed.). New York: Harper & Row, Publishers, 1978.

Belmont, L., & Birch, H. G. Lateral dominance and right-left awareness in normal children. *Child Development,* 1963, *34,* 257-270.

Benton, A. L. *Right-left discrimination and finger localization.* New York: Hoeber-Harper, 1959.

Bower, T. G. R. The visual world of infants. *Scientific American,* 1966, *215,* 80-92.

Brain, R. W.: Speech and handedness, *Lancet,* 1945, *2,* 837-842.

Bridges, W. H. Sensory habituation and discrimination in the human neonate. *American Journal of Psychiatry,* 1961, *117,* 991-996.

Chancy, C., & Kephart, N. C. *Motoric aids to perceptual training.* Columbus, Ohio: Charles E. Merrill Pub. Co., 1968.

Collins, R. L. The sound of one paw clapping: an inquiry into the origin of left-handedness. In G. Lindsey & D. Thiessen (Eds.), *Contributions to behavior-genetic analysis: the mouse as a prototype.* New York: Appleton-Century-Crofts, 1970.

Coren, S., & Porac, C. Fifty centuries of right-handedness: the historical record, *Science,* 1977, *11* (November), 631-632.

Cratty, B. J. *Perceptual and motor development in infants and children.* New York: Macmillan, Inc., 1970a.

Cratty, B. J. *Some educational implications of movement.* Seattle: Special Child Publications, 1970b.

Delacato, C. *Treatment and prevention of reading problems.* Springfield, Ill.: Charles C Thomas, Publisher, 1959.

Eagles, E. L., Wishik, S. M., Doerfler, L. G., Melnick,

W., & Levine, H. S. Hearing sensitivity and related factors in children. *Laryngoscope,* 1963, *11,* 220.

Elkind, D. Children's conceptions of right and left: Piaget replication study (Pt. 4). *Journal of Genetic Psychology,* 1961, *99,* 269-276.

Fantz, R. L. A method for studying depth perception in infants under six months of age. *Psychological record,* 1961, *11,* 27-32.

Fantz, R. L. Visual perception from birth as shown by pattern selectivity. *Annals of the New York Academy of Science,* 1965, *118,* 793-814.

Frostig, M. *Developmental Test of Visual Perception: administration and scoring manual.* Palo Alto, Calif.: Consulting Psychologists Press, 1966.

Frostig, M. *Movement education: the way and practice.* Chicago: Follett Education Corp., 1970.

Getman, G. *How to develop your child's intelligence: a research publication.* Ruverne, Minn.: G. N. Getman, 1962.

Gibson, E. J., & Walk, R. D. The visual cliff. *Scientific American,* 1960, *202,* 64-71.

Haith, M. The response of the human newborn to visual movement. *Journal of Experimental Child Psychology,* 1966, *3,* 235-243.

Harris, A. J. Lateral dominance, directional confusion, and reading disability. *Journal of Psychology,* 1957, *44,* 283-294.

Held, R., & Hein, A. Movement-produced stimulation in the development of visually guided behavior. *Journal of Comparative and Physiological Psychology,* 1963, *56,* 872-876.

Hicks, R. E., & Kinsbourne, M. On the genesis of human handedness: a review. *Journal of Motor Behavior,* 1976, *8,* 257-266.

Hildreth, G. The development and training of hand dominance. *Journal of Genetic Psychology,* 1949, *75,* 197-275.

Ilg, F. L., & Ames, L. B. *School readiness.* New York: Harper & Row, Publishers, 1966.

Kephart, N. *The slow learner in the classroom.* Columbus, Ohio: Charles E. Merrill Pub. Co., 1960.

Kessen, W., Haith, M. M., & Salapatek, P. H. Human infancy: a bibliography and guide. In P. H. Mussen (Ed.), *Carmichael's manual of child psychology.* New York: John Wiley & Sons, Inc., 1970.

Lipsitt, L. P., & Levy, N. Electrotactual threshold in the neonate. *Child Development,* 1959, *30,* 547-554.

Lockavitch, J. F. *The development and validation of a test battery for lateral awareness and directionality in elementary school children.* Unpublished doctoral dissertation, Boston University, 1977.

McCarthy, D. A. *McCarthy scales of children's abilities.* New York: The Psychological Corp., 1972.

Maccoby, E., & Jacklin, C. *Psychology of sex differences.* Palo Alto, Calif.: Stanford University Press, 1974.

Martinek, T. Perceptual motor training: a new role for the physical educator. *New Jersey Reporter, State Journal of AAHPER,* 1974, *48,* 29.

Motegi, M. A problem of cross culture between Japan and U.S.A. findings in a study on McCarthy scales of children's abilities. In F. M. Ottobre (Ed.), *International newsletter, education evaluation and research.* Princeton, N.J.: Educational Testing Service, October 1977.

Mussen, P. H., Conger, J. J., & Kagan, J. Child development and personality (4th ed.). New York: Harper & Row, Publishers, 1974.

Pick, H. L., & Pick, A. D. Sensory and perceptual development. In P. H. Mussen (Ed.), *Carmichael's manual of child psychology.* New York: John Wiley & Sons, Inc., 1970.

Wertheimer, M. Psychomotor coordination of audio-visual space at birth. *Science,* 1961, *134,* 1962.

Williams, H. G. A theoretical overview. In C. Corbin (Ed.), *A textbook of motor development.* Dubuque, Iowa: William C. Brown Co., 1973.

Zaichkowsky, L. D. Efficacy of perceptual-motor programs in elementary schools. *MAHPER Journal,* 1975, *22,* 8.

Zaichkowsky, L. D., & Smith, L. What psychological variables are important in an individual's movement? In J. T. F. Cheffers & T. Evaul (Eds.), *Introduction to physical education: concepts of human movement.* Englewood Cliffs, N.J.: Prentice-Hall, Inc., 1978.

Student projects

1. Design several activities that help to develop the following perceptual-motor abilities—
   a. listening skills
   b. body awareness
   c. laterality
   d. directionality

   What are the specific qualities of your designed activities that make each one unique in terms of helping to develop these perceptual-motor abilities?

2. Visit a school that offers a program of remedial perceptual-motor training. Does the program follow a particular theory and practice, for example, those of Kephart, Getman, or Doman-Delacato? On what basis are students selected for the remedial program? What age and sex distribution are there in the school population? Do you agree with their program offerings? What changes might you incorporate?

3. This might best be done as a class project. Several students should be responsible for collecting data on hand, foot, and eye preference for a number of age groups. By visiting day-care centers it will be possible to gather data from children as young as 3 years. Other students would be responsible for data gathering at a kindergarten and still others at elementary and junior high schools with a specific grade approximating a given age. Using the informal measures for hand (throwing, writing), foot (kicking), and eye (aiming) dominance, prepare a chart that will give you the percentage number of children at a specific age and sex with a right or left preference. Are these data consistent with those of McCarthy and Belmont and Birch?

Part two

DEVELOPMENT OF COGNITION AND COMMUNICATION

Chapter 6

COGNITIVE DEVELOPMENT

James McMullen

Although we all have our own connotations of cognitive development, it is probably safe to say that most of us interpret cognition as something that deals with thinking and intelligence; in the vernacular we might say "using your head." A perusal of the psychological literature would undoubtedly verify this definition; however, we also find that under the rubric of cognitive processes are such topics as *intelligence, language, reasoning, perception, classification, creativity, memory, attention, mediation,* and *imagery*. If we look at Guilford's (1967) structure of the intellect, we would include numerous other structures or functions of cognition or both. The term "cognition," therefore, although generally referring to mental activities, encompasses numerous "subordinate" terms. One can conclude from the many terms associated with cognition that mental activity involves both a *process* and a *product*. The product of mental activity is usually referred to as intelligence.

It is beyond the scope of this chapter to deal effectively with all of these cognitive activities. We have chosen to write on what we think are three major components of cognition: attention, memory, and logical thinking. These three areas are among the most thoroughly researched "cognitive" areas in the developmental literature.

Attention could logically have been discussed in the chapter on perceptual development. There is no question that attentional processes are a part of perception, but attention is also necessary for cognition and motor performance. Memory is another essential condition for learning in children, one that has received considerable research attention in the last 20 years. Our decision to include a discussion of the development of logical thinking was influenced by the writings of Piaget, unquestionably the foremost authority on the development of thinking in children. Our theoretical bias in this area is therefore the theory of Piaget.

The plan of this chapter is as follows: to present an overview of theory related to cognitive development; to describe the development of attention, memory, and logical thinking by using the developmental stages that have been used throughout the book; to discuss the issue of sex differences in cognitive development; to present a section on the implications of cognitive development for physical education.

Unquestionably the measurement of cognition (intelligence or IQ) is one of the most hotly debated issues both in psychology and education. The many standardized individual and group IQ tests have been able since their inception to demonstrate individual differences in intelligence. It is not the individual differences per se that are the issues (they are unequivocally acknowledged), but rather the issues surrounding the *factors* (heredity, environment) that contribute to individual differences in intelligence, namely, the nature-nurture debate. Psychologists are not in agreement about genetic and environmental contributions to intelligence. Some geneticists, led by Jensen, believe that as much as 80% of intelligence can be explained by heredity; others believe that environmental factors such as social class, schooling, and even birth order (Zajonc, 1975) affect intelligence more than heredity. For a more extensive discussion of the problems of intelligence measurement and the issues surrounding it, see Bee (1978, Chapter 10).

The developmental theories that appear to receive the greatest amount of recognition include learning theory, Werner's comparative theory, Bruner's theory, and of course the theory of Piaget. The learning theory position as described in Chapter 1 has some proponents in the development field, namely, Bijou and Baer. By and large this theory, which is characterized by such terms as stimulus, response, and reinforcement, maintains that the processes involved in learning are the same for all children regardless of age or task to be learned. Scientists with this theoretical orientation attempt to demonstrate that basic laws of learning can totally explain how children acquire skills and specific traits. The present status of learning theory orientation is perhaps best described by White, who after a very extensive review on learning theory wrote, "The learning theory tradition is waning, and the arguments against it have considerable point" (1970, p. 686).

The other three theories fall under the general rubric of "cognitive theories," since they emphasize the development of thinking rather than all of human behavior, as does the learning theory approach. It is also true that these theories have something in common. For example, all three theories maintain that during the course of development cognitive structures become more *differentiated* and *hierarchically integrated*. They also propose that children pass through "stages" in the development of cognitive processes, although these theorists do not use the same terms to describe the developmental stages. We briefly discuss the theories of Werner and Bruner before moving on to a more elaborate discussion of Piaget's.

Werner perceives development to "proceed from a state of relative globality and lack of differentiation to a state of increasing differentiation, articulation and hierarchic integration" (1957, p. 126). This differentiation process follows developmental stages, which Werner labeled sensorimotor, perceptual, and conceptual, with each successive level reflecting a higher degree of differentiation. Although Werner believes that the sequence of development is universal, at the same time he acknowledges that a child cannot be assigned to the same developmental stage for all aspects of cognitive functioning. This is a rather important departure from Piaget's theory, which does not appear to allow for this task flexibility. Werner in essence is saying that a child may switch from a conceptual stage to a perceptual or sensorimotor stage and vice versa, depending upon the task.

The fundamental developmental theme in Bruner's theory is that children change in their preference for a mode of representations of their world. More specifically, Bruner maintains that children start off in the "enactive" stage, which describes a child's dependence on sensorimotor activity for perceiving the world. As the child grows older, the emphasis shifts to the "ikonic" mode. The child is now capable of representing the world in the form of an image or schema that is relatively independent of motor activity. Cognitive growth culminates with a preference for the "symbolic" mode; the child is now able to internally manipulate symbols that are characteristic of abstract thought.

Although this brief outline of Bruner's theory does not do justice to his extensive work, our point is that the enactive-ikonic-symbolic sequence parallels the sensorimotor-perceptual-conceptual theory postulated by Werner and also the stages of Piaget.

DEVELOPMENTAL THEORY OF JEAN PIAGET

Before the description of Piaget's theory, some background information about this remarkable man is provided. Then there is a description of the concepts and specific terms that Piaget uses to develop his theory, followed by a condensed table that gives an overview of Piaget's stages of development. Finally, the cognitive changes — attention, memory, and logical thinking — that occur as a child moves from infancy to adolescence are delineated.

Piaget's background

Piaget's career had a most interesting beginning. He was born in the Swiss university town of Neuchâtel in 1896, and it was in this area that he published his first scholarly work, at the ripe old age of 10. His work was so impressive that he was offered the post of museum curator until the director of the museum found out that Piaget was still in secondary school. It was during his university years that he became interested in the philosophy of knowledge (epistemology) and ultimately the psychology of child development. His interest in children appears to have been secondary, for he was really interested in how knowledge developed. To Piaget, what better way to study knowledge development than to study children.

After completion of his doctoral work (in biology) Piaget spent three years as a postdoctoral student at Alfred Binet's laboratory in Paris. Binet at that time had a strong reputation in the area of intelligence, for he had developed the first standardized intelligence test, parts of which are still used today (Stanford-Binet). It was in Paris that Piaget became fascinated by children's answers to questions, particularly the wrong answers. He observed that as children grew older, they not only became brighter *(quantitatively)*, but the answers were *qualitatively* different. Older children not only knew more, but they were also capable of mental manipulations that simply were not available to younger children. Piaget had discovered his research material — the changing patterns of thought processes in children. To gather data on the thought processes of children Piaget relied primarily on observation, not only of his own children but of thousands of others. Many of his methodologies were most ingenious.

Piaget then began to publish his theory on the development of cognition in children. His numerous experiments and the revisions in his theory have led to an astonishing number of publications (Piaget, 1950, 1952). By 1965 it was estimated that his writings, translated into many languages, totalled some 18,000 pages (Maier, 1978). By 1978 he had been credited with over 40 books, and at over 80 years of age he is still writing. For those interested in reading Piaget's original work Maier (1978) has a bibliography of over 70 publications in English. As noted in Chapter 1, part of North America's initial reluctance in accepting Piaget's work stemmed from his rather subjective observational research methodology, as well as the lag in translation from French to English, which contributed to a misunderstanding of his now almost universally accepted theory.

Basic concepts and terminology

These concepts and terms are most easily presented in summary form.

1. Children have mental structures that are different from those of adults. They are not adults in miniature; they have their own distinct ways of determining reality and of viewing the world.

2. Children's mental development progresses through definite stages that occur in a fixed sequence (are invariant) for all children. However, not all children move from one stage to another at the same rate.

3. Cognitive development is influenced by several interactive factors, namely, maturation and experience not only with physical objects but also with people.

4. Cognitive development is the result of two basic biological characteristics that remain constant throughout development. Piaget calls these two inborn attributes *organization* and *adaptation*. Organization is the building of simpler processes such as seeing, touching, nam-

ing, and so forth into higher-order mental structures. Adaptation is simply the continuing change (adjusting) that occurs in an individual as a result of his interaction with the environment.

Piaget breaks down the process of adaptation into two distinct parts termed *assimilation* and *accommodation*. Assimilation in a general sense means to bring in or incorporate events so that they become part of a system. For example, immigrants become assimilated into a new country when they cannot be distinguished from the "natives." Likewise, knowledge becomes assimilated. When a baby sees a block and reaches for it, she is assimilating because she is utilizing abilities she already has, in this case seeing, grasping, and reaching. In accommodation the structure of the child's understanding is changed by experiences. The baby in the preceding example shows accommodation when she changes the way she holds her hand in order to grasp a particular block.

Piaget believes that one goes through a lifetime engaging in the processes of assimilation and accommodation. During the course of development, assimilation and accommodation seek some type of balance as maturation and experience bring about what Piaget terms *equilibration*. When assimilation and accommodation are in balance, the child's behavior is relatively stable and is characterized as being in a specific stage. When these attributes are unstable, there is transition or change. Whenever an individual is nudged further to more advanced thinking, the process of equilibration is going on (Maier, 1978).

Piaget used another term that is unique to cognitive psychology, the *schema*. The schema could best be described as a hypothetical construct that Piaget sees as a cognitive analogue of a bodily structure. For example, an infant begins life with reflexive schemas such as looking and hearing. Although assimilation and accommodation take place, the schemas are still reflexive actions. As the child grows older and internal representations begin, the child's schemas may be *representations* of actions or concepts. As the child grows still older and develops more complex schemas (about 7), the child is capable of what Piaget calls *operations*.

Table 6-1. Piaget's stages of cognitive development

Period	Approximate age	Characteristics
1. Sensorimotor (actually six stages)	0 to 2 years	Learning limited to simplest aspects of motor behavior and sensory perception—vision, touch, smell, taste, sound; last stage capable of using "action" symbols
2. Preoperational Preconceptual	2 to 4 years	Appearance of symbolic function and beginning of internalized actions accompanied by representation; characterized by childlike precausal thinking; unable to take perceptual viewpoint of other people
Intuitive thought	4 to 7 years	
3. Concrete operations	7 to 11 years	Beginning use of elementary logic and reason, about size, volume, numbers, and weight; capable of hierarchical classification and seriation
4. Formal operations	11 years and beyond	Capability of hypotheticodeductive logic; able to formulate laws or general principles and apply them to situations; able to manipulate symbols to solve problems; highest level of cognitive functioning

Operations are complex mental processes such as adding, subtracting, classifying, ordering, and so forth, whereby the child manipulates symbols. Operations are reversible thought processes; that is, they can be done and undone.

The main stages of Piaget's theory, the *approximate* ages of occurrence, and some of the major characteristics are summarized in Table 6-1.

AGE DIFFERENCES IN COGNITIVE DEVELOPMENT
Infancy, or the sensorimotor period

Attention. Attention refers to the ability to orient and select certain stimuli for sustained periods of time. In learning it is essential that children attend not to the total environment but to their *effective* environment. It is most difficult for infants to sustain attention for even short periods of time. Nevertheless, some things are known about what attracts the attentional processes of infants. Lights that blink on and off (show movement) and tones that are intermittent are more attention getting than continuous stimuli. Stimuli that show distinct black-and-white contrasts are more attention getting than stimuli with minimal contrast. Infants also pay more attention to a stimulus that they have some experience with and yet one that has some novelty. Kagan (1976) refers to this phenomenon as attention to discrepancy.

Kagan maintains that infants do not pay much attention to events that are very similar to "schemata" (cognitive representations of an event) they hold or to events that are completely unrelated to their present schemata. For example, infants' attention is attracted to photographs of human faces rather than random objects; however, they are particularly attracted if the faces are discrepant in some way, for example, a face having only one eye or a funny nose. Perhaps cartoons owe their attractiveness to this principle.

A 4-month-old is capable of sustaining attention to a colorful, moving mobile for five minutes or more. At 1 year of age children can be seen attending to certain toys up to 15 minutes, but by and large it is difficult to get children, even in late infancy, to sustain attention for a period as long as 15 minutes.

A summary statement regarding attention in infants might say that infants can focus attention on changing or discontinuous stimuli and on stimuli that are somewhat discrepant (novel); however, the time frame is short compared to what it is at an older age.

Memory. Memory is a factor that is very much related to attention, for a lack of attention leads to poor registration of events. There are two ways whereby children can show that they can remember something from the past. One is referred to as recognition, where the response is usually, "I recognize it" or "I don't." For us recognition memory is demonstrated on multiple-choice tests. A second way of demonstrating memory is through *recall;* that is, children are asked to reconstruct or recreate in words the events that occurred. Essay exams tax recall memory.

In addition to two ways of demonstrating memory (recognition and recall) there are also two memory types, *short-term* (STM) and *long-term* memory (LTM). STM is a temporary store for incoming information and is quite limited in capacity. With adults it has been demonstrated that the STM store is capable of holding about seven, plus or minus two, "chunks of information" (Miller, 1956). Seven chunks of information may refer to seven randomly selected words or one-digit numbers such as a telephone number. Information is held in STM for a few seconds or until attention is diverted. Some information passes into LTM, and the rest is forgotten.

LTM consists of events that are "permanently" stored; however, it is possible to forget information simply because it got "lost" in the LTM filing system or its retrieval has somehow been interfered with.

During infancy, memory is usually demonstrated only through recognition, since it relies almost exclusively on perception. Recognition memory is known to be present during the first few months of life. Recall, on the other hand, requires language skills, and according to Piaget and Inhelder (1973), this form of memory is not demonstrated until about 1½ to 2 years of age.

Both STM and LTM are restricted in infants, STM because of poor states of attention and organizational ability (coding) and LTM because of an inability to effectively code information for long-term storage. Since infants, even during the latter stages of this growth period, have limited language skills, it is difficult for them to store information in LTM.

Logical thinking. As stated at the outset of this chapter, our discussion of logical thinking is based primarily on Piaget's developmental stages introduced in Table 6-1. Piaget labeled the first time frame in cognitive development the sensorimotor period; this begins with birth

and ends when the child is able to use symbols (about 2 years). He subdivided this period into six stages, each with distinct, hierarchical functioning. Since most of what an infant does during this period utilizes sensory and motor activity, Piaget believes that these sensory experiences and motor responses serve as important foundations for cognitive processes.

During the first stage (birth to 1 month) the infant adapts to and builds from basic reflex responses. Nipple searching, although a primitive response, is in fact the beginning of cognitive growth. During the second stage (1 to 4 months), infants repeat what was initially an accidental response. For example, if the infant turned her head and accidentally brought her thumb in contact with her mouth, she tends to repeat this response. Piaget called this phenomenon the *primary circular reaction*. Stage 3 (4 to 10 months) Piaget termed the *secondary circular reaction*. The infant now repeats chance events that occurred with objects in the environment. For example, a baby might accidentally kick a mobile in her crib. However, later on the kick will be voluntary or goal directed. She now sees a causal relationship between the kicking and mobile movement.

The fourth stage of infancy (10 to 12 months) is characterized by a first attempt to use old and familiar strategies (schemas) in a new way. The infant now attempts to remove a barrier (for example, blanket) that separates her from a toy. Also at this stage the infant begins to anticipate events; for example, babies may begin to cry when they see their parents putting on their coats.

Stage 5 (12 to 18 months) occurs during the time that walking is acquired, and as a result the infant is able to explore her environment much more actively. This results in a large range of experiences, which leads to *experimentation;* for example, the infant explores new ways of holding and dropping objects, throwing objects, and so forth.

During stage 6 (18 months to 2 years), Piaget thinks, the infant develops the ability to use rudimentary symbols in thought. Actually these symbols are motor response symbols and not words. Children do not use words as symbols until after 2 years. Piaget (1952) presents an excellent example of this type of symbol use in describing the problem-solving behavior of his daughter. Piaget, while playing with his daughter, hid an attractive chain inside a small box and left a very small opening. Piaget reasoned that at this age the only schemas available to the little girl were either to turn the box over and empty it or pull the chain out of the small opening. Since neither of these alternatives worked for her, she paused briefly. Then she began opening her mouth and closing it. As though "seeing the light," she used this principle to widen the opening in the box and removed the chain. Piaget viewed this behavior as action functioning as a symbol.

Early childhood, or preoperational period

Attention. Attention appears to be much easier to assess during early childhood than during infancy because it can seemingly be observed whether children are being attentive to the effective environment, and, further, they can be asked test questions about what they should have been "absorbing." But it turns out that children are good "fakers," and even though they appear to be attending to the effective environment (parent or kindergarten teacher), they really are not. Adults are masters at this skill. This lack of attention is usually evidenced when the child fails to respond correctly to simple questions about the story or reading material.

The research literature does point out several factors that seem to determine the focus and duration of attention in preschool children. As was the case with infants, preschoolers pay more attention to events that are *slightly* different from what is familiar and expected (Jackson et al., 1976). It is also true that preschoolers are more likely to attend to loud noises or big pictures than to soft sounds or small pictures, although it is important that there be some variability. Repeated constant stimuli become boring, and the preschooler becomes inattentive.

As the preschool child increases in age, some very interesting events take place with regard to attention. Initially, young children have little ability when it comes to planning and searching for useful information. They "flip and dash"

all over in search of hidden or lost items. For example, a 3-year-old may lose a ball in the backyard, and even though it may be quite visible to an adult, the 3-year-old runs around vigorously in search of the ball. After a brief period of unsystematic wandering the child usually asks for help. With increased age the child becomes more systematic and planful in searches.

It is also true that preschool children are initially extremely distractible. They seem unable to "tune out" irrelevant stimuli, even on command. As they grow older, they are capable of ignoring "the dog that walked into the room" and focus their attention on the relevant stimuli for a surprisingly long period.

Memory. As a general rule the older children are, the better their memory skills, particularly for recall memory (Hagan, 1971). When it comes to recognition memory, children as young as 3 years of age are amazingly accurate (approximating adults) in recognizing what they have seen before (Perlmutter and Myers, 1974). It can also be said that preschool children have a limited capacity for short-term memory. As indicated earlier, adults can recall about seven, plus or minus two, chunks of information. Research with children shows that 2- to 3-year-olds can cope with no more than two or three chunks; 4- to 5-year-olds, with about four chunks; and 6- to 7-year olds, with about five chunks (Farnham-Diggory, 1972). Kagan (1976), however, provides some recent evidence suggesting that preschoolers (2½ to 3) have STM for four to five objects, but the objects must be *familiar,* for example, toys that the child frequently plays with. Kagan extends this *context specificity* to the development of cognitive competencies in general. He indicates that numerous studies now reveal that cognitive abilities such as STM, attention, and spatial reasoning are very much dependent on the context in which the competency is being manifested; that is, memory is dependent to some extent on what one is being asked to remember. This situation or context specificity is very similar to what has been advanced in studies of attitudes and motives (see Chapter 11 on attitude development).

Logical thinking. Piaget labeled the second

stage of development "preoperational," which is synonymous with prelogical. Preschool children's thinking is dominated by *perceptual* processes, by what seems to be, rather than by what logically must be. Logical operations are not mastered until the third stage.

The early stage (2 to 4 years) of the preoperational period is characterized by continued use of action symbols, and perhaps visual images are used to represent objects. During the latter part of this stage the child does in fact begin to utilize words as symbols. A child at this stage has some interesting, often humorous ways of reasoning, and these are usually influenced by what he wants. For example, it is not uncommon for a 3-year-old who does not want to take a nap to say that he took his nap simply because he momentarily lay down and closed his eyes. His reasoning is, "I closed my eyes, therefore I took my nap." He sees a causal relationship between closing eyes and taking a nap. Children at this age also reason from specific to specific. For example, if the parents serve snails for dinner and they have guests, the next time snails are being prepared the 3-year-old reasons that guests will be arriving. Piaget calls this *transductive reasoning*.

Piaget thinks that one of the dominant thought characteristics of the preoperational stage is a quality he calls *egocentrism*. He is not referring to being egotistical as we might interpret it; rather, he is referring to the fact that preschool children can only relate to experiences in terms of themselves. Piaget's method of demonstrating egocentrism was to ask children to look at objects such as toy mountains. He then placed dolls at different points around the mountain and asked the children to put themselves in the dolls' position and tell what they saw. Preoperational children could only report what they saw from their perspective. As children get older they begin to decenter; that is, they can make accurate judgments about objects even if the objects are away from their own perspective.

Classification skills, that is, the ability to put objects, events, and so forth into groups, are also only present in rudimentary form during the preoperational stage. For example, a child who takes one pile of red and blue blocks and sorts them into separate red and blue piles is classifying them. Preschool children can only classify objects on a single attribute such as size, form, color, or perhaps function. Rarely do children at this age sort objects by color and, within each color, by size.

Late childhood, or the concrete operations period

Attention. Attention to stimuli for longer periods of time becomes easier for the 6-year-old than it was for the 4- and 5-year-old. Nevertheless, during the early stages of this period children are still very easily distracted. Novel events still attract their attention and sustain it for a fairly long time. As the child grows older, attention improves. More specifically, children are much more systematic in the search for relevant stimuli. While the preschooler randomly walks around the yard in search of a lost ball, the 7- and 8-year-old uses logical thought in organizing his search. The elementary school child is also more capable of "tuning in" or "tuning out" relevant and irrelevant information. He is better able to distinguish between what needs to be known and what is incidental to the learning environment.

Another characteristic of attentional development during this period is that the child is now able to simultaneously pay attention to more than one factor, an ability we call *decentering*. It is important to note that there is no conflict or discrepancy in saying that children focus more attention and yet at the same time "decenter" attention. These are, in fact, different attentional strategies. For example, the child is now able to pay attention to the ball that she is about to catch, at the same time place her hands in a proper catching position, and perhaps attend to her present location in comparison to where the ball will come down. She is "decentering," that is, she is not only paying attention to the ball as the preschooler would, but she is also attending to hand location and possible ball trajectory. She is also capable of tuning out irrelevant factors such as room or outdoor noise.

Memory. It was pointed out in the discussion of early childhood memory that 4- and 5-year-old children had limited STM (about four chunks), but that this capacity increased with age. One of the reasons that this ability increases is that children at about age 6 or 7 begin to effectively use strategies to facilitate recall. These strategies are developmentally linked to language acquisition. Children who are 4 and 5, when asked to recall a series of pictures, words, or responses, experience great difficulty in correctly ordering the series or list. It is only when children are about 6 or 7 that they can employ recall strategies, which psychologists term "labeling strategies," "mediating devices," or "rehearsal strategies." What are these labeling strategies? Perhaps this concept of labeling can be understood better by looking at two research demonstrations. Flavell (1970) has demonstrated labeling deficiency in young children by giving them a set of pictures to remember in a particular order. After a brief delay period the child is asked to remember what he saw and reproduce the set of pictures in their correct order. The experimenter then typically listens and watches for the use of mnemonic strategies such as whispering or muttering to oneself. Flavell indicates that 4- and 5-year-olds do not use any systematic strategies to facilitate recall, whereas 6- and 7-year-olds rehearse spontaneously. Still older children are capable of "silent" rehearsals and more sophisticated memory-labeling strategies.

Zaichkowsky (1974) observed a similar increased utilization of labeling strategies with age in tasks that required the serial recall of motor responses. In this study 5-, 7-, and 9-year-old children were asked to make a series of eight hand and foot responses (pedal pressing) to a lighted stimulus. That is, when a light appeared above the pedal corresponding to the left hand, the child pressed it and continued making appropriate hand and foot responses until eight responses were made. In one case the pattern was very definite or organized, simply two clockwise hand and foot movements. A second recall task had no apparent pattern. After completing one of the tasks the child was asked to recall the correct order of responses. Results of the study showed that 5-year-old children could recall the organized pattern almost as well as the 7- and 9-year-old children. The task was simple, and they were essentially

provided with a labeling device. The 5-year-olds verified this conclusion nicely in interviews after the experiment. They indicated such things as, "The pattern looked like two circles." On the complex task, however, the 5-year-olds were unable to recall the correct order, even after 25 trials. The 7- and 9-year-olds showed increasing proficiency, primarily because they were able to provide their own labels for rehearsal in STM. When questioned about their strategies for recall, the older children indicated that they attached numbers to different responses, covertly rehearsed the muscle responses, or used some other mnemonic aid.

There are numerous other studies that demonstrate this most significant memory change. Those interested in reading more about this fascinating developmental change are referred to Flavell (1970), Flavell et al. (1966), Hagan (1971), and Robinson and London (1971).

Logical thinking. Most researchers and theoreticians in child development concur that somewhere between 5 and 7 years of age, major changes occur in the thought processes of a child. Piaget calls this transition the period of *concrete operations*. Bruner (1966) called this the symbolic stage. What both theoreticians are saying is that the child is moving away from specific-to-specific reasoning and is able to use and manipulate symbols in her thinking.

Piaget sees the period of concrete operations beginning at about age 7. The child is now capable of rather complex mental functions such as adding, subtracting, classifying, serial ordering, and so forth. The child is now able to reverse operations. For example, if water is poured from a short, "fat" glass into a tall, thin one the younger child would see the water level being higher and therefore would reason that there is more water. The child who is able to reverse operations (beginning at 5 or 6 years of age) would see that the amount of water really did not change. The operations are very much concrete; that is, they are tied to particular experiences. It is not until the period of formal operations that the child is able to imagine things not yet experienced.

The concrete operational child has advanced beyond the preoperational child in a number of ways. One task that the concrete operational child can now perform is that of *classifying* objects along several dimensions rather than just one; for example, a child can now separate circles, squares, and rectangles and can separate them by size and even by color. The development of the *class inclusion* principle also marks the beginning of the concrete operations period. Understanding the class inclusion principle permits the child to understand that things have more than one name; for example, "mothers" can also be "women," and "dogs" can also be "animals."

Another task that the concrete operational child can perform is that of *seriation,* ordering events along a single dimension. Although 3-year-olds are capable of serially ordering toy stacking rings, they do it on the basis of trial and error and perceptual understanding. Piaget calls the more mature logical understanding of seriation *transitivity.* This is the principle that if A is larger than B and B is larger than C, then A must be larger than C. Understanding transitivity makes it possible for children to cognitively place things in order without directly testing all the possible comparisons. Piaget believes that the development of serial ordering skills and transitivity is a necessary condition for solving many logical and mathematical problems (Zaichkowsky, 1975b).

Conservation also emerges during the period of concrete operations. The problem of conservation has produced the most famous of Piaget's experiments. Piaget gave children two equal balls of clay and then asked them to roll one into the shape of a sausage and the other

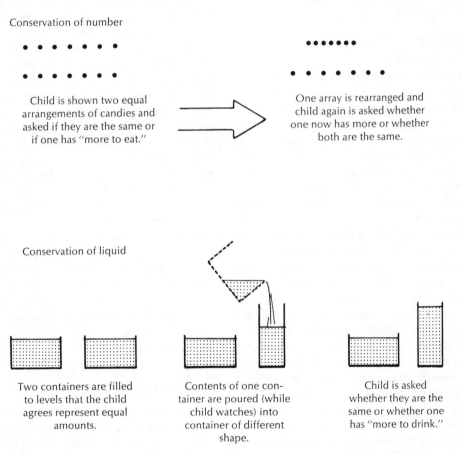

Conservation of number

Child is shown two equal arrangements of candies and asked if they are the same or if one has "more to eat."

One array is rearranged and child again is asked whether one now has more or whether both are the same.

Conservation of liquid

Two containers are filled to levels that the child agrees represent equal amounts.

Contents of one container are poured (while child watches) into container of different shape.

Child is asked whether they are the same or whether one has "more to drink."

Fig. 6-1. Examples of tests for conservation of number and conservation of liquid quantity. (From N. Jackson, M. Robinson, and P. Dale. *Cognitive development in young children: a report for teachers.* Washington, D. C.: U. S. Department of Health, Education and Welfare, 1976.)

into the form of a pancake. When asked which shape had more clay, the preoperational child typically answered "the pancake" because it is bigger. The concrete operational child answered that they were the same. Piaget has also demonstrated the principle of conservation in experiments on quantity and liquid. In the former experiment he lined up two numerically equal groups of buttons, each above the other so that the rows were of equal length. The child acknowledged that the two rows had the same number of buttons, but when one row was spread out more, the preoperational child said that the longer row contained more buttons. In the conservation-of-liquid experiment children are asked whether the amount of water changes after it is poured from a short, stout glass into a tall, thin one. Children do not master this conservation principle until they are about 7 years of age (Fig. 6-1).

Adolescence, or the formal operations period

Attention. By the time a child reaches adolescence he is quite capable of sustaining attention for long periods of time. In essence he will have mastered the ability (1) to conduct systematic searches, (2) to be selective of complex information, and (3) to ignore irrelevant information. The adolescent, nevertheless, is no different from younger children in preferring moderately novel stimulus objects to objects that are "old hat."

Memory. Adolescent children are generally capable of absorbing, processing, and retrieving information in a manner equivalent to adults. They are certainly superior to children who are in the earlier stages of development. This superiority is generally attributed to the fact that older children are capable of utilizing more effective mediating devices or labeling strategies. Pascual-Leone (1970) has recently suggested that there may be an additional reason for superior memory in older children, namely, a gradual increase in the absolute number of ideas that a child can manipulate. He theorizes that normal children have a basic memory capacity that is enhanced about one unit per year from age 5 until 11 or 12. Further, this processing capacity (M-space) grows in an all-or-none manner as a function of age. Pas-

cual-Leone thus has a different notion regarding memory superiority in older children. He believes that older children simply have a greater absolute capacity for information, a larger storehouse. To date there are no empirical data that allow any conclusion about whether Pascual-Leone's view has any more merit regarding memory development than the mediating theories. For a more extensive discussion of Pascual-Leone's theory as it relates to motor skills, see Todor (1975).

Logical thinking. The final period of Piaget's theory is formal operations, generally reached in adolescence. We say generally because unlike the preceding stages where most children achieve certain milestones, formal operations is achieved by less than two-thirds of the people of advanced cultures and even fewer in developing cultures (Bee, 1978). The child who is capable of formal operations is able to think in terms of the hypothetical and in solving problems generates a number of possible solutions, then selects the best solution without having to go through a process of trial and error. Formal operations can be said to be characterized by a shift from inductive to deductive logic. Whereas the concrete operations child can go from the particular (experiences) to the general, the formal operations child can go from the general to particular problem. Many adolescents are thus able to engage in the kind of thinking that is characteristic of scientific experimentation.

In addition, formal operations enable the adolescent to think about ideal situations and to understand metaphorical expressions. For example, if a child was asked to suppose that a "baseball was flat," he would probably reply that a "baseball is round." The adolescent, on the other hand, can accept the given premise and reason from it.

SEX DIFFERENCES IN COGNITIVE DEVELOPMENT

Most of the studies on sex differences in cognition have emanated from standardized IQ or achievement tests. The few studies that have looked at sex differences on Piagetian tasks have shown that there are no consistent differences in the development of preoperational, concrete operational, or formal operational skills (Bee, 1978). The testing research, although failing to demonstrate overall IQ differences between boys and girls at any age, has demonstrated sex differences in several components of intelligence. Based mainly on the comprehensive review of Maccoby and Jacklin (1974), the following conclusions can be made on sex differences in cognitive functioning:

1. Differences in general intelligence as measured by present IQ tests do not exist.
2. Girls tend to excel in verbal reasoning and other measures of verbal ability from infancy through adolescence and adulthood.
3. Boys tend to excel on quantitative (mathematical) tasks and on spatial problems.
4. Girls tend to get better grades in school, except for classes involving science and mathematics.
5. Ability differences are most apparent in older age levels in children.

The last conclusion may provide a tentative explanation regarding the question of why sex differences exist. The fact that sex differences become increasingly prominent with age (math and science achievement favoring boys increases from the early grades through high school) suggests that sex differences appear to be largely a function of home and school experiences and interest, rather than differences in mental ability per se.

IMPLICATIONS FOR PHYSICAL EDUCATION

How can physical educators contribute to the cognitive development of children? The answer seems obvious — engage children in games of physical activity that force them to "think." Although this seems straightforward, the truth is that few empirical studies have demonstrated that thought-provoking physical activity *directly* enhances the cognitive abilities of children. The belief that physical education can contribute to intellectual functioning is then simply that — a belief. The source of this belief is probably the early writings of such eminent philosophers and educators as Plato, Locke, Comenius, Roussea, Pestalozzi, and, more recently, Montessori, Dewey, and Piaget. All of these individuals believed that motor activity was either the basis of the intellect or that motor activity

contributed to the development of the intellect (transfer of experience and motivation).

Plato, for example, postulated that learning could take place better through play. In 380 BC he stated: "Lessons have been invented for the merest infants to learn, by way of play and fun. . . . Moreover by way of play, the teachers mix together [objects] adapting the rules of elementary arithmetic to play." In 1650, Comenius wrote: "Intellectual progress is conditioned at every step by bodily vigor. To attain the best results, physical exercises must accompany and condition mental training." The more contemporary American educational philosopher Dewey believed that play made learning much less a chore: "Experience has shown that when children have a chance at physical activities which bring their natural impulses into play, going to school is a joy, management is less of a burden and learning is easier" (Dewey, 1919, pp. 228-229).

The writings of many of these early philosophers apparently influenced the founders of the fledgling field of psychology in the late 1800s. This is evidenced by the fact that when psychologists first began to measure cognitive abilities, the tests contained items that had strong motor components. Cattell (1890), for example, included items such as rate of movement, dynamometer pressure, reaction time to sound, and time for naming colors. Although intelligence tests have changed greatly with respect to the type of items that purportedly measure intelligence, many scientists believe that there is a relationship between motor attributes and cognitive abilities as measured by a test of intelligence.

Basically, two approaches have been used to ascertain the relationship between motor ability and cognitive functioning. The first approach utilizes the technique of *correlation* to determine the magnitude of the relationship between achievement tests and motor ability tests, or intelligence and motor ability tests. The second technique is more experimental and methodologically is more sound than the correlational technique, since it attempts to ascertain causal relationships between variables of cognition and motor functioning.

The numerous correlative studies conducted over the years reveal a consistent finding: the

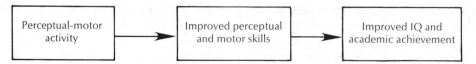

Fig. 6-2. Hypothesized chain directly linking motor activity to cognitive ability.

relationship between intelligence or academic achievement and motor ability is positive but low and usually statistically nonsignificant (Erhartic, 1977; Ismail and Gruber, 1967). This means that one's score on an IQ test cannot accurately predict one's score on a test of motor ability or vice versa.

This near-zero relationship between cognitive ability and motor ability is not universal for all populations and experimental conditions. Studies report higher correlations between IQ tests and motor ability for young children and also for low IQ children. That is to say that when "retarded" children are used as the test population, the relationship between intelligence and motor ability increases. Likewise, when infants' motor scores are correlated with infants' scores on IQ tests, the correlation increases. This is understandable because tests of infant intelligence generally have items that are predominantly motor.

Another factor that tends to increase the correlation between cognition and motor ability is the use of a complex motor-ability item in the correlational analysis. If the motor response is simple (for example, movement time of arm or standing long jump), the relationship between this score and an IQ measure will be near zero. But if the complexity of the motor response is increased (a series of body movements through a maze), then this score will be more highly correlated with an IQ score. It should be kept in mind that even though correlations between IQ and motor ability increase as the complexity of the motor task is increased and also when young and low-ability children are used, the correlations are still low (.30 to .40) and thus have very little predictive value.

The experimental studies, on the other hand, attempt to determine systematically a causal relationship between motor ability and cognitive ability. Researchers hypothesize that a chain of events takes place (Fig. 6-2). The best examples of these studies are those conducted

to test the efficacy of the perceptual-motor programs advocated by theorists such as Barsch (1965), Doman-Delacato (1959), Frostig (1964), Kephart (1960), and others (see Chapter 5). To date no researcher has provided strong support for a causal linkage between perceptual-motor training and increased intellectual functioning. Some studies have indeed demonstrated increased perceptual and academic functioning in children after experimental periods of motor training; however, methodological shortcomings have prevented causal explanations across all populations.

For example Oliver (1958), using educable retardates, found that he could improve their IQ by 25% merely by subjecting these children to an extra three hours of physical activity per day. This study thus suggests that *remedial* physical activity can enhance cognition; however, one must keep in mind that this is with a *special* population. To our knowledge perceptual-motor programs used with "normal" children —something we term *developmental* rather than remedial— have not demonstrated increased intellectual performance in children.

A methodological shortcoming of all these experimental studies is their lack of control over *intervening* variables such as motivation and self-concept. That is to say, perceptual-motor training per se may not directly contribute to increased intellectual functioning; rather, it may have an *indirect* effect. By this we mean that perceptual-motor programs may be enhancing the physical, social, and academic self-concept of children and likewise be motivating them to greater achievement, rather than simply affecting cognitive ability directly (Fig. 6-3). The correlational and experimental studies to date thus do not appear to provide much support for the notion that motor activity is the basis of the intellect (Zaichkowsky (1975a).

Although there is no evidence to say that motor activity is a necessary condition for the

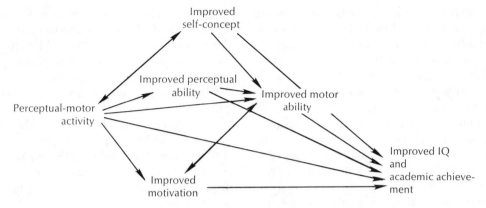

Fig. 6-3. Hypothesized model suggesting direct and indirect effects of selected variables on academic achievement.

development of the intellect, one can say that motor activity may modify the cognitive skills of children. We strongly believe that movement experiences in the form of organized physical education and sports can enhance not only the child's motor skills, but also perceptual, social, and cognitive skills. In some cases the motor experiences have a direct effect—as in motor development—and in other cases the effects are indirect, particularly in the development of cognitive skills. What is important is that educators must *specifically* structure the movement experiences so that they tax the perceptual system, encourage social interaction, and stimulate cognitive processes. Movement experiences *do not automatically transfer* to enhance these skills. We see movement experiences enhancing cognitive skills in children in the ways enumerated below.

1. Movement aids the development of intelligence if the child is encouraged to think about her movements creatively, logically, and quickly. Movement activities must be paired with cognitive concepts. The many fine texts on movement education and elementary physical education provide numerous examples of games that can enhance creative and also logical thinking (Kirchner, 1974; Miller et al., 1974). A series of books by Cratty (1971, 1972, 1973) also provides excellent ideas regarding the use of games for taxing the intellect.

2. Physical education can be used as a medium for stimulating problem-solving behavior. The problems should be structured so that they will have maximum transfer. The recent

"Adventure" and "Outward Bound" types of experiences are excellent training ground for learning problem-solving skills (Kaherl, 1978).

3. The cognitive skills of attention, short-term memory, and sequencing ability can be enhanced (within maturational limits) within a physical education environment. With STM the movement experiences must be specifically structured to develop this attribute. Cratty (1971, 1972, 1973) has some excellent ideas on games that can enhance memory and sequencing ability. Attention can likewise be increased in at least two ways. With hyperactive children vigorous games prior to sitting down for "academic" subjects may enhance attention, and with children in general, movement experiences are motivating. Because they are motivated, they will be more attentive.

4. Participation in physical education may enhance children's global self-concept; this may in turn lead to increased academic achievement. Although there is very little research support for this thesis at this point, numerous theoreticians, researchers, and educators believe that the self-concept is intricately related to academic achievement and therefore indirectly to intelligence. We think that well-planned, well-taught classes in physical education can enhance the self-concept (see Chapter 10).

5. Physical education can serve as a valuable medium for teaching concepts within the "cognitive domain," subjects such as mathematics, science, social studies, and language arts.

Humphrey (1965) initially suggested numerous ways in which various "academic" concepts could be taught to children using movement as the medium. More recently texts by Cratty (1971) and Gallahue et al. (1975) have expanded upon this methodological approach to teaching acedemic subjects. The mechanism operating here is probably that of motivation. As so many of the early philosophers mentioned, it is natural for children to play—they all enjoy playing. Thus, when math, science, and other concepts are creatively inserted into active games, children not only learn the concept, but they enjoy learning it. Rather than provide examples from Humphrey, Cratty, and Gallahue and co-workers, we recommend these texts and elementary physical education texts such as Kirchner (1974) and Miller et al. (1974) (Fig. 6-4).

We would be remiss in our implications sec-

tion if we did not return to our friend Piaget for some words of wisdom on developing cognitive functioning in children. Although Piaget does not see himself as an "applied person" (he chooses to let educators find applications for his theories), numerous writers have provided physical educators and educators in general with much Piagetian "food for thought" with respect to the teaching of children (Charles, 1974; Schwebel and Raph, 1973; and Winnick and French, 1975). We as teachers can benefit from what Piaget has provided us in the following ways.

Piaget has provided a description of children's abilities at various stages in their cognitive development. By being cognizant of a child's intellectual capabilities we can be realistic in our demands and expectations. We should painstakingly avoid going beyond their functional capabilities, an undertaking that will

Fig. 6-4. Children use perceptual modalities and movement to learn days of the month.

bring only frustration both to ourselves and the students.

Children should be encouraged to interact with other children to learn not only social skills but also language skills and the life experiences of other children.

Children learn by doing. The Chinese proverb

> I hear and I forget
> I see and I remember
> I do and I understand

probably has some truth to it, particularly the last statement. Piaget reminds us constantly of this.

The learning climate should be free and spontaneous. Children should be allowed to move and play freely, experiencing a variety of environmental stimuli. Movement education in elementary schools when structured properly fulfills this objective during the early years. Children should also share in decision making about what activities to do when, for how long, discipline, and so on. The teacher nonetheless sees to it that active, productive work is maximized.

Children learn not only by doing but also by modeling. Since the child is influenced a great deal by models, it is imperative that the teacher serve as a positive role model.

We would like to close this section of the chapter with a statement made by Larry Humm (1975, p. 7) regarding Piagetian theory and education:

Education should be a process of intellectual seduction. We should take small enough steps so that the learner feels each movement toward the goal is logical, reasonable, and natural. Alas, I feel all too often we are guilty of intellectual rape, because we know what the goal is and lack the patience to lead the student by small steps toward that goal.

References

Barsch, R. M. *A movigenic curriculum.* Madison, Wis.: State Department of Public Instruction, 1965.

Bee, H. *The developing child* (2nd ed.). New York: Harper & Row, Publishers, 1978.

Bruner, J. S., Olver, R. R., & Greenfield, P. M. *Studies in cognitive growth.* New York: John Wiley & Sons, Inc., 1966.

Cattell, J. M. Mental tests and measurements. *Mind,* 1890, *15,* 373-381.

Charles, C. M. *Teachers petit Piaget.* Belmont, Calif.: Fearon Publishers, Inc., 1974.

Cratty, B. J. *Active learning: games to enhance academic abilities.* Englewood Cliffs, N.J.: Prentice-Hall, Inc., 1971.

Cratty, B. J. *Physical expressions of intelligence.* Englewood Cliffs, N.J.: Prentice-Hall, Inc., 1972.

Cratty, B. J. *Intelligence in action: physical activities for enhancing intellectual abilities.* Englewood Cliffs, N.J.: Prentice-Hall, Inc., 1973.

Delacato, C. H. *Treatment and prevention of reading problems,* Springfield, Ill.: Charles C Thomas, Publisher, 1959.

Dewey, J. *Democracy in education: an introduction to the philosophy of teaching.* New York: Macmillan Co., 1919.

Erhartic, M. S. *Stability of global self-concepts from three different elementary schools during their first year in a regionalized jr. high school.* Unpublished doctoral dissertation, Boston University, 1977.

Farnham-Diggory, S. The development of equivalence systems. In S. Farnham-Diggory (Ed.), *Information processing in children.* New York: Academic Press, Inc., 1972.

Flavell, J. H. Developmental studies of mediated memory. In L. P. Lipsitt & H. W. Reese (Eds.), *Advances in child development and behavior* (Vol. 5), New York: Academic Press, Inc., 1970.

Flavell, J. H., Beach, D. R., & Chinsky, J. M. Spontaneous verbal rehearsal in a memory task as a function of age. *Child Development,* 1966, *37,* 283-299.

Frostig, M. *Frostig program for the development of visual perception: teaching guide.* Chicago: Follett Educational Corp., 1964.

Gallahue, D. L., Werner, P. H., & Luedke, G. C. *A conceptual approach to moving and learning.* New York: John Wiley & Sons, Inc., 1975.

Guilford, J. P. *The nature of human intelligence.* New York: McGraw-Hill Book Co., 1967.

Hagan, J. W. Some thoughts on how children learn to remember. *Human Development,* 1971, *14,* 262-271.

Humm, H. L. Piaget: overview and perspectives. In J. P. Winnick & R. W. French (Eds.), *Piaget for regular and special physical educators and recreators,* Brockport, N.Y.: State University College, 1975.

Humphrey, J. H. *Child learning through elementary school physical education,* Dubuque, Iowa: William C. Brown Co., Publishers, 1965.

Ismail, A. H., & Gruber, J. J. *Motor aptitude and intellectual performance.* Columbus, Ohio: Charles E. Merrill Pub. Co., 1967.

Jackson, N. E., Robinson H. B., & Dale, P. S. *Cognitive development in young children: a report for teachers.* Washington, D. C.: U.S. Department of Health, Education and Welfare, 1976.

Kagan, J. *Cognitive development: master lectures on developmental psychology.* Washington, D.C.: American Psychological Association, 1976.

Kaherl, K. Discovery through outdoor education. *Journal of Physical Education and Recreation, 49,* 28-32.

Kephart, N. *The slow-learner in the classroom.* Columbus, Ohio: Charles E. Merrill Pub. Co., 1960.

Kirchner, G. *Physical education for elementary school children* (3rd ed.). Dubuque, Iowa: William C. Brown, Co., Publishers, 1974.

Maccoby, E. E., & Jacklin, C. N. The psychology of sex differences. Palo Alto, Calif.: Stanford University Press, 1974.

Maier, H. *Three theories of child development.* New York: Harper & Row, Publishers, 1978.

Miller, G. A. The magical number seven, plus or minus two: some limits on our capacity for processing information. *Psychological Review,* 1956, *63,* 81-97.

Miller, A., Cheffers, J. T. F. & Whitcomb, V. *Physical education: teaching human movement in the elementary schools* (4th ed.). Englewood Cliffs, N.J.: Prentice-Hall, Inc. 1974.

Oliver, J. The effect of physical conditioning exercises and activities on the mental characteristics of educationally sub-normal boys. *British Journal of Education Psychology,* 1958, *28,* 155-165.

Pascual-Leone, J. A mathematical model for the transition role in Piaget's developmental stages. *Acta Psychologica,* 1970, *32,* 301-345.

Perlmutter, M., & Myers, N. A. Recognition memory development in two to four-year olds. *Developmental Psychology,* 1974, *10,* 447-450.

Piaget, J. *The psychology of intelligence.* London: Routledge & Kegan Paul, 1950.

Piaget, J. *The origins of intelligence in children.* New York: International Universities Press, 1952.

Piaget, J., & Inhelder, B. *Memory and intelligence.* New York: Basic Books, 1973.

Robinson, J. P., & London, P. Labeling and imaging as aids to memory. *Child Development,* 1971, *42,* 641-644.

Schwebel, M., & Raph, J. *Piaget in the classroom.* New York: Basic Books, 1973.

Todor, J. Neo-Piagetian theory: a functional model for perceptual-motor learning and development. In D. M. Landers (Ed.), *Psychology of sport and motor behavior* (Vol. 2). University Park: Pennsylvania State University, 1975.

Werner, H. The concept of development from a comparative and organismic point of view. In D. B. Harris (Ed.), *The concept of development: an issue in the study of human behavior.* Minneapolis: University of Minnesota Press, 1957.

White, S. The learning theory approach. In P. H. Mussen (Ed.), *Carmichael's manual of child psychology.* New York: John Wiley & Sons, Inc. 1970.

Winnick, J. P., & French, R. W. *Piaget for regular and special physical educators and recreators.* Brockport, N.Y.: State University College, 1975.

Zaichkowsky, L. D. The development of perceptual-motor sequencing ability. *Journal of Motor Behavior,* 1974, *6,* 255-261.

Zaichkowsky, L. D. Efficacy of perceptual-motor programs in elementary schools. *MAHPER Journal,* 1975a, *22,* 8.

Zaichkowsky, L. D. Piaget's theory of memory development: implications for motor skill learning. In J. P. Winnick & R. W. French (Eds.), *Piaget for regular and special physical educators and recreators.* Brockport, N.Y.: State University College, 1975b.

Zajonc, R. B. Birth order and intelligence: dumber by the dozen. *Psychology Today,* 1975, *8*(8), 37-43.

Student projects

1. Design a progressive series of activities that could be used to develop the cognitive skills of memory, attention, and logical thinking. What is your rationale for choosing these activities?

2. Review the literature relating to the "adventure curriculum" and textbooks that suggest ways in which we can use movement to learn about problem solving in mathematics, science, social studies, and the language arts. Experience as many of these activities as possible so that you can feel comfortable in using them to teach "cognitive" skills.

3. This (ideally group) exercise will give you an opportunity to observe the development of the conservation of mass, number, and liquid. Obtain two or three children representing each age from 5 to 10 years. You will also need two balls of clay, Play-Doh, or Plasticine, as well as the material (candy, containers, water) shown in Fig. 6-1. Begin with the two balls of clay. Ask each child, "Is there the same amount of clay in each of these balls? Are they the same?" If the child

agrees, proceed. If not, ask the child to make them the same. After the child molds the clay balls and indicates that they are the same size, proceed with the test. Say to the child, "Now I am going to squeeze this ball into a pancake." Do so, then place the two objects in front of the child and ask the child whether they are equal in amount of clay or whether the pancake has more or the ball has more. Record the answer and ask for an explanation of it. Record the response. Proceed now to the conservation-of-number task and then to the conservation-of-liquid task (Fig. 6-1). Ask your questions in a manner similar to the "mass" task. Record whether the child was capable of conservation and alo the explanations. You are now ready for data analysis. At what age were the children capable of conservation for each task? Is this consistent with your readings in the chapter and other sources? Did you learn anything about observation and experimentation, for example, giving instructions, recording responses, analyzing data?

Chapter 7

LANGUAGE DEVELOPMENT

Deutsche Presse

Language development is a complex topic. To condense the writing and research of such a large area is indeed difficult; however, this was done with an eye to the purpose and format of this book. In this chapter a discussion of theory precedes information pertaining to age and sex differences in the acquisition of language. The final section discusses the implications language development has for physical education.

The study of human speech and language behaviors has been an area of interest, observation, and speculation since late in the eighteenth century. Child language as an exact and research-oriented study began in Germany in the middle of the nineteenth century (Leopold, 1971). However, contemporary research in speech and language development can be dated from the descriptive studies of Jakobson (1939), McCarthy (1930, 1946, 1954), and Leopold (1971) in the years immediately before and after the Second World War.

Then in 1957 the publication of Chomsky's *Syntactic Structures* provided the impetus for a surge of research and writing by a new group of psycholinguists headed by Menyuk (1963, 1964a, 1964b, 1968, 1969, 1971), Brown and Bellugi (1964), Brown and Fraser (1964), and McNeill (1966). Modern psycholinguistic theory was born in the decade from 1957 to 1967. It has since altered some of the bases for educational theory and has provided a new direction for the study of cognition and learning.

Parallel to the growth of language development theory and research was the intensive psychological study of cognition and the medical investigations of the neuroanatomical and neurophysiological bases for all of human communication, normal and disordered (Geschwind, 1964, 1965, 1970, 1971, 1972; Lenneberg, 1967; Luria, 1958, 1959, 1961, 1966; Masland, 1969). The decade of the sixties witnessed a remarkable melding of the research efforts and findings of psychologists, linguists, neurologists, and educators.

Many earlier theories of language development depended heavily on the Skinnerian view

---

□ This chapter has been prepared expressly for this book by M. Margaret Read, Department of Communication Disorders, Worcester State College, Worcester, Mass.

that language behavior develops out of a conditioning relationship between the human organism and its environment, that language is "taught" by the parent to the child, that the child "learns" because of a need to be approved of and loved by the parent (Mowrer, 1960), and that the process is one of the child's "imitation" of the parental model.

The new theories hold that language is an innate, genetically endowed "potential" that is "triggered" by environmental stimulation. What children "learn" are not specific words and strings of phrase units but rather the rules that predict and regulate the patterns by which sounds and words are sequenced, the forms that determine a word's function within a sentence (noun, verb), the restrictions of form and sequence (past-future tense, singularity-plurality, and so on), and the manner and potential of attaching meaning(s) to particular sound-word sequences. It is the learning of these "linguistic universals" that enables the speaker to produce sentences never before heard and that allows numbers and varieties of verbal combinations staggering to the imagination.

These linguistic rules, which dictate the manner in which the language symbols may be manipulated by the receiver of the message, can be both common to languages in general and specific to the particular language in question. That is, all languages are similar in that they are regulated by rules of phonology, morphology, syntax, and semantics, but there are variations within these that account for the uniqueness of each language.

The mechanism that enables the human child to master the task of verbal communication is located in the brain. Though still not clearly identified and defined, certain localized areas are related to rather general language functions. For example, for most speakers, either right- or left-handed, major responsibility for both interpreting (decoding) and producing (encoding) language is mediated by the left hemisphere. Interpretation and organization for meaning of auditory language stimuli occur primarily within Wernicke's area of the left temporal lobe, and the end process by which words are sequenced and uttered occurs within the frontal lobe of the left hemisphere.

The initial assumption in language development is that the sensory receptors are functioning adequately to provide input to the central nervous system. Mere reception of the sensory stimuli at the cortex is involuntary. However, to deal with the incoming signal at any level beyond reception requires that the cortex be alerted to attend. Screening out or selecting significant stimuli and alerting the cortex to attend seems to be a function of the reticular system of the brain.

Having been discriminated from other stimuli, the incoming signal must be maintained in its temporal and spatial sequence throughout its passage from receptors, through the brain stem and deep structures of the brain itself, across the cortex to its point of reception, and then across the cortex again as it is perceived, related, and associated. In order for meaning to be attached the cortex must recall from storage and then transfer all images and information units (visual, auditory, tactile, and so on) received in the past that pertain to the new signal. Memory is based on a prior neurological fixation of information units with their associated meaning. The current signal and associated past information are then fixed in memory for response, if indicated.

The motor expression of only a single unit of meaning (one word) requires the maintenance of the auditory image of the sounds in sequence; the stimulation and coordination of several muscles each for respiratory, phonation, and articulation; the reception of auditory, tactile, and motokinesthetic feedback; and subsequent correction of production and the sequencing of subsequent units of utterance.

ENVIRONMENTAL FACTORS IN LANGUAGE DEVELOPMENT

Language is not "taught" by the environment; in fact, direct attempts to "teach" language (generally by imitative, reinforcement procedures) to young children are nonproductive. Children learn language from the environment at a rate determined by ability and neurological maturation. Given a normal nervous system with its innate ability to analyze verbal relationships, to make associations between linguistic symbols and their referents, and to produce sequences of phonemic utterances, the child proceeds to learn from the raw material provided by the "instructive" language environment. However, since each child's language environment is distinctive in model or style, it does rather directly determine level and type of vocabulary acquired, distinctive intracultural differences such as regional pronunciation and syntactic styles, and personal style such as rate, intonation, and amount of output.

Absence of environmental stimulation

Environmental stimulation for language must be present in *some* form, and it must be provided at critical times of neurological maturational readiness. Deprivation studies of animals show organic changes as a consequence of lack of sensory stimulation during critical periods. Clinical deprivation studies of children reveal behaviors that *suggest* organic changes and that indicate detrimental delays and alterations in performance. Institutionalized children from infancy to school age are clearly delayed in all aspects of language as compared with peers from both natural and foster home environments (Broadbeck and Irwin, 1946; Dennis, 1973; Goldfarb, 1943a, 1943b, 1945). When institutional environments are clinically manipulated to provide enriched language stimulation, developmental patterns increase as long as the environmental enrichment is maintained but are lost when the enrichment stops. Research with school-age deaf children shows a significant positive correlation between age of diagnosis and remedial intervention and ultimate level of language facility, both in oral communication and in written (or academic) skills. The consequences of late diagnosis and remediation appear to be permanent (Fiedler, 1969; Gallaudet College Survey, 1971; Templin, 1966).

Clearly, language acquisition depends for its existence on an environment that provides the child with experiences to analyze and from which to experiment with linguistic forms and also with reinforcement of the developing experimental utterances.

Environmental variables

Parental models. Parents or parent-figures, rather than siblings and peers, are the most significant providers of children's linguistic environments in the early years, although later, peer groups assume larger roles. Because of cultural patterns, mothers provide more language experiences than do fathers; therefore most studies of parent-child verbal interaction have related to maternal speech stimulation. These studies reveal patterns of verbal interaction that experimenters have clinically manipulated to measure effects of varying interaction styles and to identify what really happens in language analysis and learning.

Mothers use shorter sentences, slower speech, less complex grammar, fewer and more concrete vocabulary items, and more verbal redundancy in speaking with young children than with older children or adults (Phillips, 1973; Vorster, 1974).

Mothers who are the most effective in providing language stimulation do not simplify their language to baby talk or to replications of the young child's utterances. Children are more responsive to a simplified but adult form than to their own levels of output (Shipley et al., 1969; Snow, 1972; Spring, 1974).

There is no major difference in maternal styles of speaking to preverbal daughters or sons; however, there *are* differences in style and patterns between middle- and lower-class mothers (Phillips, 1973).

Parental exchanges with the very young child can be classified into four general types (Dale, 1976, after Brown and Bellugi, 1964).

Prompting. The parent asks a question, such as, "What do you want?" When there is no response, the parent alters her question to, "You want what," a form that more closely approximates the deep structure of the child's yet-to-be-expressed need.

Echoing. In response to a child's unintelligible statement, "I goin owa nah," the parent offers, "You're going where?" The parent is asking for a more intelligible utterance in a way that elicits more linguistic processing from the child than if she had merely repeated the utterance clearly or had just asked, "What?"

Expansion. If the child says, "Mommy soup," the mother responds with, "Mommy is having her soup," or, "This is mommy's soup." In this type of exchange, which reportedly occurs in approximately 30% of middle-

class parent-child interactions, the parent interprets what she thinks the child is saying and provides the full grammatical form, though not requesting a repetition from the child. At this stage the child could probably not provide an accurate repetition anyway, so the parent merely provides the presumed linguistic form by expanding upon what the child has said.

Modeling. In response to a child's utterance the parent offers a relevant question or complementary statement. For example, the child says, "I got apples." The parent says, "Do you like them?" The child responds with, "We got some more," to which the parent replies, "There are a lot in here." The parent is not offering examples of other forms for the child's utterance but is engaging in an exchange of information and content.

McNeill (1966), Menyuk (1971), and Dale (1976) have all concluded that modeling is the preferred manner of interaction. Cazden (1972) theorizes that if modeling is more productive, it is because "richness of verbal stimulation" is a more powerful factor in the child's learning of language than is the model for a specific syntactic form provided by expansion or repetition.

Rank order of birth. Research has shown that singleton children are superior to others in levels of language proficiency achieved. These children demonstrate a larger, more varied vocabulary, longer sentences, and more complex patterns of grammar (Davis, 1937; Day, 1932; McCarthy, 1930). The significant factor seems to be greater association with and exposure to an adult level of language stimulation.

First-born children show patterns of language superiority, but to a lesser degree than only children; the variations partially depend upon the number of years of singleton existence. The more older siblings there are, the less is the language proficiency, particularly at early ages. Exceptions to this pattern occur in a variety of circumstances, related to intelligence level, family dynamics, overall linguistic skill in the family, and parental efforts to minimize the pattern. Children of multiple births (twins, etc.) also tend to exhibit slower rates of speech onset, sentence development, and clarity of articulation.

Multilingualism. One of the long-standing myths of language development and language disorders is that a multilingual environment is a negative factor in the normal acquisition of language and that many communications problems are caused by the presence of more than one primary language in the home. Recent observations suggest that two languages can easily be learned simultaneously by a child with normal language processing abilities and that it is the language-disordered child of bilingual homes who cannot handle two different codes simultaneously.

Socioeconomic class. Educational and social class differences are reflected more in vocabulary than in patterns and styles of grammatical development. Vocabulary seems to be more directly related to the specific experience provided by the environment and tends to be more "teachable" than the development of syntax. Even by the age of 1 year class differences are apparent in measures of vocabulary acquisition, and the discrepancies tend to be maintained throughout maturation.

Not only is the vocabulary of the lower classes later to develop; it also reflects less variety and fewer total items than that of the middle and upper classes. This last factor may be significant in that it is related to differences in the ability to understand or to express abstractions, logical spatial and temporal relationships, generalizations, and individual feelings and differences. Since language serves as a tool for mediating new learning, problem solving, and general cognitive functioning, it is possible to theorize (though not yet possible to prove) a cause-effect relationship between the more limited vocabulary of the lower classes and their history of lesser performance on intelligence and academic achievement tests, both of which have been largely dependent on verbal, Standard American English items.

It is more difficult to define the class differences observed in grammar. Recent studies, however, describe class differences in length and complexity of sentences, use of nouns versus pronouns, and skill in decoding and encoding in functional situations.

Black English. Research of culturally "disadvantaged" language differences in the U.S. has focused primarily on the study of Black American dialect or what is termed Black English, since it is "the most widespread nonstandard dialect and the one we know most about" (Dale, 1976, p. 273).

In contrast to earlier views of it as a deviant linguistic form, Black English proves itself a highly structured and consistent, though different, language or coding system. Some of the rules involving word meanings, sentence structure, and sound production are unlike those of Standard American English, having evolved out of a distinctly different linguistic history, but the use of Black English is now judged by linguists to be a linguistic variation rather than a distorted form of basic English (Table 7-1).

In addition to the differences in linguistic rules between the two languages, there are differences in language content and style developing out of cultural and class differences in life patterns. There are class differences in total verbal output or in length of utterances. Conversational experiences such as mealtimes, trips, and social exposure are different, as are the type and amount of language-enriching experiences such as story-telling, television, and family reading habits. One can also identify differences in lexicon and slang forms.

Earlier work in the field tended to treat the speech of disadvantaged children (class or race groupings) as deviant or deficient as compared to the tests and teaching practices of a Standard American English–dominated society. The early 1960s saw the beginnings of change, due to concurrent linguistic and civil rights developments. Now there is a lesser tendency to relate ethnic/class differences with differences in conceptual and cognitive ability; tests are being developed to reduce the cultural language biases in items for ability measurement. In addition there are efforts to devise teaching programs and curricula that minimize class difference dependencies, even to the degree of teaching Standard American English as a "second language" in an attempt to provide acceptance of the class-cultural difference and yet equal opportunity for competition and social movement among and between classes. Many black speakers make the transition between the two English forms with little effort and teaching; others need the benefit of formal teaching.

Table 7-1. Examples of Standard American English and Black English*

Category	Standard American English	Black English
Negatives	Nobody saw it. I don't see it.	Didn't nobody see it. I ain't see it.
Agreement between subject and verb	He has a bike. He does his work.	He have a bike. He do his work.
Tense	He walks He is working. I have been gone.	He walk He be workin'. I done been gone.
Possessives	John's mother	John mother
Plurals	Tests Desks	Tesses Deskes
Pronominalization	David said, "Here I come."	David, he say, "Here I come."
Embedded interrogatives and imperatives	Ask Albert if he knows how to play basketball. I told you not to do that.	Ask Albert do he know how to play basketball. I told you don't do that.
Speech sound substitutions		
i/e	Pen	Pin
f/th	With	Wif
t/th	Throw	Trow
d/th	These	Dese
Speech sound omissions		
-t	Meant	Men
-l	Help	Hep

*Modified from Dale, P. S. *Language development: structure and function* (2nd ed.). New York: Holt, Rinehart & Winston, 1976; and Shuy, R. W. Language problems of disadvantaged children. In J. V. Irwin and M. Marge (Eds.), *Principles of childhood language disabilities.* Englewood Cliffs, N.J.: Prentice-Hall, Inc., 1972.

RELATION OF LANGUAGE TO COGNITION

The process of thinking is generally considered to involve the manipulation of "internal representations" of events in the external world. The problem is to define what is meant by internal representations. Are they "images" of motor and sensory perceptions of experience or coded symbols representing the experiential events, or both? At what point (or age) do sensory images become coded and thus symbolized? Both thought and language are involved in the child's conceptual organization of the environment. Are they used simultaneously or sequentially?

Piaget (1955, 1969) has been the leading proponent of the argument that thought precedes (and thus is, in effect, independent of) language in the developmental sequence. In Piagetian terms the child's first 2 years are characterized as a sensorimotor period. In the initial stages of this period the child is merely a reflexive organism, reacting involuntarily to body needs and external stimulation. Then he begins to gain awareness of his own behavior, motor and vocal, and to imitate himself. From self-awareness and imitation he progresses to awareness of others and the onset of "intention" as he begins to respond meaningfully and with intent to the actions of others. He imitates these actions, and he begins to manipulate himself and environmental objects in exploration and in preliminary attempts to achieve an end via a self-propelled means.

Midway through the sensorimotor period the child begins to organize the environment in terms of internalized perceptions of experience. To Piaget this is the beginning of symbolic function, the ability to represent one thing with another. He considers this the basis of cognition and one of the prerequisites for the emergence of language. In Piagetian terms the symbolic function refers to a level of perceptual organization rather than to the association of meaning with language symbols. According to Brown's interpretation (1973, p. 200), "The first sentences express the construction of reality which is the terminal achievement of sensory motor intelligence." Thus, language reflects rather than determines cognitive development.

In opposition to the Piagetian view is the proposition that linguistic coding provides the means (rather than the end) for the development of internal representations, that coding enables the child to establish the symbolic function. This view evolved largely from the Whorfian hypothesis (Whorf, 1956).

According to this hypothesis, since each language has its own lexicon (words and word meanings), and since these differ from one linguistic community to another, and since categorization and conceptual frameworks are based on available coding symbols, then perceptions and interpretations and thought vary among language communities. Language provides the means for experiencing the world, and it focuses and, in some ways, determines the internal representations or thoughts about the experienced reality.

Vygotsky (1962) has perhaps been the leading theorist in developing a balance to Piagetian views in relating thought and language. Vygotsky proposed that (1) thought and language have different origins, initially developing concurrently and rather independently; (2) there is a preintellectual stage in the development of speech and language and a prelinguistic stage in the development of cognition; and (3) at a certain point in development the paths of the independent skills, cognition and language, intersect and become interdependent so that thinking becomes verbal and speech reflects rational thought.

Although there is disagreement on the existence of a cause/effect relationship between thought and language and on the temporal sequence of the origins of the two, there is uniform agreement that language is the vehicle by which thought can become more abstract and that it is a major factor in learning new skills and in retaining what is learned.

Piagetian theory must be accounted for in any study of language development, whether by acceptance, modification, or rejection. Therefore let us return to a consideration of Piaget's theory and influence in the language/thought developmental sequence.

During the last 6 months of the sensorimotor period, oral language (speech) becomes a significant behavior in the young child's life. Piaget (1955) concludes that language makes its appearance concurrently with the child's readiness for internal representation. Then, as a result of the child's newly developed ability to use a verbal code to represent reality, he now has the means to recall past events and to anticipate future ones. This development relates to the emergence of such evolving concepts as object permanence (awareness that an object exists even when out of sight) and beginning perceptions of time and space.

At the age of 2 begins Piaget's preoperational stage (Phillips, 1969; Piaget, 1955). As stated by Phillips (1969, p. 54), the "essential difference between a child in the Sensorimotor Period and one in the Preoperational Period is that the former is relatively restricted to direct interactions with the environment, whereas the latter is capable of manipulating symbols that *represent* the environment." After the age of 2, there is an increasing ability to differentiate by means of a verbal code symbol what it represents. The symbols or words can now refer to an event that has happened or might happen; the words become tools for mediating thought and for dealing abstractly with the environment. Thus, this stage represents the beginning of reasoning.

Throughout the 4 or 5 years of this period language development proceeds from one- to two-word utterances to complete, grammatical sentences and a vocabulary of several thousand words. There are many changes in cognition during this period also, evolution of patterns identified by Piaget as concreteness, irreversibility, egocentrism, centering, and states versus transformations (see Chapter 6). For our purposes here it is important to highlight only egocentrism, for much of the study of egocentric thought has focused on its expression through language.

Piaget has characterized both the thought and language of the preoperational period as egocentric and has measured the maturational development of both by the diminution and ultimate disappearance of their egocentric qualities. In referring to egocentric speech he specifies that which is not intended for communication—repetitive and echoic speech and the monologue and collective monologue patterns.

According to Piaget (1955) the monologue is "verbal incontinence," thinking aloud, the overt expression of the images and symbols of the child's thought as related to the surrounding action. The words reflect her experience and then, having been expressed, serve as a feedback device to focus and direct subsequent actions. According to Piaget, the monologue does not in any way relate to a listener. According to Vygotsky (1962), however, the child is unable to distinguish between communication with others and communication with the self, but either way he assumes the presence of a listener. Thus, Piaget's "egocentric speech" is for Vygotsky inner speech vocalized for self-guidance in a social context. As the child matures, the monologues do not just disappear; they become internalized as inner (self-guiding) speech.

As the child matures through the preoperational period, he begins to use language for more "socialized" and diverse purposes. Those include (1) adapted information, in which the child begins to receive and to convey information in dialogue with his listener; (2) criticism of the styles, actions, and events of his environment; (3) commands, requests, and threats with which the child definitively manipulates his environment with words; (4) questions by which information is solicited from the environment; and (5) answers to questions and demands placed on the child by the environment (Piaget, 1955). At 3 years of age the child knows many vocabulary words but does not use them spontaneously in learning, memory, or problem-solving situations; at 5, he uses words as mediators to learning if they are provided by someone else; at 6 or 7 the child spontaneously uses his vocabulary to assist in memory and learning tasks.

At the end of the preoperational period there are major changes in both cognition and language. Between the ages of 5 and 7 the child begins to learn the concept of classification (grouping according to function or semantic clues) or categorization, largely facilitated by developments in language acquisition. He begins to see that reasoning can move not only forward but also back to the beginning of a logical consequence (reversibility). He learns the concept of conservation, that changes in shape or spatial organization need not change the quantity of an object or mass.

These developments, among others, bring the child to a level where, beginning at 7 years of age, she can learn to perform complex mental or symbolic operations such as addition, subtraction, classification, serialization, relationships, and so forth. This is the period of "systematic intellectual activity" (Piaget, 1955), which is still limited to concrete experiences. It is during this period that the child is laying the experiential and symbolic foundations for the last and highest stage of cognitive development, that which is marked by logical thinking or reasoning. In terms of language acquisition the child in the period of concrete operations has, for the most part, mastered the basic linguistic processes. She has acquired a vocabulary of several thousand words; she has learned to generate sentences of a type and complexity comparable to those of the adult; her auditory discrimination and auditory memory have attained adult-level performance; and she is well on her way to mastering the intricacies of written language.

During the formal operations period (ages 11 to 15) the young person has both the mental systems and the linguistic code to perform second-order manipulations, to think logically, sequentially, and creatively, to achieve uniquely productive thinking. During this period thought and language are irretrievably interdependent, as witnessed by the difficulty in researching and in measuring cognition without language at this level. From this point the individual adds quantity, subtle differentiation and expansion, and sophistication to his already established linguistic repertoire. He differentiates and acquires new semantic meanings; he formalizes his understanding and skill in the use of syntax; he increases his skill in using verbal symbols to perform cognitive functions.

AGE DIFFERENCES IN LANGUAGE DEVELOPMENT
Infancy

At birth the infant is capable of gross motor movements; is able to hear and to adapt motor behavior to auditory signals in limited ways; can perceive and track visual signals and produce sounds that contain rudimentary elements of the vocal language. Those sounds initially appear reflexively in a rather gross, whole-body response to environmental stimulation or to internal states of comfort or discomfort. With neurophysiological maturation and continued exposure to an environment of stimulation the reflexive behavior begins to disappear and to be replaced by more selective responses.

The earliest vocal behavior comprises largely the nasalized vowels of the infant cry and other reflexive sounds. Gradually the relatively undifferentiated sounds evolve into a more selective and experimental stage described as babbling. Babbling begins at from 4 to 6 months of age and is characterized by repetitive syllables (consonant plus vowel) that reflect some patterns and, more importantly, auditory and kinesthetic self-awareness. It is the first indication that the child can modify sounds on the basis of information received from the environment and his own nervous system.

As the child nears 1 year of age, consonants outnumber vowels in her utterances, sounds become more specific to the phonemic structure of the parent language, and vocal output diminishes in preparation for the appearance of true speech. Throughout the first year the child begins to associate between language symbols (words, gestures, facial expressions, inflectional patterns) and the things, ideas, and concepts they represent.

The child has been absorbing the sensory stimulation of his environment and has been storing information about what has been sensed. This information is received by the primary reception areas of the cerebral hemispheres, processed by adjacent "association areas," integrated with information being processed by other areas of the brain, and discriminated, sequenced, stored, recalled, and patterned; in short, it is processed for the association between the original stimulus and an idea or concept. Meaning is being established. To use Mykelbust's term, the child is beginning to develop "inner language" (Mykelbust, 1954). Evidence of this inner processing of symbolic behavior is apparent by the ninth or tenth month, at which time the child responds appropriately to such words as his name, "no," and "bye-bye." During ths period the child makes gross motor imitations of gesture, meaningful motions such as shaking the head, waving, and others.

The first word is a significant and sometimes controversial event for all concerned—child, parent, and linguistic researcher. Statistically the first word appears at approximately 12 months. By definition it is the first vocal utterance that has a meaningful referent or that refers to a specific person or thing. In appearance it is most often a bisyllabic, consonant-vowel utterance that sounds like the repetitive, syllabic babbling observed at 6 months. Thus, the "mama," "dada," "baba," "kaka" at 12 months is so much like the "mamamama," "dadadada," "bababa" of earlier vocalizations that parents often report the incidence of first word appearance at 6 months. Again, it is important to stress that in order to be considered a "word" the utterance must be used in association with a referent object or action.

Early studies of first words described them merely as verbal labels, naming devices. However, recent research suggests that they are much more than simple names, that instead they represent early sentence forms or holophrases. Some of these are recognizable words marked by stress or intonational patterns or both that aid in distinguishing them as a question, request, statement, and so forth. Others are sequences of sounds or unrecognizable words also accompanied by stress and intonational markers that identify the utterances as sentence-like, though unintelligible, forms (Menyuk, 1969).

The child is processing and comprehending the nature of the sentence form but lacks the linguistic skill to reproduce the form exactly. Thus, at this stage the child is producing an immature version of a functional unit, with the syntax conveyed by a combination of single words and accompanying intonational markings.

Linguistic competence (comprehension of the rule) precedes linguistic performance (expression of the specific linguistic form); that is, the child comprehends linguistic form prior to development of the maturational skill of expressing it (Chomsky, 1965). Thus at each level of language acquisition, from the emergence of the first word at 12 months to the basic mastery of the sentence form at 8 years, the child relies on an elementary expression of a more complex form.

Sometime between the ages of 18 and 24 months most children make their first attempt at two-word phrases, or what are commonly judged the first actual "sentences." The observed two-word sentences are imperfect examples of either imitated or internally generated grammar. Children do not hear their parents say "bye-bye car" or "Rick go" or other often-quoted examples. Some believe that these sentence forms appear as they do because of the child's limited auditory memory. Others believe that the young child develops an early ability to group words according to functional classes such as noun, verb, and adjective. The concept of linguistic competence-performance again can be applied.

The child does not learn to repeat whole sentences to be understood at a later time. He does not repeat only what he remembers from what he has heard. From his linguistic environment he analyzes and learns structural relationships, which allow him to generate utterances at this level of linguistic competence (Chomsky, 1957; McNeill, 1966; Menyuk, 1963, 1969; Slobin, 1966). Thus, when he hears a sentence such as "Let's take your shoes off," he replies with "shoe off," a reduction of the parental model, retaining word order and functional relationships but reduced to a more ele-

mentary level of understanding of the grammar of the language.

The child's earliest sentences (18 to 24 months) generally consist of a subject and a predicate (S + P) plus modifiers or determiners (noun phrase and verb phrase) that do not basically alter the functional S+P relationship. The early modifiers tend to be articles, possessive pronouns, cardinal numbers, demonstrative adjectives and descriptive adjectives, that is, my coat, more cookie, two mans, big dog, a milk, the mans (Brown and Bellugi, 1964). The basic S + P form exists even when one of the component structures is merely implied (Menyuk, 1969, p. 31):

> (I am) big boy
> (I want) more milk
> (I will) go car
> (It did) fall down
> (This is) mommy chair
> Light (is) on
> Shoe (is) off

With increasing knowledge of grammatical relationships, the child's sentences lengthen to three and four words as they indicate:

1. Agent (subject)—Action (predicate)—Object
   Boy hit ball.
   Me want ball.
2. Agent—Action—Location
   Me go up.
3. Agent—Action—Object—Location
   Me take kitty bed.

One can observe that in all of the early sentence reductions, word order of the retained words is maintained. Words retained from the parental model tend to be nouns, verbs, and adjectives. They are words that have easily teachable referents, are more frequently present in the child's environment, convey more semantic content, and receive more intonational stress. Omissions tend to be those words that serve a more functional, connective purpose and receive less vocal stress in the parental model.

Early childhood

As the child generates more and more of these utterances, she adds new grammatical classes of words, again without altering the basic structure of the sentence. She expands the sentence without changing its form (modified from Menyuk, 1969, p. 33):

Articles	Wash a dishes.
	I makin a cakes.
Prepositions	Put in head.
	Goin on floor.
	He goin up in the ladder.
Pronouns	Turn it off the light.
	I show you again.
Adjectives	The boy saw the girl.
	The happy boy saw the pretty girl.

As children acquire new classes of words and new syntactic forms, they go through a period of experimentation and practice with the new acquisition that often results in redundancy and inappropriate selectivity. The acquisition process goes through three basic stages: (1) acquisition of the vocabulary word, grammatical class, or syntactic string; (2) overgeneralization of the newly acquired item or rule resulting in errors in form; and (3) differentiation of use into more specific and selective situations, allowing for utterances closer in form to the parental model. The stages represent periods of rule induction and hypothesis testing. For example, in "turn it off the light," the child is using the indefinite pronoun "it" but is not convinced that "it" substitutes adequately for "light" and so uses both.

Piaget and others have stressed that language before the age of 3 aids the child in exploring her environment and in clarifying for herself what it is that she is seeing and doing. The child thinks and explores aloud in egocentric monologues of verbal strings. Therefore during this time verbs are expressed primarily in the present tense; there is no time except now. Tense markers come in late in this period.

In addition to the development of grammatical structures 2- and 3-year-old children demonstrate their most rapid acceleration in vocabulary acquisition. As shown in Table 7-2, the number of lexical (meaning) units doubles in that year. Children of that age also achieve perhaps the greatest improvement in clarity of articulation (McCarthy, 1954; Templin, 1957). By 2½ years the child uses practically all of the

vowel sounds and two-thirds of the consonants present in adult speech (Chen and Irwin, 1946).

Vocabulary acquisition or semantic growth is a complicated process, for it involves both lexical (dictionary meaning) and semantic properties as determined by function in a sentence, or semantic properties that themselves dictate function in a sentence. These semantic markers serve as selectional restrictions in a determination of when and how a word is to be used in a sentence, and they must be learned in order both to comprehend and to formulate sentence strings.

Some sentences are ambiguous; that is, their surface structures may have more than one potential meaning to be conveyed. The listener must have knowledge of the possible selectional restrictions in order to assign the correct meaning from context. Likewise, a speaker must be knowledgeable in the selectional restrictions related to semantic relationships in order to formulate meaningful sentences.

By the age of 3 there are major changes in the development of syntax or sentence structure. In Menyuk's (1969) study, she found that all of her 3-year-olds were using all of the classes of grammatical structures needed for what are described as "base structure rules," those rules which enable a child to express a complete, single underlying sentence. They contain grammatical relations, syntactic order, and syntactic classes. Although 3- to 4-year-old children are using all the classes in the base structure rules, they may be using them with deviations in grammatical form. They may have acquired the linguistic rules but are applying them in inappropriate situations, incomplete form, or a redundant manner.

Table 7-2. Development of vocabulary*

Age	Number of words
1 year	3
2 years	272
3 years	896
4 years	1,540
5 years	2,072

*Modified from Smith, M. E. An investigation of the development of the sentence and the extent of vocabulary in young children. *University of Iowa Studies in Child Welfare*, no. 5, 1926.

Less than half of the youngest of Menyuk's population were performing transformations on more than one underlying string or meaning at a time. However, by the end of the period (age 7) more than three-fourths of them were performing operations on two or more underlying sentence strings. In other words they had learned to lengthen and modify their structures by performing gradually more complex transformational manipulations on the word sequences.

Between the ages of 3 and 5 the child uses both egocentric monologue speech as an interpersonal communication characterized by questions, requests, and commands, most often related to her immediate environment and those activities in which she is engaged. This communication serves largely to satisfy immediate needs and to explore and clarify her developing concepts. It is during the latter part of this period that the child begins to develop concepts of number, time and space, and causality. This interactive communication reveals her gathering of information and her reflection on her enlarging world.

After approximately 4½ years of age verbal utterances reflect awareness of past and future and other types of distance from the child's immediate experience. The child demonstrates increasing knowledge of tense, number, person, and gender (Berko, 1958).

In first grade there is an increase in the number of compound words in the child's vocabulary and in the number of compound and complex sentences possible with the new rules of transformation. Vocabulary is more specific and more selective; verbal categorization becomes a vehicle for academic and conceptual learning. The ability to abstract becomes more evident, both cognitively and linguistically.

Late childhood

The age of 8 years represents an extremely significant milestone in the child's development of language. The "normal" 8-year-old child has acquired adult-level abilities in auditory memory and discrimination. His tactile discrimination and fine motor proficiency and dental development have enabled him to master all of the necessary articulatory adjustments for precise speech sound production. He has acquired thousands of semantic units for use in comprehension and expression in both auditory-oral and visual modalities. And, except for the most subtle and complex of the linguistic rules, he has mastered most of the grammatical and syntactic forms of the language.

During late childhood and early adolescence there will be refinement of all the currently existing linguistic forms and processes. Vocabulary units continue to accumulate by means of new additions and by subtle differentiation of semantic definitions already learned. Basic sentence forms acquire variation and sophistication by means of new skills in surface structure transformations. There is increasing facility with and dependence on written language forms as a means to acquire new knowledge and to express new ideas. There is experimentation and mastery of new coding systems in mathematics, foreign languages, and computer sciences.

The first short 8 years provide the child with the basic skills of communication with which she can join the adult population in cognitive and social-psychological interaction and exploration (Fig. 7-1).

SEX DIFFERENCES IN LANGUAGE DEVELOPMENT

Early research among white American children showed a slight difference in favor of girls in nearly all aspects of language development: greater frequency of vocalization and mean number of phoneme types in infancy, earlier appearance of first words and first sentences, clearer articulation, greater complexity of language output, and so on (McCarthy, 1930; Smith, 1926). Studies of cognitive abilities (Goodenough, 1927; Monroe, 1932; Terman, 1916) also showed a slight superiority of girls in intelligence as measured with the usual tests, which were heavily loaded with verbal items. Existing sex differences seem to be more marked among children of the lower socioeconomic classes than among those of middle and upper economic groups (Davis, 1937; Young, 1941).

Later research has continued to support some of these findings but has provided a more selective, carefully identified profile of the variables

"Mamamama."

"Bye-bye?"

"No go nigh-nigh"

"Can we go swimming after school today?"

Fig. 7-1. Various stages of language development. **A,** 6-month-old babbling. **B,** 18-month-old with beginnings of speech. **C,** 30-month-old using rudimentary sentence structure. **D,** 5-year-old with correct language use.

involved, including age of measurement, socio-economic class, tools of measurement, and specification of language or cognitive function under study.

Girls continue to demonstrate superiority in *early* language skills (though no differences are observed in the first year). To be specific they use words sooner, acquire vocabulary more quickly, and develop articulatory proficiency at earlier ages than boys. At early ages girls show an advantage in sentence length or mean length of response, a measure that McCarthy considered the most "objective and reliable" quantitative measure to use for comparisons of the sexes.

However, as shown in Tables 7-3 and 7-4, boys' scores equal or surpass those of girls in both vocabulary and mean length of response by the age of 5 or 6. In addition, studies of sentence complexity and rate of grammatical transformations do not reveal any sex-related discrepancies (Menyuk, 1969; Templin, 1957). Girls, however, do continue to demonstrate a

superiority in clarity of articulation and memory for verbal context with age.

The pattern of measurable (though, according to McCarthy, not statistically significant) differences in early acquisition followed by equalization of scores by the age of 6 is largely attributed to the differential rate of neuro-anatomical maturation, which clearly favors girls in the years from birth through 6 years of age.

One must, however, deal with the ongoing research and clinical data (including the reports of teachers) showing that girls outperform boys in linguistic skills related to later academic success in verbal-related tasks. The problem can be approached from two perspectives, neuroanatomical and environmental. There is organic evidence of more rapid, thus earlier, establishment of cortical dominance for language in girls. There is also long-standing evidence of increased male vulnerability to various types of disease processes and developmental disorders. The figures consistently show a 4:1 preponderance of stuttering, speech disorders, and language and learning disabilities in males over females. Speech and reading ultimately depend on firmly established cerebral dominance, usually of left over right hemispheres, and neurological integration of motor control. If these are late to occur or if they are susceptible to interruption, one expects to see delayed or terminated development in linguistic skills.

Table 7-3. Vocabulary estimates

Age (years)	Boys	Girls
2	304	743
3	822	920
4	1,571	1,576
5	2,181	2,058
6	2,606	1,964

Table 7-4. Mean length of sentence in spoken language*

Researcher	Date	Group	N	1½	2	2½	3	3½	4	4½	5	6	7	8
Smith	1926	Boys	64		1.3	2.2	3.3	4.4	4.1	4.8	4.7			
		Girls	60		2.2	2.4	3.5	3.8	4.4	4.7	4.6			
		All	124		1.8	2.2	3.4	4.3	4.2	4.7	4.6			
McCarthy	1930	Boys	67	1.0	1.4	3.2	3.1	4.2	4.3	4.6				
		Girls	73	1.3	2.1	3.1	3.8	4.4	4.4	4.7				
		All	140	1.2	1.8	3.1	3.4	4.3	4.4	4.6				
Templin	1953	Boys	120								5.35	6.73	7.34	7.25
		Girls	120								6.11	6.35	7.16	7.85
		All	240								5.74	6.53	7.26	7.55

*Modified from McCarthy, D. Language development in children. In L. Carmichael (Ed.), *Manual of child psychology* (2nd ed.). New York: John Wiley & Sons, Inc., 1954.

If one considers that the male child, who is demonstrably slower in some aspects of early language acquisition and thus deprived of equal amounts of practice and accumulation learning effect compared to his female counterpart, enters an academic situation and is placed under equally competitive expectations and stress, one might expect these environmental factors to compound the originally inequitable situation. Thus, clinically, one can find male academic problems clearly related to delayed maturation or organic disorganization, the stress of unfair competition, or both. One can also demonstrate that there continue to be culturally differentiated expectations of male and female children in terms of amount and type of language expression and academic learning.

The research of Maccoby and Jacklin (1974) proposes, in summary, that there are three age-related patterns of sex-related language differences. The first, in support of the older research, is the slight advantage for girls over boys up to age 3 or slightly beyond, with boys having caught up by early school years. The second phase is that of the elementary school years; at this time, except for children with specific problems and for more vaguely reported patterns of lesser language and academic skills in males, it is difficult to prove any significant differential in performance on the basis of specific measures of linguistic skill. The last phase begins at adolescence and continues through college; during this time girls regain and maintain a small but statistically significant superiority in measures of verbal skills such as spelling, comprehending written material, logical relations expressed verbally, and some measures of verbal creativity.

IMPLICATIONS FOR PHYSICAL EDUCATION

Recent theory suggests that the child's perception of sound or phonemic sequences depends on his awareness of the neuromuscular patterns of articulation, or proprioceptive feedback (Berry, 1969; Mysak, 1976). This awareness of motor behavior apparently mediates acoustic information received about the speech signal in such a way as to make possible the early learning of contrasting phonemic markers (Jakobson, 1939). Thus, the child hears and feels the sounds as defined by their acoustic patterns and articulatory placement and is able to learn speech sounds by phonemic categories.

Although the first "true" words and the first independent steps appear at approximately the same age, 12 months, vocalizations tend to decrease during periods of early motor development (reaching for objects, sitting alone, mastery of walking), followed by a rapid spurt in vocabulary acquisition after walking is established (Brigance, 1934; Shirley, 1933; Smith, 1926). The child seems to need to focus his energy on the mastery of one major motor skill at a time.

Movement and position in space, including the concept of laterality and the establishment of cerebral dominance, have been viewed as the underpinnings of visual-spatial perception, number concepts, visual-motor problem solving, and consequently such skills as reading and writing. Thus, a theory has developed that the cause of many academic learning disabilities is the failure of a child to establish dominance and to attain "neurophysiological integration" through the early developmental sequences of gross motor behaviors. The consequent remedial programs involve eye exercises, eye-hand coordination activities, and, the most inclusive, Doman and Delacato's (1963) "patterning." In patterning the objective is to establish cerebral dominance through passive exercises, positioning in sleep, and creeping and crawling.

It is held that by superimposing on the defective organism a regimen of "normal" neuromuscular developmental behaviors that it failed (for whatever reason) to experience or to integrate at the usual ages and the usual sequences, improved, if not normal, levels of perceptual-motor and cognitive functioning can be achieved. Remedial programs based on this premise "have in common the idea that training in basic perceptual and motor functions is a necessary prerequisite for higher cognitive functions, and furthermore, that such functions will be facilitated indirectly, that is, without direct remedial attention, once the perceptual motor foundation is thoroughly established" (Kessler, 1970, p. 144).

In assessing such an approach in terms of its value in treating delays and disabilities in linguistic processing—including speech comprehension, reading, and spelling—it is important to review what is known about neurological maturation and age of established dominance as they relate to language acquisition and to look more closely at the descriptive studies of neurological processes as related to language pathology.

As has been stated earlier, language acquisition occurs for the most part between the ages of birth and 8 years, with particularly significant growth patterns observed between 1 and 3 years. This pattern of acquisition largely parallels and is related to neurological maturation, specifically, the process of myelination of nerve fibers.

The young brain displays a greater tendency toward plasticity and flexibility in terms of focal responsibility for language tasks than does the more mature brain. Indeed, some authors refer to this tendency as a state of equipotentiality, that is, the equal ability of portions of the brain to adapt themselves to the performance of specific functions. Geschwind (1971, 1974) cites research cases of near-complete recovery or acquisition of language function following left hemispherectomy or serious destruction of the left hemisphere, particularly before the ages of 6 to 8 years. In normal neurological development clear left-hemispheric dominance

for language is established by the ages of 6 to 7, with girls demonstrating a clear neuroanatomical advantage in speed of maturation and with demonstrable neuroanatomical asymmetries between left and right hemispheric tissue and pathways. Clinical studies of older children and adults reveal that cortical damage after the age of 8 or so results in permanent language disability, depending on the loci and extent of the lesion and the age of the individual. Clinical studies also reveal diminishing therapeutic and educational gains working with the neurologically impaired population as age increases.

With this in mind and with the view of language and symbolic processing as a function dependent on much more than visual-spatial-motor organization, it is imperative that there be more definitive research to establish the validity of all therapeutic and educational approaches in terms of what is actually being accomplished and the nature of the learning process. Motor activities, in and of themselves, may or may not facilitate cognitive growth, learning, and academic skills. What then is the physical educator to keep in mind in terms of developing programs for the ''normal'' as well as the deviant child?

Language as a measure of maturation

It is important for all educators to recognize and accept the level of performance capability of each child, regardless of age or grade place-

Table 7-5. Early linguistic developmental milestones*

Milestone	Age
Prelinguistic vowel and consonant utterances	Birth to 2 months
Cooing and response to human voice	2 to 4 months
Pleasure vocalizations	3 to 7 months
Variety in syllabification (babbling)	4 to 6 months
Beginning sound imitation	6 to 10 months
''Listening'' to familiar words	8 months
Differential responses to different words (Auditory comprehension)	9 to 10 months
Responses to gestures and to ''bye-bye''	9 to 12 months
First word (vocalization with a referent)	11 to 15 months
Two or more sequential words	18 to 24 months
Naming of single objects and pictures	18 to 24 months
Phrases, sentences, pronouns, and prepositions	18 to 24 months

*Modified from McCarthy, D. Language development in children. In L. Carmichael (Ed.), *Manual of child psychology* (2nd ed.). New York: John Wiley & Sons, Inc., 1954.

ment. We must meet the child "where she is" and take her from there. Language performance is one of the significant indicators of neurological maturation, readiness for academic learning, the environment from which the child comes, the breadth of experiences, and, indirectly, the level of cognitive functioning. Therefore, it is necessary for the educator to be aware of the stages of language development and of illustrative examples of the levels of linguistic expression, and to be able to recognize signs of deficits in the coding process. Table 7-5 provides a listing of some of the early developmental milestones in language development.

Language as a tool for affective growth

Language is the primary means of relating to other people. It is the vehicle with which one acknowledges and explores one's own physical, mental, and emotional states. Language is a tool for the acquisition of new learning, for the control of behavior (one's own and others), and for the modification of the environment. It is a means by which one expresses and solicits friendship and love.

Mothers of young deaf children frequently notice a reduction of anger and frustration observed in their children as language comprehension and expression begin to be established. McCarthy (1954) reports increased facility with behavioral control related to increased comprehension of spoken language; she also discusses changes in social behavior with peers when verbal instead of physical interactions are possible.

The physical educator can assist the child in achieving better affective development through language in a variety of ways:

1. Provide ample opportunity for verbal interaction one to one and in groups.
2. Establish yourself as an available and skilled listener, both individually and in group activities.
3. Utilize verbal expression as a means of clarifying misunderstandings about rules of the game, judgments about performance, and general dissatisfactions.
4. Allow children the opportunity for verbal leadership at their own level in officiating, giving directions for an activity, taking attendance, and in whatever activities are feasible for individual verbal expression.
5. Create opportunity for verbal expression even when one does not easily exist.

Language as a modality for teaching

It has been demonstrated that language is a device for self-direction and self-monitoring, that it aids in focusing attention on and identifying component parts of the learning task, and that it facilitates storage and recall of information to be retained.

Language, then, is a specific tool for teaching and for learning. Within the physical education curriculum it is possible to teach by combined verbal and motor demonstration and to have the children express the following for themselves.

1. Spatial concepts related to prepositions:
   in front of, behind
   above, under
   up, down
2. Relative spatial and size concepts related to adjectives and adverbs:
   higher, lower
   highest, lowest
   faster, slower
   fastest, slowest
   larger, smaller
3. Directional concepts:
   right, left
   around
   circular
   straight
4. Action concepts expressed by verbs:
   run
   walk
   jump
   bend
   touch
   throw
5. Names of objects and games, materials, and so on

Carry-over into home and classroom use can be managed by activity sheets shared with parents and teachers and by closer questioning of the other adults in the child's experience as to the child's performance levels and needs in all areas of life.

Physical educators should use their creativity

and ingenuity to integrate the language arts with physical education. Although the primary objective of activity programs is not the development of language skills, there are numerous *teachable moments* in physical education classes for the concomitant development of language art skills. Gallahue et al. (1975, Chapter 13) provide some very good suggestions for the teaching of language art concepts.

Language is learned from the childs' environment; therefore, the environment must provide ample and consistent experiences in language comprehension and use. Learning is facilitated by language; therefore, the environment must take advantage of the relationship by learning to use language as a teaching device. The language environment is everywhere—home, school, playground. The opportunity to participate is there for every adult who is part of the child's experience.

References

Berko, J. The child's learning of English morphology. *Word*, 1958, *14*, 150-177.

Berry, M. F. *Language disorders of children*. Englewood Cliffs, N.J.: Prentice-Hall, Inc., 1969.

Brigance, W. N. The language learning of a child. *Journal of Applied Psychology*, 1934, *18*, 143-154.

Broadbeck, A. J., & Irwin, O. C. The speech behavior of infants without families. *Child Development*, 1946, *17*, 145-156.

Brown, R. *A first language: the early stages*. Cambridge, Mass.: Harvard University Press, 1973.

Brown, R., & Bellugi, U. Three processes in the child's acquisition of syntax. *Harvard Educational Review*, 1964, *34(2)*, 32-57.

Brown, R., & Fraser, C. The acquisition of syntax. In U. Bellugi & R. Brown (Eds.), The acquisition of language *Monographs of the Society for Research in Child Development*, 1964, *29*, 43-79.

Cazden, C. *Child language and education*. New York: Holt, Rinehart & Winston, 1972.

Chen, H. P., & Irwin, O. C. Infant speech: vowel and consonant types. *Journal of Speech Disorders*, 1946, *11*, 27-29.

Chomsky, N. *Syntactic structure*. The Hague: Mouton Publishers, 1957.

Chomsky, N. *Aspects of the theory of syntax*, Cambridge, Mass.: The M.I.T. Press, 1965.

Dale, P. S. *Language development: structure and function* (2nd ed.). New York; Holt, Rinehart & Winston, 1976.

Davis, E. The development of linguistic skill in twins, singletons with siblings, and only children from age five to ten years. *Institute of Child Welfare Monograph* (No. 14). Minneapolis: University of Minnesota Press, 1937.

Day, E. J. The development of language in twins: a comparison of twin and single children. *Child Development*, 1932, *3*, 179-199.

Delacato, C. H. *The diagnosis and treatment of speech and reading problems*. Springfield, Ill.: Charles C Thomas, Publisher, 1963.

Dennis, W. *Children of the creche*. New York: Prentice-Hall, Inc., Century Psychology Series, 1973.

Fiedler, M. F. Developmental studies of deaf children. *American Speech and Hearing Association Monographs* (No. 3). Washington, D.C.: American Speech and Hearing Association, 1969.

Gallahue, D. L., Werner, P. H., & Luedke, G. C. *A conceptual approach to moving and learning*, New York: John Wiley & Sons, Inc., 1975.

Gallaudet College Survey. Survey of hearing impaired children and youth. *Gallaudet College Office of Demographic Studies*, ser. D. no. 9, 1971.

Geschwind, N. The development of the brain and the evolution of language. In C. I. J. M. Stuart (Ed.), *Monograph series on language and linguistics* (Vol. 17). Washington, D.C.: Georgetown University Press, 1964.

Geschwind, N. Disconnection syndromes in animals and man. *Brain*, 1965, *88*, 237-294; 585-644.

Geschwind, N. The organization of language and the brain, *Science*, 1970, *170*, 940-944.

Geschwind, N. Neurological foundations of language. In H. Mykelbust (Ed.), *Progress in learning disabilities* (Vol. 1). New York: Grune & Stratton, 1971.

Geschwind, N. Anatomical evolution and the human brain. *Bulletin of the Orton Society*, reprint 41, *22*, 1972.

Geschwind, N. Selected papers on language and the brain. In R. Cohen & M. Wartofsky (Eds.), *Selected papers on language and the brain*. Boston: D. Reidel Publishing, 1974.

Goldfarb, W. The effects of early institutional care on adolescent personality, *Journal of Experimental Education*, 1943a, *12*, 106-129.

Goldfarb, W. Infant rearing and problem behavior. *American Journal of Orthopsychiatry*, 1943b, *13*, 249-265.

Goldfarb, W. Effects of psychological deprivation in infancy and subsequent stimulation. *American Journal of Psychology*, 1945, *102*, 18-33.

Goodenough, F. L. Consistency of sex differences in mental traits at various ages. *Psychological Review*, 1927, *34*, 440-462.

Jakobson, R. *The sound laws of child language and their place in general phonology: selected writings*. The Hague: Mouton Publishers, 1939.

Kessler, J. W. Contributions of the mentally retarded toward a theory of cognitive development. In J. Hellmuth (Ed.), *Cognitive studies* (Vol. 1). New York: Brunner/Mazel, Inc., 1970.

Lenneberg, E. H. *Biological foundations of language*. New York: John Wiley & Sons, Inc., 1967.

Leopold, W. The study of child language and infant bilingualism. In A. Bar-Adon & W. Leopold (Eds.), *Child language: a book of readings*. Englewood Cliffs, N.J.: Prentice-Hall, Inc., 1971.

Luria, A. R. Brain disorder and language analysis. *Language and Speech*, 1958, *1*, 13-21.

Luria, A. R. The directive function of speech in development and disolution. *Word*, 1959, *15*, 341-352.

Luria, A. R. *Human brain and psychological processes* (Vol. 1). Moscow: Izdatelstvo Akademii Pedagogicheskikh Nauk Russian S.F.S.R., 1963. (English translation by B. Haigh. New York: Harper & Row, Publishers, 1961.)

Luria, A. R. *Higher cortical functions in man* (1st ed.). Moscow: Moscow University Press, 1962. (English translation by B. Haigh. New York: Basic Books and Plenum Press, 1966.)

McCarthy, D. The language development of the preschool child, *Institute of Child Welfare Monograph Series* (No. 4). Minneapolis: University of Minnesota Press, 1930.

McCarthy, D. Language development in children. In L. Carmichael (Ed.), *Manual of child psychology*. New York: John Wiley & Sons, Inc., 1946.

McCarthy, D. Language development in children. In L. Carmichael (Ed.), *Manual of child psychology* (2nd ed). New York; John Wiley & Sons, Inc., 1954.

Maccoby, E. E. & Jacklin, C. N. *The psychology of sex differences*. Palo Alto, Calif.: Stanford University Press, 1974.

McNeill, D. Developmental psycholinguistics. In I. Smith & G. A. Miller (Eds.), *Genesis of language*. Cambridge, Mass.: The M.I.T. Press, 1966.

Masland, R. L. Brain mechanisms underlying the language function. In National Institute of Neurological Diseases and Strokes, *Human communication and its disorders: an overview*, Monograph no. 10. Washington, D.C.: U.S. Department of Health, Education and Welfare, 1969.

Menuyk, P. Syntactic structures in the language of children. *Child Development*, 1963, *34*, 407-422.

Menuyk, P. Comparison of grammar of children with functionally deviant and normal speech. *Journal of Speech and Hearing Disorders*, 1964a, *7*, 109-121.

Menuyk, P. Syntactic rules used by children from preschool through first grade. *Child Development*, 1964b, *35*, 533-547.

Menuyk, P. The role of distinctive features in children's acquisition of phonology. *Journal of Speech and Hearing Research*, 1968, *11*, 138-146.

Menuyk, P. *Sentences children use*. Cambridge, Mass.: The M.I.T. Press, 1969.

Menuyk, P. *The acquisition and development of language*. Englewood Cliffs, N.J.: Prentice-Hall, Inc., 1971.

Monroe, M. *Children who cannot read: the analysis of reading disabilities and the use of diagnostic tests in the instructions of retarded readers*. Chicago: University of Chicago Press, 1932.

Mowrer, O. H. *Learning theory and the symbolic processes*. New York: John Wiley & Sons, Inc., 1960.

Mykelbust, H. *Auditory disorders in children*. New York: Grune & Stratton, 1954.

Mysak, E. D. *Pathologies of speech systems*. Baltimore: The Williams & Wilkins Co., 1976.

Phillips, J. L. *The origins of intellect: Piaget's theory*. San Francisco: W. H. Freeman & Co., Pubs., 1969.

Phillips, J. R. Syntax and vocabulary of mother's speech to young children: age and sex comparisons. *Child Development*, 1973, *44*, 182-185.

Piaget, J. *The language and thought of the child* (2nd ed). New York: World Publishing, 1955.

Piaget, J., & Inhelder, B. *The psychology of the child*. New York: Basic Books, 1969.

Shipley, E. F., Smith, C. S., & Gleitman, L. R. A study in the acquisition of language: free responses to commands. *Language*, 1969, *45*, 322-342.

Shirley, M. M. Intellectual development. *The first two years: a study of twenty-five babies* (Vol. 2). *Institute of Child Welfare Monographs* (No. 7). Minneapolis: University of Minnesota Press, 1933.

Slobin, D. I. The acquisition of Russian as a native language. In F. Smith & G. A. Miller (Eds.), *The genesis of language*. Cambridge, Mass.: The M.I.T. Press, 1966.

Smith, M. E. An investigation of the development of the sentence and the extent of vocabulary in young children. *University of Iowa Studies in Child Welfare* (No. 5). Ames, Iowa: University of Iowa Press, 1926.

Snow, C. E. Mother's speech to children learning language. *Child Development*, 1972, *43*, 549-565.

Templin, M. Certain language skills in children: their development and interrelationships. *Institute of Child Welfare Monographs* (No. 26). Minneapolis: University of Minnesota Press, 1957.

Templin, M. Vocabulary problems of the deaf child. *International Audiology*, 1966, *5*, 349.

Terman, L. *The measurement of intelligence*. Boston: Houghton Mifflin, 1916.

Vorster, J. *Mothers' speech to children: some methodological considerations*. Instituut voor Algemene Taalwetenschap, Universiteit van Amsterdam, 1974.

Vygotsky, L. C. *Thought and language*. Cambridge, Mass.: The M.I.T. Press, 1962.

Whorf, B. L. *Language, thought, and reality*. New York: Wiley and Technology Press, 1956.

Young, T. M. An analysis of certain variables in a developmental study of language. *Genetic Psychology Monographs*, 1941, *23*, 3-141.

Student projects

1. Arrange to observe in preschool, kindergarten, and second-grade classrooms. Tape record language samples at each age level and compare collected observations with the theoretical models described in this chapter.

2. Interview the parents of a preschool child to obtain the following ages at which the child first:

a. Sat alone
b. Walked unsupported
c. Babbled (repetitive syllables)
d. Responded to verbal instructions (without gestural cues)
e. Used the first meaningful word
f. Combined words into two- and three-word phrases

Do the times that the parents remember corre-spond with those milestones indicated in this chapter?

3. Tape record a ten- to fifteen-minute conversation with a third-grade child and analyze the recorded language sample in terms of the following criteria:
   1. Average number of words per sentence
   2. Variety of verb forms
   3. Use of possessives
   4. Variety of sentence forms
   5. Estimated size of vocabulary

Part three

AFFECTIVE, OR SOCIAL-PSYCHOLOGICAL, DEVELOPMENT

Chapter 8

SOCIALIZATION

Socialization is generally considered the process by which an infant becomes an adult in a specific cultural setting. When a child is born, she is embarking on a road of many and varied social encounters. These assist her in learning commonly accepted behaviors and attitudes of the society in which she will be functioning. Socialization is commonly, and inappropriately, associated with the very young child and the learning of behaviors dealing with such things as feeding habits, toilet training, and the control of aggression and sexuality. Socialization, however, is a lifelong process, and as people vary their social environment, they must learn to adapt to new situations.

This process involves learning how to behave in a cultural setting, that is, interacting with other people and understanding what kind of behavior is expected or appropriate in different contexts. Most people can recall many new experiences when they felt very anxious—the first day of school, moving to a new place, the "first date," and so forth. These anxious feelings in part were caused by not knowing what would be expected of them in the new situation. Therefore, if socialization is defined as "the modification of one's attitudes and behavior to conform to the expectations with whom one interacts" (Secord et al., 1976, p. 12), it is necessary to describe how to go about learning to conform to expectations. How does one find out how to act in varied situations? There are three general concepts that will help to better understand the structure of the social system. These concepts are expressed in the terms status, roles, and norms.

STATUS, ROLES, AND NORMS

A *status* refers to a position in society. The same person can hold many positions in society—educator, mother, daughter, friend, swimmer, and so on—in the course of a week or even a day. Some of these positions are simply a function of age or sex, that is, mother, adult, daughter. Others, such as educator or swimmer, may be a function of expertise or experience in a particular area. As a person holds or aspires to a particular status, she learns to play the role associated with it.

A *role* is the particular, individual behavior that a person uses in carrying out a status or the way a person interprets a status. It is the dynamic aspect of the status. In all athletic contests there is a particular position played by each participant. There is a "job description" that goes with that position; for example, a tackle in football is expected to be able to block well, among other things. However, various individuals bring their own style of play to a position. Who can forget the way Bobby Orr played defenseman with a very definite offensive style or the various moves of Julius Erving when he handles the basketball?

As people continue to interact with one another, they build up role expectations. A person who has a particular status should enact his role in a predictable fashion: a teacher should act like a teacher, and a doctor like a doctor. These expectations can also be called norms. A *norm* is a standard of behavior that would be expected from all members of a given group or even an entire society. Roles, then, are individualistic, whereas norms are standardized behaviors. Certain behaviors are associated with mothers and certain behaviors with fathers, regardless of the specific individuals.

Some norms are shared by a few groups, a particular geographical area, or an entire country. Basketball players' shaking hands with their opponents prior to the beginning of the contest is a norm that is particular to athletic contests in general. A geographical norm is exemplified by "southern hospitality." Southerners are thought of as warm and friendly people. An example of a societal norm is the "norm of reciprocity." When Mary does a favor for Matthew, Matthew is expected to return the favor. Mary and Derek hold and turn the jump rope while Matthew jumps. It is expected that Matthew will also hold and turn the jump rope while Mary and Derek take their turns.

Holding statuses and learning about the roles associated with those statuses is how one becomes socialized. We will discuss two general ways roles can be learned.

The work of Skinner (1969) is usually associated with the use of reinforcement contingencies as a learning strategy. This particular mode of learning looks at the type of reinforcement used in relation to a response; this has an effect on the probability of the response's occurring again. The types of reinforcement have been labeled positive and negative reinforcement; both kinds increase the chance of a particular response's occurring again. Many times people confuse punishment with negative reinforcement. They can be differentiated by remembering that reinforcement is supposed to strengthen a response, while punishment is supposed to eliminate it. Reinforcement is viewed as a better way than punishment to enhance learning, and positive reinforcers are considered more desirable than negative ones.

This can be demonstrated easily in the family or educational setting. When a child starts to take his first wobbly step, encouragement or reinforcement in the form of praise is offered,

thereby strengthening the response. The child continues to try to walk. In school teachers use the word "good" to indicate that a particular response was appropriate and should be used again.

Some theorists object to the Skinnerian view of learning and indicate that other factors need to be taken into account when a person is attempting a new skill. These people are concerned with learning that occurs via modeling or imitation. These terms, although not synonymous, are used to indicate the same process. The work of Bandura and Walters (1963) is commonly associated with this theoretical approach to learning. According to Bandura there are four processes involved in modeling. A person must: (1) attend to the other person's behavior, (2) remember it, (3) have the capa-

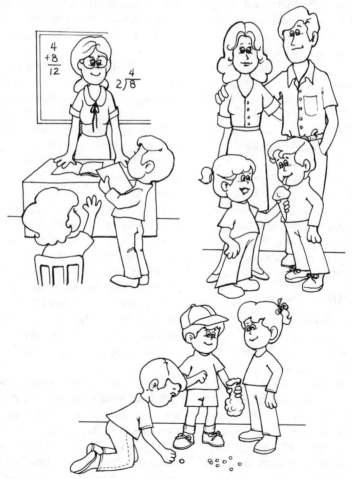

Fig. 8-1. Three important socializing agents in the life of a child: school, family, and peer group.

bility to perform it, and (4) be motivated to do so. One factor to keep in mind is that the imitation of the behavior does not need to immediately follow its observation. Modeling could occur in the following manner. Dawn is watching Dorothy Hamill perform the free exercise routine in skating that culminated in the receipt of a gold medal at the Olympic Games. A few days later Dawn decides to go ice-skating, and as she is skimming over the ice she remembers a particular jump that Dorothy had performed. She wants to try a jump, too. She remembers what the jump looked like and with this thought in mind attempts the jump. The success or failure of her performance will be dictated by her ability to perform that particular movement.

It is important to note that models may be chosen from a variety of sources, with the family an early primary source and age-mates, relatives, teachers, coaches, athletes, and television and film stars other rich sources. As children imitate these models, they are assuming the roles of the models. Children in their play many times assume adult roles, that is, mother, father, doctor, pilot, parachutist, dancer. This role playing assists children in making the transition from childhood to adult status. This occurs as a child "tries on" a particular role without having to meet any of the role obligations.

Socialization occurs through the learning of social roles. These roles consist of particular patterns of behavior that are expected of people who fill the same place in society. Certain behaviors are expected of people who fill the role of "parent" or "teacher" without specific reference to a particular parent or teacher. There are many factors that interact in the entire socialization process; some have been explained in this chapter. For further discussion see Hollander (1976).

There are many conditions under which one learns the social roles that are necessary to become a competent person in society. One may learn about cooperation through playing with friends, about competition by competing for grades, about morals by becoming active in a religious group, about politics by being involved in the community, and about love by sharing loving relationships in the family. Some of the major socializing agencies are the family, the school, the church, the peer group, and the community. Three of these important agencies will be considered—the family, the school, and the peer group. These agencies have varying amounts of influence, depending on the age of the individual. The family is of prime importance in the early years, but the school and peer group take on added importance as age increases. The socialization process is illustrated in Fig. 8-1.

THE FAMILY AND SOCIALIZATION

The first 6 months of life are mostly an asocial time for the infant. Much time is spent in sleeping and eating. Indeed, one author (Rheingold, 1969) views this as a time when the child socializes the wife and husband into mother and father by teaching them to respond to specific needs and wants. The child indicates his desires, and the caretaker responds by changing, feeding, playing, or putting the child to bed, depending on the circumstances.

Even though the first 6 months and sometimes the first year may be considered asocial times by those with a more intellectual orientation, people involved in the discipline of human movement consider this a time when initial contact through physical movement plays a major part in the socialization process. The first smile, the first rollover to the stomach, the first time the infant sits up, and the first attempts at crawling, creeping, and walking normally occur by the age of 1 year. Certainly all of these movements or accomplishments are accompanied by some type of reaction by the parents or other siblings. The child is encouraged to do all of these activities and is rewarded by others or by herself simply by the satisfaction derived from the movement itself. It is during this time that a child starts to form an impression of herself as a distinct being. Piaget places a great deal of importance on physical movement as a source of learning. This is clearly exemplified in his first stage of cognitive development, called the sensorimotor stage.

The time until the commencement of school is spent mainly with the family. The child becomes acquainted with the adult world through the behaviors, attitudes, and values of the family members, particularly the mother, father, and other siblings. Other inputs into these behaviors, attitudes, and values occur as the child enters school.

THE SCHOOL AND PEER GROUP IN SOCIALIZATION

It is very difficult to separate the influence of these two agencies on socialization because the peer group is often formed in the school setting. Schools may be viewed as the formal socializing agent and the peer group as the informal one. With neighborhood schools the groups formed in the school are quite similar to those play groups found in the nieghborhood.

The school, as a socializing agency, is expected to help the student learn the skills that are necessary for efficient functioning in society. Our society expects the school to be mainly concerned with cognitive skills, although affective ones (morality, attitudes, inerpersonal relations) have recently claimed their share of time in the school structure. The school operates in a formal way in that classroom groups are formed by certain prescribed standards, be they aptitude, intelligence, age, or other categories.

The peer group, the informal socializing agency, is closely, if not integrally, connected with the school. The peer group many times arises from the associations made in the schools, particularly if the schools are attended by people in the same neighborhood. Havighurst and Neugarten (1975) have noticed that peer groups have certain characteristics in common regardless of age. These characteristics are as follows:

1. The child is treated as an equal, on the same level as playmates. No adult authority figure makes them feel inferior.
2. The relationships tend to be transitory— groups change as a result of the child's own needs and interests.
3. Influence tends to become more important as age increases.

They further state that these groups serve three basic functions. The first is *learning the culture,* that is, learning about the prevailing standards of the adult society, which include among other things competition, cooperation, sex roles, honesty, and responsibility. The peer

group also aids in *social mobility*. This is thought of in terms of upward mobility, and it has been demonstrated that a student's desire to attend college or the likelihood that this will occur is strongest if the student's best friend plans to go to college (Alexander and Campbell, 1964). Last, the peer group serves as a *reference group* and helps the child achieve independence from adults, particularly parents.

AGE DIFFERENCES IN SOCIALIZATION

What are some of the things one needs to know to adapt to the environment? Havighurst (1972) sets forth the developmental tasks of education, and his work has been chosen as the guideline for this chapter specifically for that reason. Havighurst (1972, pp. 9-17) lists the developmental tasks of infancy and early childhood as follows:

1. Learning to walk
2. Learning to take solid foods
3. Learning to talk
4. Learning to control the elimination of body wastes
5. Learning sex differences and sexual modesty
6. Forming concepts and learning language to describe social and physical reality
7. Getting ready to read
8. Learning to distinguish right and wrong and beginning to develop a conscience

He goes on to list the tasks of middle childhood, which for him includes the ages of 6 through 12 (pp. 19-35):

1. Learning physical skills necessary for ordinary games
2. Building wholesome attitudes toward oneself as a growing organism
3. Learning to get along with age-mates
4. Learning an appropriate masculine or feminine social role
5. Developing fundamental skills in reading, writing, and calculating
6. Developing concepts necessary for everyday living.
7. Developing conscience, morality, and a reality of values
8. Achieving personal independence
9. Developing attitudes toward social groups and institutions

There is continuing refinement of some of the developmental tasks from one period to the next. Tasks for adolescence include (pp. 43-82):

1. Achieving new and more mature relations with age-mates of both sexes
2. Achieving a masculine or feminine social role
3. Accepting one's physique and using the body effectively
4. Achieving emotional independence of parents and other adults
5. Preparing for marriage and family life
6. Preparing for an economic career
7. Acquiring a set of values and an ethical system as a guide to behavior—developing an ideology
8. Desiring and achieving socially responsible behavior

Table 8-1, adapted from Havighurst, indicates which socializing agents are responsible for developmental tasks.

Most of the physiological needs (infancy and early childhood) that occur in the early years are met by the principal caretaker in the family. However, those tasks that deal with readiness to perform certain activities are accomplished through the peer group and school as well as the family. The concepts of language and cognitive development have been discussed in previous chapters, and moral development will be investigated in a subsequent one. In this chapter the focus will be on the development of physical skills and masculine or feminine social role development.

The task of learning a feminine or masculine identity is probably very important for people concerned with physical activity. With the increasing emphasis on equality of sexual opportunity (sports programs, employment, and privileges and responsibilities) there is greater awareness of those behaviors necessary to help people become competent and comfortable in their identity as woman or man.

Infancy and early childhood

The family has been the primary socializing agency, but as societies have shifted from agrarian to industrial, it has been found that the family cannot teach all the skills necessary for a child to become a productive member of society.

The family, which is the first socializing agency, provides a comfortable environment for the child in which to grow and to learn the attitudes, values, and beliefs of parents and other siblings, as well as age-mates. One medium through which the child is socialized is movement. The very first responses and interactions between parents and child are physical. Motoric activity is the main way in which the child learns about himself and the surrounding environment. Attempts to reach out and touch objects, to propel the body through space, and to manipulate toys are the beginning interactions with the environment and parents. Toys are used to enhance a child's awareness. A rattle, stuffed toy, and perhaps even a ball are some common items seen in the cribs and playpens of infants. The parents play with the

Table 8-1. Socializing agents involved in tasks of middle childhood and early adolescence*

Task	Agent		
	Family	Peers	School
Get along with peers		X	X
Learn masculine or feminine role	X	X	X
Develop intellectual skills			X
Choose and prepare for an occupation	X	X	X
Develop attitudes toward social groups and institutions	X	X	X
Become independent of parents and other adults		X	X
Develop conscience and moral judgment	X	X	X
Develop physical skills		X	X

*Modified from Havighurst, R. J. *Developmental tasks and education* (3rd ed.). New York: David McKay Co., Inc., 1972.

child—sing songs, pat-a-cake, peek-a-boo—and are the caretakers for the necessary chores of feeding, changing, and dressing during the first year of life.

Other children (age-mates, siblings) interact with the child during early childhood. Hugging, squeezing, and kissing are common behaviors seen at this age. As time goes on, the type of play changes. These changes, in effect different patterns of play behavior, have been categorized by Parten (1932). They are solitary, parallel, associative, and cooperative play. *Solitary play* is that in which the child acts alone. The child is engrossed and involved in her own activity without concern for others. This type is more common among children in the 2 to 2½ group. *Parallel play* is quite similar to solitary play. The child may be in the presence of other children, and the toys may be similar or identical to those of the other children, but the play is alongside, not with, other children. This type is common between the ages of 2½ and 3½. *Associative play* occurs when children start using social interaction as a basis for play. Two children may use the same toys and initiate some type of game. Follow-the-leader and invitation-type activities are seen at this time. The age span for this type of play is 3½ to 4½. *Cooperative play* between children is purposeful. Some goal for the activity is probable. The play group may have one or two leaders who direct and select the activities of the group. This type of behavior is seen around the ages of 4 and 5 (Fig. 8-2).

These four categories demonstrated in early childhood parallel the types of changes that are also occurring in other developmental domains. A child is able to play with others once he is able to be less "egocentric" and more able to place himself in another's shoes. This corresponds to Piaget's movement from the sensorimotor to pre-operational stage. As the child progresses through these stages (which end at approximately 7 years of age), he becomes less and less egocentric. As the play or peer group increases in importance, the family decreases in importance on some socialization tasks.

Late childhood

As previously mentioned, physical movement sets the stage for later development. The dependence upon the family during the early years of life is gradually reduced by associations with age-mates in play activities and subsequently through school associations. There is some concern that the amount of time spent in constructive play activity has been diminishing. Parten's study (1932) in which preschool children were observed indicated that in the older age groups a good share of time was spent in play involving other children. A more recent study (Barnes, 1971) indicated that this same age group now spends a good share of its time just watching activity and less than one-half as much time in cooperative activities.

Other studies (Devereux, 1972; Sutton-Smith and Rosenberg, 1961) have found a decreasing appearance of spontaneous game activity participated in by the youth of this country. Devereux attributed this change to the increased incidence of television watching. Another explanation may be that *organized sport* (Little League, Pop Warner) takes up a great deal of time. For example Skuberic, as early as 1955, found that with a sample of Little Leaguers about one-half of the free time of boys was utilized in practicing baseball skills.

Play activities take up a sizable amount of time during childhood, and this time is spent in physical activity–related groups (unorganized and organized) that can enhance the opportunity to develop and learn physical skills. As one acquires those basic physical skills that are necessary for participation in more complex activities later and as basic motor skills increase in relationship to ability to perform, play patterns become more complex. People play cooperatively and with more structure because they have become more proficient in physical and intellectual abilities, thus allowing games to be more complex. It is possible to interact more easily using running, throwing, and other basic skills. Acceptance by the peer group may be based on physical attributes and abilities—"being able to play the game" (Broekhoff, 1976; Martens, 1975, Chapter 6).

As physical activity evolves from play to

Fig. 8-2. Four types of play. **A**, Solitary. **B**, Parallel. **C**, Associative. **D**, Cooperative. (C Courtesy Boston University Photo Service.)

games to sport, there is an increasing emphasis on the competitiveness of the activity—the desire to win. Orlick (1975) and Orlick and Botterill (1974) have expressed the concern of many professionals about the value of "competitive sports" at very young ages. These authors report feelings of dissatisfaction with organized athletics from very young participants. These are the athletic "dropouts." The pressure to win placed on players by the parents and coaches has been given as one reason for dropping out. It has been noted that players would rather play for a mediocre team than sit on the bench for a winning one.

Is this competitive behavior observed only in children of the United States and Canada? Are North American children more competitive than cooperative? It has been demonstrated that different cultures socialize youth differently in relation to cooperation and competition. Israeli kibbutz children who are group reared are more cooperative than urban Israeli children (Shapiro and Madsen, 1969). Russian children reared in day-care centers show more cooperative behavior than children in the United States (Bronfenbrenner, 1970). This competitiveness seems to increase with age, as demonstrated in a study by Webb (1969). Students in grades six, eight, ten, and twelve were asked to respond to a questionnaire about certain objectives of playing a game. The choices were to play as well as you can, to beat the opponent, or to play the game fairly. The results indicated that as the age increases, the choice of "beating the opponent" increases.

Can physical educators work in some way to tone down this competitiveness? The work of Sherif and others (Sherif et al., 1961; Sherif and Sherif, 1953) has pointed out that it is possible to develop cooperative endeavors. This concept has been promulgated with "no win" sports (Flaegelman, 1976; Orlick, 1978). Participants simply play the game with no emphasis on score but with emphasis on developing physical attributes and enjoying the activity.

Adolescence

During adolescence the importance of the peer group increases and in some instances runs counter to the values of the adult world. This seems to be a particular problem with students in high school, where the values of achieving good grades and continuing in educational pursuits at a good school are not high-priority items. Studies by Coleman (1961) and Gordon (1957) have indicated the importance of the peer group and reflection of its values on the behavior of school students. These studies indicated that the athletic subculture had high prestige, while scholars were perceived in a lower-prestige group. This pattern has also been demonstrated in the elementary school (Buchanan et al., 1976).

If athletes are the more popular students, what are the implications for achievement and educational aspirations? There is some evidence that athletes have higher educational aspirations than nonathletes and achieve more academically. In a review of the literature Stevenson (1975) cites eight studies that support higher academic achievement for athletes. However, he also indicates that there are two research studies that did not find this result. A study by Schafer and Armer (1968) found also that there seemed to be a greater positive effect on the academic performance of "blue-collar" athletes.

Rehberg and Schafer (1968), Spady (1970), and Spreitzer and Pugh (1973) have shown that the educational aspirations of sports participants are high and not detrimental to academic pursuits. It was particularly noted that the effect seemed to be greatest for those who would not otherwise attend college. Spady contends that the recognition received in a high-status peer group tends to make a person have higher educational aspirations; however, the skills necessary for achieving those expectations (college attendance) are not necessarily taught or learned by those who initially have low "resources; that is, financial, attitudinal, intellectual, and academic attributes are initially low. A more recent study (Hanks and Eckland, 1976) agrees that low-ability students might enhance their academic performance by participation in athletics but states that other extracurricular activities may be just as important, if not more so, as athletics in helping people achieve educational aspirations. It seems that participating in athletics does not develop those skills necessary for a successful place in the adult world to as great an extent as do leadership positions in other types of extra-curricular activities.

Play, games, and sports do play a part in the socialization of youth in that they allow children to gain some skills that enable them to feel competent and good about themselves. Physical activities give opportunities for much interaction and diversity in role playing; these enhance a person's ability to handle a variety of experiences. It has been shown that when activities such as group games, cards, and checkers are provided, rather than toys for individual play (crayons, clay), more complex social interaction occurs (Quilitch and Risley, 1973). The opportunity for physical educators to enhance the socialization of youth is present and can be capitalized on by a teacher who is genuinely concerned about students.

SEX DIFFERENCES IN SOCIALIZATION

Very few topics are presently generating more interest and conversation than appropriate behaviors, occupations, and child-rearing responsibilities of the two sexes. The discussion is leading to the redefinition of responsibilities and appears to be having a broadening effect on the flexibility allowed to men and women in performing their various roles and functions in society. What are the sex differences? Are they innate or learned? What part do play, games, and sports contribute to the development of appropriate masculine and feminine identities? First let us discuss the question of learning about sex roles.*

There are three basic explanations for the learning of appropriate sex-role identity and behavior. These are psychoanalytic, social-learning, and cognitive-developmental theory.

Psychoanalytic theory, which is based on the work of Freud, explains the acquisition of the proper sex role through identification with the same-sex parent. This entails adopting all the qualities of the parent. A girl's identifi-

---

*We have depended upon the work of Bee (1978) concerning theories of sex-role development for preparing this section of the chapter.

cation flows easily from her primary loving attachment to her mother; however, the boy usually does not have a strong emotional attachment to the father. Therefore, Freud explains the sex-role identification of the son through the resolution of the Oedipal conflict; that is, even though the son wants to be close to his mother (in a sexual sense), he fears the power of his father (castration of son) and therefore identifies with him. If he is like his father in all respects, he does not have to fear that his father will castrate him.

Another view of sex-role behavior is that of the social-learning theorists. Mischel (1966) has contributed the most definitive statement on the theory. In learning a sex role the child first has to *discriminate* between the patterns of behavior of the two sexes, then *generalize* from the specific circumstances to new situations, and finally *perform* the appropriate behavior. The major way of learning these behaviors is through imitation. The child models herself after those persons who are nurturant, have power in the area of giving rewards, and appear to be effective in performing their own roles.

Once a child performs a particular behavior, the reaction that behavior elicits in the form of reward, punishment, or no response is likely to determine the future occurrence of that behavior. A girl who gains approval for playing with dolls has a tendency to repeat that behavior, just as will a boy who gains recognition for being able to throw a baseball.

This theory suggests that the treatment of the sexes at very early ages would be different, with girls being rewarded for "feminine" behaviors and boys for "masculine" ones. However, Maccoby and Jacklin (1974) report that there are few differences in the preschool years in how parents treat their children. The evidence does not indicate that children under the age of 4 or 5 are differentially rewarded for sex-appropriate behaviors or that they choose the same-sex models for imitation. However, as Bee (1978) has pointed out, by the age of 6 the child knows his own sex, has begun to show a preference for toys and activities appropriate to that sex, and does imitate an adult of the same sex.

A further explanation of sex-role development is offered by the cognitive-developmentalists. Kohlberg (1966) is one of the proponents of cognitive-developmental theory concerning sex-role development. According to this theory, once children learn the label boy or girl and use it appropriately for their own sex—that is, realize that a person's sex is a permanent condition—they begin to value and emphasize those things which are feminine or masculine. The crux of this approach is that once a child reaches the concrete operational stage of cognitive development, which includes the concept of consistency, appropriate sex-role development begins. A differentiation of the social-learning and cognitive-developmental approaches to sex-role behavior is exemplified in the following remarks by Kohlberg (1966, p. 89):

Social-learning	I want rewards, I am rewarded for doing boy things, therefore I want to be a boy.
Cognitive-developmental	I am a boy, therefore I want to do boy things, therefore, the opportunity to do boy things (and to gain approval for them) is rewarding.

Infancy and early childhood

When babies are born, there seem to be few sex differences other than those already discussed in reference to physical growth and development (Chapter 2). These—such as physical maturity, musculature, and physical stress differences—lend support to the notion that heredity plays a part in determining the variation between the sexes. The evidence of boys' being more aggressive than girls (discussed in Chapter 12) lends support to the idea that boys and girls are genetically different on emotional traits. However, the more popular view about those sex differences, which are identifiable in adults, is that they are the result of differential socialization, not heredity.

In learning sex roles—that is, the culturally approved characteristics for a particular sex—during the period from 3 to 7 years of age, the child realizes that there is a difference in the behavior of boys and girls, women and men, wives and husbands. This learning occurs by noticing certain characteristics of the sexes in relation to dress, physical attributes, posture at the toilet, and characteristic behaviors in the kitchen, yard, or basement (Kagan, 1964). This learning is consistent with both the social-learning and cognitive-developmental theories concerning sex-role development.

Late childhood

By the time children enter elementary school they have a clear idea of their own sex and of the stereotypical male and female roles and the behaviors associated with them. In addition it seems that nurturance is an important factor in adopting the appropriate sex-role identity. Both father-son and mother-daughter interactions that were seen as nurturant were more likely to produce highly masculine or feminine sex-typed behaviors. These behaviors are labeled by some people either instrumental or expressive. Instrumental or masculine traits consist of such things as tenacity, aggressiveness, curiosity, ambition, responsibility, competitiveness, and others. The expressive or feminine traits were kindness, friendliness, obedience, and affection.

Adolescence

During the school years, particularly to the beginning of adolescence, girls outperform boys academically; in late adolescence and adulthood boys catch up and in some cases surpass girls (Boocock, 1972, Chapter 5; Kagan, 1964).

Bee (1975, p. 352), in summarizing the literature concerning sex differences, states that at adolescence sex differences become much more sharply defined. The characteristics shown by boys and girls at this time are the following:

Boys	Girls
More aggressive	Less aggressive
Less nurturant	More nurturant
Less affiliative	More in need of contact with others
Less suggestible	More suggestible
Better at mathematical reasoning tasks	Poorer at mathematical reasoning
Less anxious	More anxious
Better at measures of spatial ability	Poorer on tasks of spatial orientation

More field independent	More field dependent
More analytic in style	Less analytic in cognitive style
Less likely to do well in school	More verbal

She continues by stating that in most cases differences are small. Aggression and spatial ability are generally the areas of greatest discrepancy, with physical strength differences also becoming quite large after adolescence. Generally, sex differences in personality, cognitive skills, and behavior become more noticeable as children grow older.

The manner in which these sex differences occur is in dispute. Some say they depend on biological differences (basically hormonal), while others attribute the differences to environment (differential treatment of the sexes). These two points of view are many times considered an either-or proposition. A more logical explanation is the interactive nature of biology and environment.

Role of physical activity in sex-role development

In the family setting it has been noted that boys receive much stronger negative sanctions from parents for effeminate behavior than girls do for masculine behavior (Maccoby, 1976). Sutton-Smith and Rosenberg (1961) have analyzed children's play over 60 years and found that the game preferences of girls have become more like boys', but that the play of boys has become even more limited; this implies that there is less social stigma attached to the display of masculine behavior by girls than feminine behavior by boys.

The type of play behavior elicited by children also seems to be differentiated according to sex. Rubin et al. (1976) found with preschoolers that girls engaged in more educational solitary play and that boys were involved in physical action play. A study by Lever (1976) indicated that fifth-graders' playtime activity equipped girls with the social skills better suited for family careers and boys with the social skills needed for occupational careers.

In early and late childhood there are differences in the way boys and girls perceive and are rewarded for their play activities. There is also some evidence that boys and girls view participation in athletics differently at grades three, four, five, and six, with females showing increased favorability in attitudes (both those who were and were not sport participants) and some males showing decreased favorability (participant males viewed women's involvement in sports more negatively with increasing grade level) (Selby and Lewko, 1976).

As children enter adolescence, boys and girls perceive physical activity differently. For boys the leading crowd in high school is the athletic crowd, whereas being the most popular is important to girls (Coleman, 1961). For men it is quite in keeping with their sex-role identity from infancy through adolescence to participate in some type of physical activity to gain recognition and acceptance in society. Although it is questionable how desirable this is in terms of positive personality traits (Schendel, 1965), particularly as boys progress up the competitive ladder, athletics is perceived as an acceptable and desirable way to gain the recognition of society. The athletic role contains those characteristics listed as instrumental. Therefore, participation by boys and men in athletics is very much in keeping with their sex-role identity and does not cause any role strain.

The case for the woman, however, is not so simple. For a woman to show those characteristics associated with success in sports (aggressiveness and achievement orientation) is in direct conflict with the role she is "expected" to play, that is, expressive. Indeed, female athletes have been shown to be higher in the personality traits of independence, aggression, achievement orientation, and dominance than female nonathletes (Harris, 1971). How do female athletes contend with this situation? Felshin (1974) suggests that the female athlete emphasizes her femininity while making a strong commitment to sports participation; that is, female athletes work hard to affirm the feminine values of society. Malumphy (1968) suggests that women athletes see themselves as instrumental in sports situations by expressive in social situations. Kukla and Pargman (1976) found that women athletes were concerned with the way others saw them.

Dietz and Breen (1975) list 11 ways in which female athletes attempt to deal with role strain. Some of these are "ostrich"—what problem; "just-a-hobby"—this is just a way to occupy my time; "peter pan"—I can participate in sports till I grow up; "one-of-the-boys"—I'm just part of the gang; "gorgeous female"—I can't be an athlete, I'm too good-looking.

An increasingly popular way of viewing male-female differences in the area of research in sex-role development is to look at the androgyny of the individual; that is, a person is representative of neither femaleness nor maleness. Bem (1974) has stated that typical measures polarize masculinity and femininity and therefore make it impossible to recognize those people who perceive themselves as both instrumental and expressive.

Sports' being viewed as an instrumental activity then would be likely to draw the highly male sex-typed male and the masculine to androgynous female. A study by Duquin (1977) supported this hypothesis and noted that female athletes scored higher on the feminine side of androgyny than did female physical education majors. Duquin was quick to point out, however, that the athletes were predominantly gymnasts and swimmers. These activities are considered traditionally feminine sports.

Although there now appears to be some shift away from viewing successful participation in physical activity as a strictly masculine enterprise, it is still doubtful that stereotypical views of masculinity and feminity will change drastically in the near future. The implementation of Title IX should speed up the process, after the initial resistance of compliance to the federal legislation wears off.

IMPLICATIONS FOR PHYSICAL EDUCATION

There can be no doubt that participation in play, games, and sports has a potent effect on the development of a person from infancy to adulthood. The level of activity as well as the sex of the person plays a significant part in the way physical activity is involved in the unfolding developmental process. This process is depicted in Fig. 8-3. This illustration is designed to show that as age increases, skill in physical activity becomes more important for the boy than for the girl, and that some activities are viewed as more acceptable for girls and others are considered more appropriate for boys. What seems clear is that physical activity can contribute to the socialization process. Whether this is a positive or negative influence depends very much on the situational factors that go into making up the physical activity "climate." Factors such as the philosophy of teachers, students, coaches, and players, as well as community influences, certainly have an effect on the outcome of the activity.

In considering two major developmental tasks of socialization—developing appropriate skills for participation in physical activity and accomplishing an adequate sex-role identity—it can be seen that through early participation in playtime activities and later in organized educational experiences (physical education classes) the opportunity to develop and practice physical skills is available. Physical educators teach and build on basic motor skills by incorporating them into games with increasingly more formalized rule structures and increasingly more complex motor skill patterns. This entails allowing children to participate in many different positions (roles) and games in which many skills can be learned, not just a specialized few. How many times has the only person who can throw a ball (pitcher) played in that position for the entire class period? Why is it that in games one so often sees the weaker players in positions in which they can do the "least damage"? A conscious effort must be made to allow children to experience a diversity of activities and to give them the chance to learn about their own abilities.

One interesting study (Polgar, 1976) that looked at play patterns in the context of the school and peer group demonstrated that when boys were engaged in free play with the peer group, mostly during recess and lunch time, the type of play that occurred was more egalitarian and concerned with the means of the play (to play for play's sake). In the physical education class the authoritarian model was observed, as well as play that was concerned with ends (practicing a particular skill to become proficient in sport). The teacher imposed the

Fig. 8-3. Participation in physical activity varies as age of child increases; sex also affects type of activities selected. **A,** Early childhood. **B,** Late childhood. **C,** Adolescence.

rules on the group, whereas in the free-play situation the group made and changed the rules as they went along. The implication is that teachers need to be concerned about producing a climate in the gymnasium that is conducive to student as well as teacher input.

In addition the question arises why people participate in physical activity. A popular way of approaching this issue is to see whether people participate to "play"—that is, to play fairly and to play well—or to "win"—beat the opponent. A study by Maloney and Petrie (1972) indicated that the level of participation is instrumental in whether people take part to play or to win. They used students in grades eight, nine, ten, and twelve and found that those people involved in sports at a casual or intramural level were more play-oriented than those involved in combinations of casual, intramural, and interscholastic activities, who were more win-oriented. This means that the higher a person's involvement in athletic endeavors, the greater the possibility of the idea that winning is an important aspect of the game. Perhaps a higher degree of skill makes success a much more salient factor in the minds of the participants.

One of the desirable outcomes of physical education is to have people participate in physical activity so that they are able to enjoy it later in life. If there is emphasis on the play aspect of activity, perhaps the chances of success would be greater. Work by Loy and others (1976) showed that women are also more interested in playing a game fairly and playing it well than in beating the opponent. Using college students of both sexes who participated in sports, they found that female intramural participants were more concerned with the play aspects of the activity and that male varsity athletes were more concerned with the win aspect. However, the play orientation was chosen by a majority of subjects surveyed, both female and male, with only the highly involved male athlete concerned with the win aspect of the activity.

One example of this "win" orientation in sports is demonstrated in youth football leagues. In this particular league there was a rule that all players on the team would play at least a specified number of minutes per game. To comply with this rule one coach would send in two substitutes every three or four plays. The people who enforce the rules could then determine that each player was getting the required amount of playing time. However, the "watchers" did not see that one of the players who went in as a substitute also returned from the huddle without actually getting in any playing time. This kind of practice teaches the participants that "winning isn't everything, it's the only thing." Loy et al. (1976) state that people mistakenly use play as an arena for the development of desirable qualities such as "good sportsmanship," while ignoring the research that reports results to the contrary.

We think it is important for physical educators and coaches to become acquainted with the types of outcomes that are being promoted and to look at these to determine whether they are in line with the skills that young people need to become fully functioning members of society.

References

Alexander, N. C., & Campbell, E. O. Peer influences on adolescent aspirations and attainments. *American Sociological Review*, 1964, *29*, 568-575.

Bandura, A., & Walters, R. H. Social learning and personality development. New York: Holt, Rinehart & Winston, 1963.

Barnes, K. E. Preschool play norms: a replication. *Developmental Psychology*, 1975, *5*, 99-103.

Bee, H. *The developing child*. New York: Harper & Row, Publishers, 1975.

Bee, H. *The developing child* (2nd ed.). New York: Harper & Row, Publishers, 1978.

Bem, S. The measurement of psychological androgyny. *Journal of Consulting and Clinical Psychology*, 1974, *42*, 155-162.

Boocock, S. S. *An introduction to the sociology of learning*. Boston: Houghton Mifflin Co., 1972.

Broekhoff, J. Physique types and perceived physical characteristics of elementary school children with low and high social status. In J. Broekhoff (Ed.), *Physical education, sports and the sciences*. Eugene: Microform Publications, University of Oregon, 1976.

Bronfenbrenner, U. Two worlds of childhood: U.S. and U.S.S.R. New York: Russell Sage Foundation, 1970.

Buchanan, H. T., Blankenbaker, J., & Cotten, D. Academic and athletic ability as popularity factors in elementary school children. *Research Quarterly*, 1976, *47*, 320-325.

Coleman, J. S. *The adolescent society*. New York: The Free Press, 1961.

Devereux, E. C. *Some observations on sports, play, and games in childhood*. Paper presented at Eastern Association for Physical Education of College Women, Philadelphia, October 1972.

Dietz, M. L., & Breen, M. Strategies used by women athletes to cope with role strain. *Mouvement*, October 1975, pp. 389-393.

Duquin, M. E. Perceptions of sport: a study in sexual attraction. In D. M. Landers & R. W. Christina (Eds.), *Psychology of motor behavior and sport* (Vol. 2). Champaign, Ill.: Human Kinetics Publishers, 1977.

Felshin, J. The social view. In E. Gerber, J. Felshin, P. Berlin, and W. Wyrick (Eds.), *The American woman in sport*. Reading, Mass.: Addison-Wesley Publishing Co., 1974.

Flaegelman, A. *The new games book*. San Francisco: The Headlands Press, 1976.

Gordon, C. W. *The social system of the high school*. Glencoe, Ill.: The Free Press, 1957.

Hanks, M. P., & Eckland, B. K. Athletics and social participation in the educational attainment process. *Sociology of Education*, 1976, *49*, 271-294.

Harris, D. V. *The social self and competitive self of the female athlete*. Paper presented at the Third International Symposium on the Sociology of Sport, University of Waterloo, Waterloo, Ontario, Canada, 1971.

Havighurst, R. J. *Developmental tasks and education* (3rd ed.). New York: David McKay Co., Inc., 1972.

Havighurst, R. J., & Neugarten, B. L. *Society and education* (4th ed.). Boston: Allyn & Bacon, Inc., 1975.

Hollander, E. P. *Principles and methods of social psychology* (3rd ed.). New York: Oxford University Press, 1976.

Kagan, J. Acquisition and significance of sex typing and sex role identity. In M. L. & L. W. Hoffman (Eds.), *Review of child development research* (Vol. 1). New York: Russell Sage Foundation, 1964.

Kohlberg, L. A cognitive-developmental analysis of children's sex-role concepts and attitudes. In E. E. Maccoby (Ed.), *The development of sex differences*. Palo Alto, Calif.: Stanford University Press, 1966.

Kukla, K. J., & Pargman, D. Comparative perceptions of psychological well-being as influenced by sport experience in female athletes. *Research Quarterly*, 1976, *47*, 375-488.

Lever, J. Sex differences in the games children play. *Social Problems*, 1976, *23*, 479-488.

Loy, J., Birrell, S., & Rose, D. Attitudes held toward agonetic activities as a function of selected social identities. *Quest*, 1976, *26*, 81-93.

Maccoby, E. E. *Sex differentiation during childhood*, Master lectures on developmental psychology. Washington, D.C.: American Psychological Association, 1976.

Maccoby, E. E., & Jacklin, C. N. The psychology of sex differences. Palo Alto, Calif.: Stanford University Press, 1974.

Maloney, L. T., & Petrie, B. M. Professionalization of attitudes toward play among Canadian school pupils as a function of sex, grade, and athletic participation. *Journal of Leisure Research*, 1972, *4*, 184-185.

Malumphy, T. Personality of women athletes in intercollegiate compeition. *Research Quarterly*, 1968, *36*, 610-620.

Martens, R. *Social psychology and physical activity*. New York: Harper & Row, Publishers, 1975.

Mischel, W. A social-learning view of sex differences in behavior. In E. E. Maccoby (Ed.), *The development of sex differences*. Palo Alto, Calif.: Stanford University Press, 1966.

Orlick, T. D. The sports environment: a capacity to enhance—a capacity to destroy. In B. Rushall (Ed.), *The status of psychomotor learning and sport psychology research*. Dartmouth, Nova Scotia: Sport Science Associates, 1975.

Orlick, T. D. *Winning through cooperation—competitive insanity; cooperative alternatives*. Washington, D. C.: Hawkins & Associates, 1978.

Orlick, T. D., & Botterill, C. *Every kid can win*. Chicago: Nelson-Hall, Publishers, 1975.

Parten, M. B. Social participation among pre-school children. *Journal of Abnormal and Social Psychology*, 1932, *27*, 243-269.

Polgar, S. K. The social context of games: or when is play not play? *Sociology of Education*, 1976, *49*, 265-271.

Quilitch, H. R., & Risley, T. R. The effects of play material on social play. *Journal of Applied Behavior Analysis*, 1973, *6*, 573-578.

Rehberg, R. A., & Schafer, W. E. Participation in interscholastic athletics and college expectations. *American Journal of Sociology*, 1968, *63*, 732-740.

Rheingold, H. L. The social and socializing infant. In D. A. Goslin (Ed.), *Handbook of socialization theory and research*. Chicago: Rand McNally & Co., 1969.

Rubin, K. H., Maioni, T. L., & Hornung, M. Free play behaviors in middle- and lower-class preschoolers: Parten and Piaget revisited. *Child Development*, 1976, *47*, 414-419.

Schafer, W. E., & Armer, M. Athletes are not inferior students. *Trans-action*, 1968, *6*, 61-62.

Schendel, J. S. Psychological differences between athletes and non-participants in athletics at three educational levels. *Research Quarterly*, 1965, *36*, 52-67.

Secord, P. F., Backman, C. W., & Slavitt, D. R. *Understanding social life: an introduction to social psychology*. New York: McGraw-Hill Book Co., 1976.

Selby, R., & Lewko, J. H. Children's attitudes toward females in sports: their relationship with sex, grade, and sports participation. *Research Quarterly*, 1976, *47*, 453-463.

Shapiro, A., & Madsen, M. C. Cooperative and competitive behavior of kibbutz and urban children in Israel. *Child Development*, 1969, *40*, 609-617.

Sherif, M., Harvey, O. J., White, B. J., Hood, W. R. & Sherif, C. W. *Intergroup conflict and cooperation: the robbers cave experiment*. Norman: University of Oklahoma Press, 1961.

Sherif, M., & Sherif, C. W. *Groups in harmony and tension*. New York: Harper & Row, Publishers, 1953.

Skinner, B. F. *Contingencies of reinforcement*. New York: Appleton-Century-Crofts, 1969.

Skuberic, E. Emotional responses of boys to Little League and Middle League competitive baseball. *Research Quarterly*, 1955, *26*, 342-352.

Spady, W. G. Lament for the letterman: effects of peer status and extracurricular activities on goals and achievement. *American Journal of Sociology*, 1970, *75*, 680-702.

Spreitzer, E., & Pugh, M. Interscholastic athletics and educational expectations. *Sociology of Education*, 1973, *46*, 171-182.

Stevenson, C. L. Socialization effects of participation in sport; a crictical review of the research. *Research Quarterly*, 1975, *46*, 287-301.

Sutton-Smith, B., & Rosenberg, R. G. Sixty years of historical change in the game preferences of American children. *Journal of American Folklore*, 1961, *74*, 17-46.

Webb, H. Professionalization of attitudes toward play among adolescents. In G. S. Kenyon (Ed.), *Aspects of contemporary sport sociology*. Chicago: The Athletic Institute, 1969.

Student projects

1. Go to a day-care or preschool playground and observe the children at play. Observe as many children as possible and classify the types of play behavior observed. Is there a predominant type of play behavior? What type of play behavior is reflected at what age? Do your observations compare with those of Parten?

2. In class make a list of stereotypical behaviors that might be displayed by men or women in a physical education class. For example, during a gymnastics unit one might typically expect males to be performing more difficult tasks than females. After the list is complete:
   a. Make it into a checklist
   b. Observe physical education classes of recently graduated teachers and teachers that are "old pros" and place check marks after the types of behaviors found in each class
   c. Categorize your observations according to the following and discuss your results

Behavior	Recent graduates		"Old pros"	
	Male	Female	Male	Female
1.				
2.				
3.				
4.				

Chapter 9

MORAL DEVELOPMENT

When we speak of moral people and moral behavior, we typically think of people who stand up for what they believe in, do the right thing, and are able to control their behavior in many different situations. Historically there have been three major assumptions underlying the basic definition of "man." These are the concepts of "original sin," "innate purity," and "tabula rasa." Each of these concepts is represented by a particular approach to moral development (Hoffman, 1970). The concept of original sin is based in religious doctrine and assumes that adult intervention based on sacred notions is the way to redeem the "lost soul." The innate-purity orientation assumes that man is basically good and that the corrupt adult society should be kept from the child, particularly in the early years. The *tabula rasa* view posits man as a blank tablet on which neither good nor bad is written, but which is impressionable. The first view is represented in the psychoanalytic approach to moral development; the second, in the humanistic vein represented originally by Rousseau and carried on by the cognitive-developmentalists. The third assumption belongs to the learning theorist or behaviorists. All three approaches to moral development will be discussed, but the main emphasis will be on the cognitive-developmental, which has provided most of the impetus in recent years for moral education.

According to Freudian or psychoanalytic theory identification with the same-sex parent is the way one learns moral behavior and other attitudes. As discussed in Chapter 8, the child believes that if he makes himself like the parent, then the parent will love him. When a child identifies with a parent, he takes on the behavior, attitudes, and values of the parent. The assumption of morality is included in this identification process. The "inner parent" tells a person whether his behavior is right or wrong. In Freudian terms this is called superego, or conscience development. According to psychoanalytic thinking there are also internal and external standards of moral behavior. Shame is considered externally controlled, and guilt is associated with internally controlled behavior (McCandless and Evans, 1973). The prevailing thought is that a truly moral person operates on

an internalized system. Some indicators of this internal system are summarized by Hoffman (1970) as follows:

1. Resistance to temptation: not cheating although you know you will not be caught
2. Guilt over deviation: feeling bad about misbehavior
3. Independence of actions from external sanctions: behaving in a moral fashion because the standards are one's own
4. Confession and assumption of responsibility for one's actions: taking the consequences of one's behavior, as in the case of going to jail when protesting civil injustices

Personal morality, according to psychoanalytic theory, is determined by parents, and moral identification is generally exhibited in children by the age of 5 or 6. It is difficult to see how this is possible, since many moral behaviors are internal and not readily observable. In addition, a child may adopt some behaviors and not others because some behaviors are easier to identify than others; such behavior would leave the process of moral development incomplete. The evidence does not seem to support this theory, as it appears that the child may not internalize the standards of right and wrong (Hoffman, 1970).

Another viewpoint concerning the development of morality is offered by the learning theorists. In this approach the contingencies of reinforcement play a part in the development of moral behavior, which is viewed as a process whereby one makes increasingly finer discriminations about appropriate behavior on the basis of the types of rewards and reinforcements received. One might simplistically say that an immoral person has been rewarded for immoral behavior and a moral one for moral behavior.

A different learning theory approach suggests that moral development is acquired through imitation. A child sees how other children and adults act in various contexts, and her behavior is shaped in accordance with what she has seen (Bandura and MacDonald, 1963). Therefore, one learns what morality is by observing moral people, imitating their behavior, and subsequently internalizing those behaviors. One of the prevalent sayings of adults, and particularly parents and teachers in our society, is, "Do as I say, not as I do." However, there is some indication that the quotation should be, "Do as I do, not as I say." Rosenhan (1972, p. 354) states:

If the model behaves charitably, so will the child—even if the model has preached greed. And conversely if the model preaches charity, but practices greed, the child will follow the model's behavior. . . . Behavior in the pro-social area is mainly influenced by behavior, not by words.

Research evidence (mostly experimental) concerning imitation as applied to moral development shows that after seeing a model who yields to temptation, the observer is more likely to exhibit the same type of behavior. However, it is not clear what effect the model's behaving in a "moral" manner has on the observer. According to Hoffman (1970) evidence supports the view that imitation can undermine past socialization processes (regarding the child's inclination to yield to temptation) rather than contribute to positive moral development; that is, one may not enhance a child's moral development through observation of an appropriate model, but a child can be harmed by exposure to a poor model or one who yields to temptation.

These two theories (reinforcement and modeling) do not contribute much to explaining how moral behavior occurs or is enhanced. Perhaps other factors need to be considered, such as the type of parental discipline used and the warmth of the parent in relation to the child.

The third approach to moral development is that of the cognitive-developmentalists such as Piaget and Kohlberg. This approach places the greatest emphasis on cognition in its claims that changes in intellectual ability allow a person to understand other aspects of his world. Moral development does not occur solely as the result of maturation but is an interactive process between biological and environmental influences.

Piaget and Kohlberg are interested in moral judgments rather than moral behavior. As Bee (1978, p. 349) states, they are more interested in the question, What kind of morality do you operate with? than the question, How moral

are you? The latter is more the concern of the learning and psychoanalytic theorists.

Basically Piaget's work (1932) was the precursor for Kohlberg's work dealing with stages in moral development. Piaget was concerned with a person's respect for rules dealing with the social order and a person's sense of justice. His work proposed a two-stage system of moral development. The earlier stage (ages 3 to 10), commonly called *heteronomous morality* or *social realism,* refers to an obligation to comply with rules because they are sacred and unalterable. They come from a higher authority (parents). Behaviors are viewed as either right or wrong, and the child believes that everyone views these behaviors in the same way. Another characteristic of this stage is that the "rightness" or "wrongness" of an act is established on the basis of the magnitude of the consequences, whether punishment is involved, and whether it conforms exactly to established rules.

The second stage (9 to 10 and older) is called *autonomous morality* or *morality of reciprocity.* During this stage a child does not see rules as unchangeable but as established and maintained through social agreements. A child begins to see diversity in views of right and wrong, and these judgements about good or bad are based on the person's intentions rather than the consequences of the act. In addition, peer expectations and being able to place oneself in another's shoes play a larger part in defining moral obligations. The type of punishment for a misdeed should be appropriate for the crime.

Piaget and his followers have tried to show that the progress of morality goes through age changes parallel to those of cognitive theory. Six of the characteristics that seem to be supported by the research are listed by Kohlberg (1964) and shown in Table 9-1.

Piaget views moral development as an active learning process that involves the development of certain cognitive skills interacting with environmental experiences to allow people to broaden their perspective about authority (Hoffman, 1970). A child needs to progress through the stage of perceiving authority as absolute to one of relativism or being able to "walk in

Table 9-1. Characteristics of moral development*

Aspect of moral judgment	Age changes	Example	Results
Intentionality	Act initially viewed as bad in terms of physical consequences; older child views in terms of intent to do harm	Who is worse? 1. Child who breaks five cups helping mother set table 2. Child who breaks one cup stealing jam	Most 4-year-olds say 1 is worse Most 9-year-olds say 2 is worse
Relativism	Act initially viewed as totally right or wrong with all people having same viewpoint; older child aware of diversity of opinion	Children told story in which a lazy pupil is not supposed to receive any help with homework (decree by teacher); friendly classmate helps; children asked: 1. Would friendly classmate think he was right or wrong 2. Would lazy pupil think classmate was right or wrong 3. Would teacher think classmate was right or wrong	Most 6-year-olds expected only one judgment on which all would agree Most 7-year-olds recognized more than one perspective of the moral issue
Independence of sanctions	Act viewed as bad because it elicits punishment; older children say act is bad because it violates a rule, does harm to others, and so on	Older brother was asked to watch a younger brother while mother was away; child did as told, but when mother returned she spanked child; was child good or bad?	Many 4-year-olds simply say child was bad Mature 4- to 5-year-olds invent some other bad behavior to account for punishment By age 7 a majority say child was good even though punished
Use of reciprocity	Younger children do not use "putting yourself in another's shoes" as a consideration in judgment; older children do	Children asked, "What would the Golden Rule say to do if a person came up and hit you?"	Age 10 (concrete reciprocity): "Hit him back. Do unto others as they do unto you." Age 11 to 13 (ideal reciprocity: see other person's viewpoint and make judgments in that light
Use of punishment as restitution and reform	Young child advocates severe punishment after misdeed; older child favors punishment leading to restitution of victim and reform of culprit	What should happen to a person who steals money from another?	Young child would want to see person physically punished; older child may demand that robber repay the money.
Naturalistic views of misfortune	Young children tend to view misfortunes after misdeed as punishment willed by God ("immanent justice"); older children do not confuse natural misfortunes with punishment	Child falls down and breaks an ankle after breaking a window by throwing a baseball through it.	6- to 7-year-old would consider this punishment for breaking the window; older child would not make this assumption.

*Based on work of Kohlberg, L. Development of moral character and moral ideology. In M. L. Hoffman and Y. W. Hoffman (Eds.), *Review of child development research* (Vol. 1). New York: Russell Sage Foundation, 1964, pp. 396-398.

KOHLBERG'S MORAL STAGES*

I. Preconventional level

At this level the child responds to authority, generally the parents. What is right or wrong is absolute and is determined by whether a person is punished or not; not the intent of the act.

Stage 1: *The punishment-and-obedience orientation.* The type of punishment incurred is used as the basis of determining right or wrong. At this point the child is trying to avoid punishment and responds to the "power" of adults.

Stage 2: *The instrumental-relativist orientation.* A person acts on the basis of "what feels good." Something that brings pleasant results is right and what brings unpleasant results is wrong. What a person does is in relation to what he receives in return; "you scratch my back and I'll scratch yours."

II. Conventional level

At this level one is interested in acting in relation to the expectations of the family, peer group, or greater society. Responding to the needs of these groups is of value in its own right.

Stage 3: *The "good boy"–"nice girl" orientation.* A person wins approval by doing that which pleases other people. Children now start to judge actions by intention—"she means well." There is still conformity to group norms.

Stage 4: *The "law and order" orientation.* One's behavior is controlled by doing what is right according to the rules of society. What the law says is right is right for the person.

III. Postconventional, autonomous, or principled level

At this level the person tries to determine what is right and wrong apart from authority (parents or society). The person deals with moral values that are apart from the group norms.

Stage 5: *The social-contract, legalistic orientation.* What is right is what is agreed upon by the whole society. A person realizes that the law is capable of being changed within the system. For behavior not regulated by law, right and wrong is a personal matter, but it is important that agreements and contracts have a binding quality.

Stage 6: *The universal-ethical-principle orientation.* Right or wrong is determined by the conscience of the individual but mediated within the framework of what is logical, consistent, and universal (for example, the Golden Rule, the categorical imperative). At the basis of this stage is the dignity of humanity as individual people.

*From Kohlberg, L. From is to ought. In T. Mischel (Ed.), *Cognitive development and epistemology.* New York: Academic Press, Inc., pp. 164-165.

another man's shoes" before making judgments.

Kohlberg has extended and refined the work of Piaget in relationship to moral development. Using his doctoral dissertation (Kohlberg, 1958) as a base, Kohlberg devised a set of "moral dilemmas" that were used to ask each subject about what the main character in the dilemma should do. Two of the most commonly cited dilemmas are the following:

A European woman was near death. One drug was available that might save the woman's life. The druggist who invented it was charging ten times more than it cost him to make. The husband could raise only half the money, and the druggist insisted on full payment. Should the man steal in order to save her life?

Should a doctor commit a mercy killing of a fatally ill woman who is begging for death because of her pain?

From this work Kohlberg derived a scheme of three major levels of development with two stages in each level. This work is shown above.

There are certain statements that can be made about the characteristics of a stage approach to moral development. Kohlberg and Hersh (1977, p. 54) state the following:

1. Stages are organized systems of thought. People are consistent in their level of moral judgment.
2. Stages form an invariant sequence. Movement is always forward, stages are not skipped. This is true across all cultures.
3. Thinking at a higher stage includes within it lower stage thinking.

In reference to the first and third statements above it has been noted that a person may function at two or three levels at the same time, but a majority of the responses come from one stage and a few others at one stage above or below the prime one. A person may function at stage three most of the time, but some responses are at stage two and some at stage four. Turiel's

(1966) research has demonstrated that a person can usually handle moral reasoning one stage above his functioning level better than two stages above. Turiel (1973) also suggests that children reject as inadequate statements about moral judgments made below the child's functioning level.

Research supporting the second statement has been shown in cross-cultural studies (Kohlberg and Kramer, 1969). This research has indicated that moral developmental stages are achieved sequentially across cultures, but that the rate and end stage are achieved differently. In studies of people in Taiwan and Mexico and in isolated villages in Turkey and the Yucatan it was found that in the isolated villages the highest stage reached was the fourth at the age of 16. In contrast, stage six was achieved by approximately 8% of the 16-year-olds in the United States. It must also be noted that very

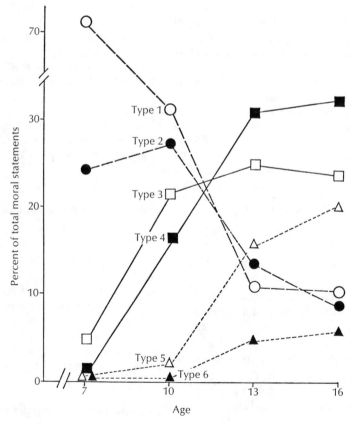

Fig. 9-1. Mean percent of total moral statements at each of six moral judgment types at four ages. (From L. Kohlberg. The development of children's orientation toward a moral order. I. Sequence in the development of moral thought, *Vita Humana,* 1963, *6,* 16.)

few people reach the sixth stage of moral development, rather, most people are at stage four to four and one-half. The percentages of moral judgments at each of the six levels and at four different ages are shown in Fig. 9-1.

CHILD-REARING ANTECEDENTS OF MORAL DEVELOPMENT

What kinds of influences are important in attempting to enhance a person's moral development? What can we do to help a child select the ''right'' behaviors and avoid the ''wrong'' ones? How can we help a child to develop an internalized sense of appropriate behavior? One obvious influence on conscience development is the kind of home environment that a child is exposed to or how a child is socialized in relation to morality. One particular aspect of the environment is the way in which a child is disciplined. Hoffman (1970), after an extensive review of the literature, divides discipline into three categories. These categories are as follows:

Power assertion techniques which include physical punishment, taking away material objects, and the use of force or the threat of using these techniques. The adult attempts to control the child through physical means. This technique is externally oriented as opposed to non-power assertive techniques which are described below.

Love-withdrawal techniques include those in which there is a non-physical expression of a parent's anger over a child's undesirable behavior. Some of the more common techniques are ignoring the child, turning one's back on the child, not speaking to the child, or threatening to leave the child. This type of punishment is similar to power assertive techniques in that it is punitive and may cause emotional problems rather than physical ones. When a child is punished physically the encounter is usually quickly enacted and dissipated. The child has been punished and it is over and done with. However, with love-withdrawal techniques there is no specific time limit for the end of the punishment and the punishment usually lasts longer.

Induction includes those techniques in which the adult gives some type of reason or explanation to the child why she did not behave in the appropriate manner. This includes pointing out the harmful effects of her behavior on herself and others. Adults try to convince a child to change behavior rather than

being punitive and directing a behavior change. ''You should'' as opposed to ''you will.'' This technique is considered helpful in allowing a child to control and internalize her own behavior. A type of induction is called *other-oriented induction*. This technique is used in an effort to point out the implications of a child's behavior for another person. Comments such as, ''If you bite your brother, it hurts him; If you throw the baseball through the Swift's window, someone may get hurt; When you disobey a rule in the game of tennis, the other player is being cheated;'' are examples of other-oriented induction.

The type of discipline that seems to be more effective in producing moral behavior includes those techniques which are non-power-assertive. Parents who are power assertive seem to show less affection toward their children; this leads some researchers to believe that power-assertive techniques could be effective in promoting moral development if the people who used them also had an affectionate relationship with the child.

The love-withdrawal technique has not proven as effective as the inductive method of discipline in promoting moral behavior. There is some debate about why love withdrawal is not as effective in producing moral behavior in children as might be supposed. The assumption is that the child conforms to the expected behavior because he is anxious about losing his parents' love. One explanation for the ineffectiveness of this technique is that parents may not express enough affection to make it obvious to the child that there is something to lose. If a child does not love a parent, it makes no difference that love withdrawal is used as a punishment for bad behavior. There is a similarity to the lack of affectional bond cited as a reason for the relative ineffectiveness of power-assertive discipline techniques.

The evidence is not clear concerning why love withdrawal has not been an effective technique. Hoffman (1970) thinks that the bond between parent and child based on love may be a background variable that is important to the child in establishing rapport with parents and in turn makes the child more receptive to parental influence.

It seems clear that power-assertive techniques by parents are associated with weak moral development and induction is associated with advanced moral development. Love-withdrawal techniques did not seem to show any consistent relationship to moral development.

DOES MORAL BEHAVIOR FOLLOW FROM MORAL DEVELOPMENT?

The research of Hartshorne and May in the late 1920s was among the first in a series of studies to shed some light on whether moral behavior results from moral thought. Children in this study were given tests under conditions that would and would not be conducive to cheating. It was found that people who cheat in one situation may not cheat in another. If the chance of getting caught is almost nil, almost all the children cheat; whereas if the chance of getting caught is high, few people cheat. The results of this study led researchers to further investigation of the question.

Kohlberg (1970) has conducted research indicating that the higher the moral level of the person (stage five or six) making the moral judgment, the more likely the person is to act in line with his principled level of moral development. On a cheating test 75% of those children below stages five and six cheated, while only 20% at stages five or six did so. Similar results were also found with college-age students. Kohlberg in addition reports about Milgram's (1963) experiment, in which subjects were told to administer increasingly severe electric shock to victims (confederates of the experimenter) in a contrived situation. It was found that of those people who were at stage six, 75% refused to shock the victim, whereas only 13% at lower stages refused.

In the area of politics Haan and co-workers (1968) found that in relation to student protests (sit-ins at the administration building) a majority of people in stage five or six were likely to participate in the protest movement. However, it was also found that 60% of stage two people were likely to sit in. The evidence is far from definitive, but it seems that the higher a person's moral stage, the more likely that behavior matches moral judgment.

MEASUREMENT OF MORALITY

Measuring morality is difficult. Continuing argument over the validity of field studies and the generalizability of experimental studies on which conclusions are based produces conflicting results. One problem is exemplified in the experiments showing that induction and affection are positively associated with moral development. The difficulty is that the conclusions are based on field studies that commonly use self-report measures, in which assuring the accuracy of the statements made by the subjects is problematic.

Much of the work done concerning moral development is in the form of field studies, in which indicators of morality (resistance to temptation, guilt, confession after transgression, and restitution) have been subjective statements of the subjects involved. The "inconclusiveness" about the type of parental discipline that affects moral development may be indicative of methodological problems inherent in these field studies. However, even though these studies have methodological weaknesses, experimental or laboratory studes are faulted because they cannot adequately take into account the parent-child interaction or affectional bond. A "reality situation" in the laboratory cannot necessarily be produced.

Measuring moral judgments

Kohlberg is one of the few researchers who has developed an interview schedule to determine the moral judgment stage of the subject. He uses a technique called a moral dilemma (such as a woman dying of cancer and mercy killing) in which he rates the responses of a subject as falling into one of his six stages. The important part of this technique is determining why a person thinks as he does and what stage of thinking is represented by that judgment. Although Kohlberg has developed a very structured research tool, the following moral dilemma might be used in eliciting responses that a physical education teacher might encounter:

A fitness class has as one of its objectives the 12-minute run for distance. During this run each student is supposed to cover as much distance as possible. All the students know that their final grade will be based, in part, on the amount of improvement that is shown on this run. Justin, who is in good physical condition, wants to get a good grade

Table 9-2. Hypothetical responses to a moral dilemma (categorized by stage)

Stage	Response
Stage 1 Punishment-and- obedience orientation	Justin should run as fast and as far as he can because the teacher told him to.
Stage 2 Instrumental- relativistic orientation	Justin should run as fast and as far as he can because the teacher will realize what a good athlete he is and give him a good grade.
Stage 3 "Good boy—nice girl" orientation	Justin should perform as well as he can because the teacher is counting on him to set an example and motivate the other students in the class to do well.
Stage 4 "Law-and-order" orientation	Justin should run to the best of his ability because he should not cheat or lie. According to society's standards that kind of behavior is wrong.
Stage 5 Social-contract, legalistic orientation	Justin should run to the best of his ability because he knows that he would not be happy with himself if he cheated or lied about his performance.
Stage 6* Universal-ethical- principle orientation	There is no justification for cheating or lying under these circumstances. No greater good would be served by not performing to the best of his ability.

*The distinction between stages five and six is difficult. In a recent personal communication (Center for Moral Education, Harvard University, June 1978) we were informed that those people who had been studied had not exhibited stage six moral reasoning. It was indicated that indeed stage five may be the upper limit and that most people are at stage four to four and one-half.

in the class. He knows that he could easily run two miles in the 12 minutes but that he would then not have much room for improvement. Additionally he is responsible for keeping accurate records and telling the teacher the distance that he has run. What should Justin do?

Table 9-2 indicates some hypothetical responses, with each stage represented by one response even though there can be many different responses to a moral dilemma that indicate the same level of moral judgment.

VALUES CLARIFICATION AND MORAL DEVELOPMENT

Thus far three basic theories of moral development have been discussed. The next step is to integrate the related concept of values clarification. Values clarification is largely based in the humanistic education model and is characterized by emphasizing the development of self-worth and the opportunity to engage in decision making.

Louis Raths is the originator of the term values clarification. His work was based on the philosophical writings of John Dewey. Raths et al. posited their ideas about values clarification in 1966. They were primarily concerned with the educational setting and how schools could help students develop and clarify their own ideas about life. Raths et al., like Piaget and Kohlberg, are more concerned with the process of "valuing" than with what is valued. It is important for a person to be able to think through a values situation and to deal with it in respect to his own particular needs as well as respecting the rights of others. This is done through the processes of *choosing, prizing,* and *acting*. There are seven subprocesses that go into the process of valuing (Raths et al., 1966, pp. 28-30):

Choosing

1. Choosing freely
2. Considering alternatives
3. Considering the consequences

Prizing

4. Prizing and cherishing
5. Publicly affirming when appropriate

Acting

6. Acting upon the choice
7. Acting repeatedly, consistently

Fig. 9-2. Person needs to "clarify values" in relation to many everyday issues.

Kirschenbaum (Kirschenbaum et al., 1977) has expanded this original work into five dimensions of the valuing process with 18 subprocesses—

Thinking

1. On many levels
2. Critical thinking
3. Divergent thinking
4. Moral reasoning

Feeling

5. Being aware of one's feelings
6. Discharging distressful feelings
7. Experiencing positive self-concept

Choosing

8. Goal setting
9. Data gathering
10. Considering alternatives
11. Considering consequences
12. Choosing freely

Communicating

13. Sending clear messages, including public affirmation
14. Empathic listening
15. No-lose conflict resolution

Acting

16. Repeatedly
17. Consistently
18. Skillfully, competently

As a person progresses through this process, an idea of what is important emerges; from this one can select various alternative ways of dealing with the idea, choosing and being able to communicate it, and finally arriving at a place where a person is comfortable with her choice. This results in actions' coinciding with feelings about what is important, right or wrong, good or bad. Simon et al. (1972) have put out a handbook that suggests a variety of activities that can be used with the values clarification procedure. This is a good source for the interested teacher.

Perhaps one of the biggest criticisms of the use of values clarification is that it is not strongly based in any theoretical framework. In replying to this charge Kirschenbaum et al. (1977) state that the theory and research that support such topics as critical thinking, self-concept, moral reasoning, and so forth would be supportive of the valuing process inherent in values clarification. Kirschenbaum (1977) and Superka and Johnson (1975) cite studies that lend support to the use of values clarification in education. Although the results are not definitive, there is evidence to indicate that students who use values clarification have a greater sense of personal value and social constructiveness. Studies also indicate that students are less apathetic, conforming, and overdissenting after the use of values clarification.

AGE DIFFERENCES IN MORAL DEVELOPMENT

There do not seem to be rigid time periods in which a specific stage of moral reasoning is achieved. Indeed, according to Kohlberg, adolescents and adults may be functioning anywhere from stage two to six. There are, however, some gross generalizations that can be made. During infancy and early childhood identificatory and imitative processes are used in acquiring basic moral standards, and the child's conscience is well developed by 5 years of age. After that time there appears to be a refinement and reorganization of the original structure of morality through the interaction of the environment and the individual's own biological make-up.

Up until the age of 7 or 8 the child's sense of justice is derived from external-parental authority (heteronomous). Between the ages of 8 and 11 the child is making the transition from heteronomous to autonomous, and between 11 and 12 the person becomes autonomous. Lickona (1977) in applying Kohlberg's framework to the educational setting states that stages one and two are dominant in the primary grades and are present in some children long beyond that time. Stage three reasoning appears during the upper elementary years and may be the major level through the end of high school. Stage four begins to emerge in adolescence, and only one in four people continues to higher levels in late adolescence and adulthood.

SEX DIFFERENCES IN MORAL DEVELOPMENT

It is commonly assumed that girls are more moral than boys, and the evidence seems to bear this out. For example, the figures on juvenile delinquency and crime show a lower proportion of girls involved in violation of the rules of society. McCandless and Evans (1973, pp. 279-280) suggest that some of the reasons that girls are more conventionally moral (conform more readily) than boys are the following:

1. Social conformity pressures are greater for girls.
2. Girls are generally less willing to admit to unconventional or immoral thoughts or action.
3. Biology plays a part in that conventional morality involves the issue of aggression. Because of the aggressiveness of boys they are more likely to "get into trouble."
4. The sexual behavior of boys is more likely to lead to morally ambiguous sexual situations, but their transgressions are not taken as seriously as those of girls.
5. In our society property is power and power is more important to males than females. Thus, boys may be more likely than girls to steal in order to gain power.

Whether these differences continue to hold up in light of the increased emphasis on freedom of the individual to deviate from expected cultural sex-typed expectations remains to be recorded.

IMPLICATIONS FOR PHYSICAL EDUCATION

As early as 1831 educators were trying to find methods that would use sports as an avenue for teaching morality. One suggestion was that teachers participate in physical activity with the students. "There is no place where a teacher may better study the characteristics of his pupils than on the playground. . . . He may mould (sic) their characters there more truly, more thoroughly, more permanently, than . . . by all other means put together" (Common School teacher as cited in Albertson, 1976, p. 30).

The value of physical activity for developing good sportsmanship and building character has long been espoused by physical educators and the public. An article by Ogilvie and Tutko (1971) entitled, "If You Want to Build Character, Try Something Else," reveals the fallacy of that idea, which is also exemplified by books such as *Meat on the Hoof* (Shaw, 1972) and *Out of Their League* (Meggysey, 1970). These books were exposés about the athletic subculture. A more recent trend is demonstrated in interscholastic sports. The University Interscholastic League (UIL), the governing body for interscholastic sports in the state of Texas, ruled that no disciplinary action would be taken against five basketball players even though they admitted to stealing ($150 and jewelry) prior to winning a fifth state Class AAA championship. "If we start getting ourselves involved in morals," says UIL director Bailey Marshall, "we will be getting hammered to take a student off the team for having speeding tickets" (*Sports Illustrated*, 1978, p. 10).

Up to this point there has been only one published study (Jantz, 1975) of which we are aware that has looked at moral judgment in the physical activity context. However, this study only investigated the appearance of stages according to the Piagetian model. Studies that would be of interest include those which would investigate the manner in which physical activity might enhance moral development. Questions that we would like to see answered are the following:

1. Does a physical education setting have particular characteristics that might be more conducive to moral development than other educational settings?
2. What techniques can be used in a physical education context to enhance moral development?
3. Are participants in extracurricular physical activities at a higher moral level than the normal population?
4. Are athletes functioning at higher moral levels than nonathletes?

A great deal has been written about applying the cognitive-developmental and values clarification approaches to an educational setting. Although these two are supposed to be vastly different, Stahl (1976) indicates that values clarification is subsumed under the moral reasoning or cognitive-developmental approach, and there are some common characteristics and variables that an educator should be familiar with before attempting to enhance the moral development of students.

According to Kohlberg (1970), the only way to deal with moral education is in a school in which there is full student participation, in other words, a "just school." Realizing that this is not a highly probable event, he indicates that to enhance moral development the teacher needs to create dissatisfaction in a person about her present knowledge of what is good and expose her to disagreements and arguments about these situations with her peers. Stahl (1976) expands upon how to promote movement from one stage to a higher stage of moral

reasoning. He enumerates these ideas. *Social interaction* is a necessary component. The student must be exposed to others and their ideas and also be involved in role-taking experiences. *Cognitive dissonance* must be aroused in that people must be confronted with data that cause them to think about their current conceptions of morality. *Stage plus one reasoning* must be present. Students can assimilate moral reasoning that is one stage above their own, so this type of argument must be present to encourage moral development. *Restructuring* based upon a student's own experiences is needed. A person's thinking is based on reactions to social and environmental influences; one has to be allowed the opportunity to make his own decisions. Ready-made solutions to problems do not promote this self-structuring process.

What part does or can a teacher play in the process of helping students develop higher levels of moral judgment? Duska and Whelan (1975) suggest the following:

1. Establish the classroom as a place where participants can be respected and feel secure.
2. Allow students an opportunity to help in establishing classroom rules.
3. Explain the effect of a person's action on the group and choose a punishment which fits the offense.
4. Provide chances for group work and help students consider the feelings of others (either real or fictional characters).
5. Use role-playing so that pupils can see the event from a perspective other than their own.
6. Make an attempt to provide discussions that will involve the use of the moral judgmental process. Use as many varied sources as possible.

These suggestions indicate to us that the physical education teacher must make a concerted effort to help students deal with moral issues. We need to move from a solely externally controlled environment (teacher-centered) to an internally controlled situation—in Piagetian terms, from a heteronomous to an autonomous environment. Exposing children in the elementary school to these experiences may enhance the stage transition periods. Adults or authority figures need not make all the decisions about what goes on in the gymnasium. Allowing students a chance to make their own rules and voice their opinions may create an environment that will enhance their development. Perhaps it would even be to our advantage to construct hypothetical or "real life" moral dilemmas that could be used in the physical education class. Stahl (1976, pp. 26-27) provides the following criteria for constructing these dilemmas:

1. It presents a real conflict for the central character.
2. It must include a number of moral issues or conflicts for consideration.
3. It should generate a number of differences among the students regarding the appropriate response of the central character.
4. It generates student responses in terms of what the character should have done in the situation.
5. It must create cognitive conflict within the students such that it stimulated their need to seek higher stage reasons to resolve the conflict.

A hypothetical dilemma might be the following. It is the last quarter of the football game and the score is tied. The end runs a pass pattern and is in the end zone as the pass is thrown. When he attempts to catch the ball, his back blocks the view of the official. The official indicates a touchdown. The player making the catch has fallen to the ground. He hears the cheers of the crowd and realizes that he has been credited with a pass completion; however, he is also aware of the fact that he did not catch the ball in accordance with the rules. What should he do?

A "real life" dilemma could include a specific happening in the gymnasium immediately after its occurrence. For example, Jennifer and Laurie are kicking a playground ball back and forth to one another so that they will have the kicking and ball-stopping skills necessary for a "real" game. John and Neil decide they want to use the playground ball, so they simply walk over and take it from the girls saying, "Girls don't need to practice because they will never be any good at games." What should the boys have done? Why?

There are certainly many other happenings that can be made into moral dilemmas with resultant meaningful discussion as they occur in the gymnasium. Conflicts over taking turns, whether students should assume responsibility for officiating their own matches, being a good sport, playing cooperatively, being competitive at all times, and so forth can certainly be the focus of the dilemmas. The students must be allowed a chance to talk about, deal with, and make decisions about what is right and wrong. Teachers do not need to teach their own values, but rather to encourage students to deal with value questions and make their own judgments.

The approaches of both Kohlberg and Raths do not intend to state what "values" should be taught; rather, the student should have the opportunity to deal with the valuing or decision-making process. The student needs to be allowed to explore, define, clarify, and decide for herself what is valuable. The effect of the classroom and the total environment in which children are raised are significant factors in their development. Dorothy Law Nolte (1963) says it well:

If a child lives with criticism
   He learns to condemn.
If a child lives with hostility
   He learns to fight.
If a child lives with ridicule
   He learns to be shy.
If a child lives with tolerance
   He learns to be patient.
If a child lives with encouragement
   He learns confidence.
If a child lives with praise
   He learns to appreciate.
If a child lives with fairness
   He learns justice.
If a child lives with security
   He learns to have faith.
If a child lives with approval
   He learns to like himself.
If a child lives with acceptance and friendship
   He learns to find love in the world.*

References

Albertson, R. *The 1831 athletic controversy; New England educators' dilemma.* Paper presented at Fourth Annual Conference of North American Society of Sport History, Eugene, Oregon, June, 1976. (ERIC Document Reproduction Service No. ED 129 823)

Bandura, A., & MacDonald, F. H. Influence of social reinforcement and the behavior of models in shaping children's moral judgments. *Journal of Abnormal and Social Psychology,* 1963, *67,* 274-281.

Bee, H. *The developing child* (2nd ed.). New York: Harper & Row, Publishers, 1978.

Duska, R., & Whelan, M. *Moral development: a guide to Piaget and Kohlberg.* New York: Paulist Press, 1975.

Haan, N. M., Smith, M. B., & Block, J. Moral reasoning of young adults: political-social behavior, family background, and personality correlates. *Journal of Personality and Social Psychology,* 1968, *19,* 83-201.

Hartshorne, H., & May, M. A. *Studies in the nature of character.* Studies in deceit (Vol. 1); Studies in self-control (Vol. 2); Studies in the organization of character (Vol. 3). New York: Macmillan, Inc., 1928-1930.

Hoffman, M. L. Moral development. In P. H. Mussen (Ed.), *Carmichael's manual of child psychology* (3rd ed.) (Vol. 2). New York: John Wiley & Sons, Inc., 1970.

Jantz, R. K. Moral thinking in male elementary pupils as reflected by perception of basketball rules. *Research Quarterly,* 1975, *46,* 414-421.

Kirschenbaum, H. *Advanced values clarification.* La Jolla, Calif.: University Associates, Inc., 1977.

Kirschenbaum, H., Harmin, M., Howe, L., & Simon, S. In defense of values clarification. *Phi Delta Kappan,* 1977, *58,* 743-746.

Kohlberg, L. *The development of modes of moral thinking and choice in the years 10 to 16.* Unpublished doctoral dissertation. University of Chicago, 1958.

Kohlberg, L. The development of children's orientation toward a moral order (Pt. 1). Sequences in the development of moral thought. *Vita Humana,* 1963, *6,* 11-33.

Kohlberg, L. Development of moral character and moral ideology. In M. L. Hoffman & L. W. Hoffman (Eds.), *Review of child development research* (Vol. I). New York: Russell Sage Foundation, 1964.

Kohlberg, L. Education for justice: a modern statement of the platonic view. In N. F. Sizer & T. R. Sizer (Eds.), *Moral education: five lectures.* Cambridge, Mass. Harvard University Press, 1970.

Kohlberg, L. From is to ought. In T. Mischel (Ed.), *Cognitive development and epistemology.* New York: Academic Press, Inc., 1971.

Kohlberg, L., & Hersh, R. H. Moral development: A review of theory. *Theory Into Practice,* 1977, *16,* 53-59.

Kohlberg, L., & Kramer, R. Continuities and discontinuities in childhood and adult moral development. *Human Development,* 1969, *12,* 93-120.

Lickona, T. How to encourage moral development. *Learning,* 1977, *5* (March), 37-40; 42-43.

McCandless, B. R., & Evans, E. D. *Children and youth: psychosocial development.* Hinsdale, Ill.: The Dryden Press, 1973.

Meggysey, D. *Out of their league.* Berkeley, Calif.: Ramparts Press, 1070.

Milgram, S. Behavioral study of obedience. *Journal of Abnormal and Social Psychology.* 1963, *67,* 371-378.

Nolte, D. *Children learn what they live.* Forest Falls, Calif.: Living Scrolls, 1963.

Ogilvie, B., & Tutko, T. If you want to build character, try something else. *Psychology Today,* 1971, *5,* 61-63.

Piaget, J. *The moral judgment of the child.* New York: Harcourt Brace, 1932.

Raths, L., Harmin, M., & Simon, S. *Values and teaching.* Columbus, Ohio: Charles E. Merrill Pub. Co., 1966.

Rosenhan, D. Prosocial behavior of children. In W. W. Hartup (Ed.), *The young child: reviews of research* (Vol. 2). Washington, D.C.: National Association for the Education of Young Children, 1972.

Shaw, G. *Meat on the hoof.* New York: St. Martin's Press, Inc. 1972.

Simon, S. B., Howe, L. W., & Kirschenbaum, H. *Values clarification: a handbook of practical strategies for teachers and students.* New York: Hart Pub. Co., Inc., 1972.

Sports Illustrated. Morality play, April 10, 1978, p. 15.

Stahl, R. J. *Values/moral education: a synthesis model.* ERIC Clearinghouse on Teacher Education, 1976. (ERIC Document Reproduction Service No. ED 129 719)

Superka, D. & Johnson, P. *Values education: approaches and materials.* ERIC Clearinghouse for Social Studies and the Social Science Education Consortium, 1975.

Turiel, E. An experimental test of the sequentiality of developmental stages in the child's moral judgments. *Journal of Personality and Social Psychology,* 1966, *3,* 611-618.

Turiel, E. Stage transition in moral development. In R. M. W. Travers (Ed.), *Second handbook of research on teaching.* Chicago: Rand McNally & Co., 1973.

Student projects

1. Select three people within the age range of 10 to 16 (try to get a 10-year-old, 13-year-old, and 16-year-old) and ask them to respond to the following moral dilemma:

   A fitness class has as one of its objectives the 12-minute run for distance. During this run each student is supposed to cover as much distance as possible. All the students know that their final grade will be based, in part, on the amount of improvement that is shown on this run. Justin, who is in good physical condition, wants to get a good grade in the class. He knows that he could easily run 2 miles in the 12 minutes but that he would then not have much room for improvement. Additionally, he is responsible for keeping accurate records and telling the teacher the distance that he has run. What should Justin do?

a. Classify the responses you get according to Kohlberg's stages (Table 9-2).
b. Do the stages represented correspond with the data illustrated in Fig. 9-1?
c. How can you explain the agreement or disagreement with the Kohlerg data?

2. Select a person (of approximately the same age) from each of the following three levels of physical activity participation: physical education class, intramural, and interscholastic. Present the moral dilemma stated in Project 1 to these people and classify the results. Discuss the types of responses from the different levels of competition.

Chapter 10

SELF-CONCEPT DEVELOPMENT

Self-concept has become a focal point for the social and psychological sciences during the past few decades. Unquestionably, it is one of the most important components of a child's psychological makeup. Educators have become more sensitized to the internal workings of a child and, thus, have recognized the influence self-concept has on academic performance and social involvement. In this chapter we examine some of the theoretical aspects of self-concept, look at how self-concept develops in boys and girls, and discuss the implications for physical education.

A review of the literature concerning self-concept shows that a great deal of confusion exists over what self-concept is. Besides the term self-concept, there are other terms such as *self-esteem, self-image, self-regard, phenomenal self,* and so on. Many of these terms have overlapping definitions, and the theories associated with them are ambiguous and incomplete. Thus, when the teacher attempts to study self-concept in the school setting, he or she is faced with the dilemma of not knowing what to study. Creelman's (1954) definition describes self-concept as a multidimensional construct that covers and includes the total range of one's perceptions and evaluations of oneself. It is hoped that a clearer picture of self-concept results from our presentation of various conditions that affect the development of a positive self-concept.

In order to fully understand the dimensions of personality, it is first necessary to explore the historical development of self-concept theory. By doing this one can see that personality is a child's awareness of himself and his relation to the world.

One of the earliest investigations of self-concept was originated by William James in the late nineteenth century (Anderson, 1949). James, a philosopher-psychologist, believed that the ego was the core of an individual's identity. The significance of James's contribution is the belief that the person's perception of himself is an important variable in the understanding of human behavior. He theorized that whenever two people meet, there are actually six people present: the person who he thinks he is, the person who he really is, and the person

other people think he is. From this perspective the view each person has of himself is different from reality, but is equally important for understanding (Felker, 1974).

The *dynamics* of self-concept were further hypothesized through the ideas and writings of Sigmund Freud. Unlike James, Freud focused on those individuals with acute psychological dysfunctions. Freud relied heavily on the belief that behavior results from unconscious motivation. Freud's role for the *ego* was that of a mediator between natural forces of the *id* and the cultural forces of the *superego*. The ego was the ultimate influence on an individual's behavior. According to Freud, the ego, superego, and id are the three major components of personality. When all three systems are working in harmony, the result is a healthy personality.

Lecky (1951) discussed the importance of inner consistency as a mechanism that maintains the cognitive stability of the self-concept. It can be thought of as an individual's flexibility in adjusting his self-concept in all situations. For children the achievement of inner consistency is not simple. Often it requires continuous movement between commitment and questioning, thrusting ahead and retreating, and self-initiation and conformity. The strength of the child's self-concept is based on his ability to adjust to such changes in life. For example, the honor student who receives straight "A's" may experience failure one day and thus may have to readjust to the general concept of himself. Such changes cause a psychological dissonance or an uncomfortable feeling, but with inner consistency there is strong motivation to re-establish equilibrium and thereby feel comfortable again.

The dimension of cognitive flexibility (or rigidity) may thus describe an aspect of an individual's self-concept. An extremely rigid self-concept involves excessive use of defense mechanisms that ultimately result in a gross distortion of the "real" self (McDavid and Harari, 1974). The child who is excessively rigid resists realignment of the self-concept and as a result may experience considerable difficulty in personal adjustment. On the other hand, excessive flexibility in the self-concept that causes erratic changes in the face of each new situation is also limiting in achieving consistency in a changing world. The child who feels that she is a genius every time she gets an ''A'' on a paper and an idiot when she gets an ''F'' is demonstrating inconsistency. She lacks a stable and operable estimate of herself as a frame of reference for future planning and decision making.

In contrast to Freudian theories Abraham Maslow and Carl Rogers have proposed a humanistic approach in defining self-concept. Both of these ''humanists'' make assumptions that man controls the development of his self-concept. Each individual possesses an inner drive for self-fulfillment and personal growth. Rogers (1951) contends that an individual grows despite various environmental influences. However, he stresses the need for helping individuals to move through stages of self-evaluation and motivation in order to gain a greater awareness of self. His classic, nondirective ''client-centered'' therapy is considered a major contribution to the reshaping of the individual's concept of himself.

Maslow (1954) was concerned with the process of ''self-actualization'' in the molding of an individual's personality. A person's ability to achieve self-actualization depends on whether certain lesser needs can be met—physiological, safety, love and belonging, and esteem. These needs are organized in a hierarchy and are dealt with in a sequential order of importance (Fig. 10-1).

For teachers the necessity to provide children with the opportunities to meet these needs should be a prime concern. Although each child possesses some level of self-motivation in meeting these needs, such motivation can quickly deteriorate as a result of a teacher's failure to foster growth and development in all learning situations. The relationship of Maslow's theory to education can best be expressed in his own words:

What I am really interested in is the new kind of education which moves toward fostering the new kind of human being that we need, the process person, the creative person, the improvising person, the self-trusting, courageous person, the autonomous person. (1971, p. 100)

Fig. 10-1. Maslow's needs hierarchy.

MEASUREMENT OF SELF-CONCEPT

Various theoretical and practical means for psychological measurement have converged upon ''the self.'' The inability of psychologists and educators to make accurate objective assessments of an individual's self-concept has remained a problem. Most researchers believe that many of the psychological measuring tools currently available are at a relatively low level of precision. Wylie (1974) thinks that the biggest problem with self-concept measurement lies with the lack of properly validated instruments.

Many of the contemporary instruments used to measure self-concept employ self-referent techniques. Much of the rationale for the use of self-referent techniques lies in the assumption that feelings of self are known only by the individual. Consequently, individual attitudes are beyond the observation of someone other than oneself. Projective techniques and self-report measures have been used in this way. Projective instruments have been most commonly employed as self-referent measures in which an individual can consciously or unconsciously project inner feelings about self to persons or situations other than self. The problem with this technique is the skill needed in interpretation and the amount of time consumed with the actual testing procedure. On the other hand when one uses self-report techniques, by far the most common measure of self-concept, there are often influences that distort the responses of the individual so as to prevent a true assessment of the self. A person may "fake" her responses in order to intentionally reveal only what she wishes. A person may fake "good" or "bad" depending on the circumstances. In many cases it has been found that adult populations fake "bad" in an effort to gain attention or as a way to get out of some unwanted situation. Children, on the other hand, are assumed to be less knowledgeable about any benefits resulting from a low score, and, consequently, any low score produced may be a reflection of a low self-esteem and should be treated with concern. Responses may also be distorted by an individual's inability to look introspectively or by her merely misinterpreting the intended meaning of the test items given.

The testing situation alone lends itself to problems of proper motivation. Some individuals may find it difficult to respond honestly to items of a test given within a group situation. Many psychologists feel that a "one-to-one" testing situation is more apt to produce a greater number of valid responses. The rapport between the examiner and examinee also exerts an influence on the self-concept test score. The student may be inhibited in responding, thereby invalidating the data.

Problems in self-concept measurement among children

The assessment of self-concept in children has been a bewildering topic for many years. Two of the issues have been the stability of the self-concept over time and the types of instruments used for testing the phenomena under discussion. It can be stated that attitudes toward the self do not become generalized until about 8 years of age. Up until that time they are more a function of the immediate situation. Prior to adolescence self-acceptance comes from the way one sees himself accepting a social role appropriate to his age. During adolescence the individual becomes more conscious of the variety of social roles he performs and eventually establishes himself in a selected role that is

fairly well-defined. At this stage of life the self-concept appears to become stabilized.

The same criticism applied to self-concept measures in general also apply to measuring self-concept in children. One problem, which may be unique to young children, is the fact that most instruments used to measure self-concept are verbal. Because these scales require reading skills, children with low verbal and reading aptitude may be unable to give true responses about themselves, simply because they do not understand the question. Related to this is the problem young children have with attention span. If the items are numerous and also difficult to understand, the child fails to portray herself accurately.

One further problem that must be mentioned is that of the type of scale used. Many of the self-concept tests have engendered difficulties when children are asked to respond to items that must be answered along a continuum, such as, "always, most of the time, sometimes, never." It has been found that younger children have a difficult time distinguishing several values for responses and their position to each other (Bryant, 1974; Coopersmith, 1967; Creelman, 1954). One solution is to present absolute values. For example a child is able to comprehend the relation of dichotomized responses such as "yes-no" rather than trying to discriminate between a series of responses. However, Piers (1969) cautioned against the use of dichotomized responses in that children may tend to develop acquiescence by answering "yes" or "no" to all questions. This is relatively easy to minimize by balancing the number of positively and negatively worded items when constructing a self-referent inventory.

Self-concept measures for children

Coopersmith (1967) developed one of the first verbal scales to measure self-concept (SEI). Over the years it has undergone modification for use with children. However, Wylie (1974) advises that more measures of validity and reliability be conducted before using it in self-concept research.

Piers and Harris (Piers, 1969) provide a scale that measures the global self-concept of children who are at least at the third-grade reading level. The Piers-Harris Scale (PH) comprises 80 items containing statements that relate to feelings a child has about himself. The derivation of the items is the collection of children's statements, compiled by Jersild (1969), about what they liked and disliked about themselves. The items are answered "yes" or "no" depending on how a child generally feels about himself. In addition the positive and negative items are balanced so as to control any acquiescence that may appear in the responses. Wylie (1974) believes the PH is one of the more worthy self-concept tests used in research. Despite its value, however, a child is required to have at least a third-grade reading aptitude in order to take the test independently; herein lies the importance of nonverbal tests for children's self-concept.

Recognizing this shortcoming, Creelman (1954) designed one of the early nonverbal instruments used with kindergarten children. She prepared a multiple-choice picture test series that included 24 cards with eight pictures on each card. Each card depicted different situations commonly experienced by children. All pictures depicted children who were representative of Western culture. A child taking the test was asked to choose pictures that she

liked or disliked most, pictures that she considered "bad" and "good," and pictures that she thought were like and unlike her.

Woolner (1966) later developed a test similar to Creelman's that consisted of ten plates with paired pictures on each plate. The pictures represented personal characteristics that preschool children attribute to themselves. These characteristics were illustrated as bipolar adjectives from which a child was required to choose. The child first was asked to select the picture that he thought was like him. Next the child was directed to go through the same set of pictures to select the picture that represented something that he would like to be. Answers to the first ten choices represented the child's self-concept; answers to the second ten choices represented his ideal self-concept. From these scores Woolner was able to measure discrepancies between these concepts and thus ascertain incongruency between the child's self and ideal self-concept.

A set of 50 cartoon-like picture cards was developed by Bolea and co-workers (1970) to reflect Jersild's (1969) categories of self-concept. In the original development of the instrument a panel of psychologists and human development specialists ranked the items from 1 to 50 on a continuum from positive to nega-

Fig. 10-2. Sample item from Martinek-Zaichkowsky nonverbal self-concept scale for children. (From T. Martinek and L. Zaichkowsky, *Manual for the Martinek-Zaichkowsky self-concept scale for children.* Jacksonville, Ill.: Psychologists and Educators, Inc., 1977.)

tive evaluations of self-concept. The mean ranking of the judges was assigned to each card as a weighted value of the card. The child being tested was asked to sort the cards into three piles according to whether the figure on the card was like him, sometimes like him, or not at all like him.

The most recent nonverbal self-concept scale is that developed by Martinek and Zaichkowsky (MZSCS) (1977). Since the scale is nonverbal, it requires little or no reading ability and can be administered to non-English-speaking groups. It consists of 25 items that measure attributes such as appropriate behavior, and intellectual, social, and physical aspects of a child's phenomenal self-concept. The MZSCS items are portrayed by a pair of cartoon pictures. Each pair of pictures shows a bipolar representation of that item to facilitate a forced-choice response by the examinee. Each set of pictures shows a boy or girl in a separate situation. For example one of the pictures shows a child who is happy, while the other picture shows the same child sad. The child being tested is asked to identify which would be most like herself. An illustration of the MZSCS is shown in Fig. 10-2.

AGE DIFFERENCES IN SELF-CONCEPT

By the time a child comes to school personality patterns have been shaped by influences of early family experiences. He enters school with a self-concept of his own. Furthermore, each child comes with a set of learnings and self-attitudes that ultimately determine how well he integrates into the new world of the classroom. For the teacher this represents a challenge to help the child with a positive self-concept, to further master developmental tasks inherent in formal schooling. For the child who comes to school with negative views of self, the opportunity to reteach a new feeling of self-worth becomes an even larger challenge. Since self-concept is relatively stable during the middle elementary years, changing negative self-concepts is not an easy task. However, a better understanding of where and how self-concepts are learned offers teachers the opportunity to effect change. If teachers are to be instrumental in changing the negative views children have of themselves, they find it helpful to view the self from the

perspective of the initial influences of early periods of infancy through the volatile years of adolescence.

Infancy and early childhood

An individual's self-concept is learned. The formation of the total personality is the result of an organized structure of various concepts that have a social and cultural reference. During infancy this process of self-awareness is initially based on acquiring a sense of security. The security that an infant feels is the result of having a variety of needs attended to. This security shows itself in a number of observable behaviors. Smiling, for example, which is evident shortly after birth, has been called the first externalized form of behavior that reflects the infant's feeling of well-being and adequacy (Thorne, 1962). When others, especially the mother, respond to this movement, a conditioned reaction is formed and is, in most cases, continually reinforced. This and other simple forms of interaction with the parents and other family members eventually lead to complex patterns of self-concept in later years.

The fact that the parents provide comfort instead of pain tells the infant that he is of value. A sense of importance is further confirmed by both verbal and nonverbal expressions of love and affection. This parental reinforcement provides the infant with a sense of belonging, which subsequently provides an early sense of competence. The achievement of competence is a constant struggle for all individuals. This struggle is intensified in early childhood because a child is always experiencing new learning tasks. Since his life is full of learning experiences, he must try to view each learning task in a positive way in spite of the incompetencies that are felt. If the child is going to develop a sense of competence, significant others around him should emphasize the newly learned things and promote further learning rather than accentuating the incompetencies (Felker, 1974) (Fig. 10-3).

Parents who have higher levels of expectations find that the child passes from infancy to the toddler stage with his new set of behaviors easily cast into the ''big boy'' role. At the same time he begins to find other inter-

Fig. 10-3. Sense of competence is developed in relationships with significant others.

ests outside his parental contact and outside himself. He begins to interact with other children and to find a new social identity outside the family group. From these experiences he forms new competencies with a totally new frame of reference. The concept of self begins to acquire a new look. His "mirror images" reflect his interpretations of people's attitudes and behavior toward him. Because of the young child's inability to see below the surface of others' words and actions, he often fails to understand their meaning. The parents should be encouraged to provide extra help to clarify this confusion and thus ease any undue stress (Brandt, 1957).

The most important thing, however, is that the child must learn that she belongs to a group of friends and to a world that is larger than her family. She must learn that the world can be filled with good and bad experiences. It is critical at this stage of development that the child select those reference groups that continue to foster a positive "mirror image."

The significant consideration here is the continuity with which the child can integrate those concepts formed from family influences and those concepts formed from her own reference groups. For example a child brought up in a home where she is given everything has to modify her self-concept in environments where this condition does not prevail.

Late childhood

During the second grade a child begins to shift the frame of reference from home and family to school and teacher. The child begins to identify with acquaintences either in school or outside home and school. A child begins to develop the ideal image of himself from sources such as movies, television, historical figures, contemporary affairs, or even comics. Much of the dependence between parent and child is lost once the child enters the new world of school. The child develops independence and identity within a new setting, with new friends and with newly established self-ideals. Felker (1974) summarized the impact of this transition from home to school as follows:

The changes brought about by starting school are dramatic both for mother and child, and the changes are of tremendous importance in the development of the child. The changes brought about by school-child interactions produce new and exciting consequences in the development and enhancement of the child's self-concept. (1974, p. 59)

The teacher now becomes a new primary model for the child. Frustration results from this when parents find the teacher is the newly found resource for the child's questions. The parents' opinions are no longer the "word of law." The child begins to quote words of wisdom from a higher authority, Ms. Jones. Although the parents may feel they are playing a secondary role, the school is merely assisting the parents in educating their child. At the same time the child is gaining increased independence as a result of school experiences (Fig. 10-4).

The school also presents new pressures for the child. These pressures result from objective evaluation criteria (grades, red marks on paper, and so on) that eventually determine academic success for the child's entire school life. Martinek and Zaichkowsky (1977) found that this kind of evaluation of the child's performance in the elementary grades may lead to a general decrease in self-concept from the second grade through the sixth. The fact that the child is now told "what to do" and "how to do it" provides little freedom for testing new competencies.

Another interesting dimension to developmental influences of the school is in the perceived teacher expectations of the child. In other words if a teacher expects a child to perform well or poorly in school and begins acting toward that child in certain ways, the student may, in fact, live up to the teacher's expectation and actually become a high or low achiever (Rosenthal and Jacobson, 1968). Purkey (1978) suggests that these perceptions have an appreciable influence on the child's self-concept and are evident in the early school years. In a recent study by Martinek and Johnson (1979) 170 fourth- and fifth-grade children were rated by their teachers according to how they were expected to perform in physical activity. The results of the study showed that not only did the high-expectancy students have significantly higher self-concepts than low-expectancy students, but more contact time, encouragement, and acceptance were given to this group.

Many researchers have suggested that the child's self-concept stabilizes around grade three. However, this stability depends on how well the child has been able to assimilate those early experiences into healthy expectations for her role in society. The family, school, and peer group relationships are means to the development of a positive self-concept. In reality each one of these groups has some influence on the child's developing self-concept. If one's interactions with one of these groups are weak during the developmental years, it becomes increasingly difficult to form a realistic attitude of the self.

Adolescence

The adolescent in our society abruptly faces a period in life when he is expected to come to terms with himself. A good self-concept becomes a vital possession for a smoother and easier transition. During childhood instability changes to stability. Most of the child's energies are expended in learning certain behaviors that lead to control and consistency. By adolescence an individual has developed well physically, thereby making possible a good measure of body control and coordination. Reference groups have been well established, with each member reflecting common characteristics.

The onset of adolescence, however, causes a dramatic upheaval in the developing child. This period represents a time in which total social, physical, and emotional readjustment takes place. Along with this readjustment comes a reorganization of the self-concept. Martinek and Zaichkowsky (1977) found that several factors can dramatically affect this reorganization during the period of adolescence: satisfaction and happiness, home and family relationships and circumstances, and physical ability in sports and games.

The volatile years of adolescence frequently cause periods of unhappiness and dissatisfaction. It is during this time that feelings are increasingly sensitive. The young adolescent vacillates between periods of happiness and depression. New interests in the opposite sex further compound feelings. The mind of a child has suddenly become encased in an adult body. This results in conflicting desires. On the one hand the adolescent wants to look good for the

Fig. 10-4. Various influences on development of self-concept.

opposite sex, and on the other hand he wants to hide those physical attributes of which he is ashamed. Tight-fitting clothes, for example, which are too revealing but are the "in thing," may be a source of constant worry. This concern could be reflected in the situation in which the individual refuses to be in front of a class when giving a report. This self-consciousness is also seen with members of the same sex; take, for example, the great lengths adolescents will go to avoid taking showers after a physical education class. In most instances this latter feeling is developed as a result of a lack of parental and teacher guidance for the child during entrance into adolescence. For girls the sudden increase in body weight only causes a desire to hide this "new weight" by wearing loose-fitting clothes. There are girls who refuse to stand erect and slouch or slump in order to be less revealing. On the other hand, there are some girls who go to extremes in wearing tight-fitting clothing and other accentuating apparel in order to show off their new maturity. According to Horrocks (1969), both attitudes are misdirected and may be the result of faulty education about the true meaning of physical change. Parents and teachers may do their children more good if they prepare them for such physical change by explaining its meaning, as well as guiding them toward a better understanding of their own bodily functions.

The attainment of self-satisfaction becomes an even greater problem with new ambiguities entering into the requirements for social acceptance. Membership in a particular social group is far more complex for the adolescent than for the child. For example the young child has few requirements to meet for joining in social and play activities with other children. She may even choose to play with other groups with little concern for set rules of acceptance. During adolescence, however, unhappiness and frustration often accompany new peer group pressures. New reference groups have a discriminating set of criteria, which may leave the adolescent frustrated in her attempts to meet them. Thus, a "lost" feeling, a sense of not "belonging," creeps in. Since the individual measures her performance in terms of well-defined role expectations, such ambiguities may

cause confusion and dissatisfaction with self.

The home and family were a focal point of interest for the child. The family, according to Moulton et al. (1966), provides the socializing system in which the child learns appropriate behaviors. Family relationships are a crucial and important force that helps a child develop an inner feeling of autonomy. This autonomy is needed in order for the child entering the adolescent period to be able to successfully assimulate new social roles independent of parental domination. Horrocks (1969) points out that parental domination is probably the leading obstacle in the normal course of adolescent emancipation from parental control. This eventually prevents an adolescent from acquiring the ability to take her place as a mature individual in the economic and social world. For many parents the child's move to independence may be threatening and uncomfortable. The parents should realize that such desires are natural and common aspects of the adolescent period. Hurlock (1964) cautions, however, that even though parental behavior should encourage self-sufficiency and self-reliance, this should not exclude reasonable dependence on parents in appropriate areas and acceptance of a healthy parent-child relationship.

SEX DIFFERENCES IN SELF-CONCEPT

Sex typing begins at birth. The label "boy" or "girl" is quickly given to the infant and provides gender identity. From this comes the basis of what McCandless and Evans (1973) call an "abstract self-concept." This gender identity of sex self-concept thereafter serves as an organizer and determinant of future attitudes and values. In infancy the child learns a set of appropriate behaviors and learns to inhibit behaviors that are considered out of character with the sex role. Boys are taught that they are to play with footballs and baseballs and not with dolls. Many parents are unaware of these influential subtleties. Felker (1974) reported that by the age of 2, children are capable of identifying male and female items with 75% accuracy, and by age 3 they can judge a wide range of activities according to sex appropriateness.

Santrock (1970) believes in the importance of "mother" and "father" models so the child can identify with masculine and feminine behaviors. In most cases it has been found that the father is most frequently absent in broken families. This is a significant disadvantage for the small boy who lives without the father model during his first 5 years. This absence results in feminine characteristics in the boy's personality. This can have depressing effects on achievement and self-concept, especially during the early and middle years (Biller, 1970). These findings have special significance in light of the escalation of divorces during the past decade. Of course in many cases the negative effect on a child's self-concept due to an absent father can likely be offset if a positive father substitute is available (McCandless and Evans, 1973).

For the most part, sex differences in self-concept for males and females have proven to be small for elementary-age children. Piers (1969) reported that there was little sex difference in male and female samples when measured on a global self-concept scale. Only slight differences were found on items pertaining to behavior and anxiety, with boys scoring more positively than girls. Felker (1974) found in a group of first graders tested that girls had a higher self-perception than boys. The reason for this sex difference is that school is seen by the young boy as a predominantly female place. Chalk, blackboards, chairs, desks, and books were perceived by boys as female articles. Another reason for the difficulty in adjusting for boys was the slower developmental rate in comparison with girls. Although this trend is most clearly characterized by earlier onset of the pubescent period for girls, it is still apparent during the developmental years. Studies (Erhartic, 1977; Martinek and Zaichkowsky, 1977; and Zaichkowsky et al., 1975) have also shown little in the way of sex differences between boys and girls. Fig. 10-5 illustrates the slight decrease in self-concept with age; although there appear to be slight differences favoring the girls at most age levels, the differences are not statistically significant.

The self-concept for both sexes falls during puberty. For girls this time of psychological change occurs around 11 years of age. For boys 14 years of age is the average time. Since there

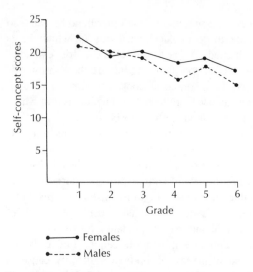

Fig. 10-5. Age and sex differences on measure of self-concept. (Data from the Martinek-Zaichkowsky self-concept scale for children.)

is often emotional turmoil associated with the onset of the pubescent period, the ability of a child to adjust to this change is largely dependent on the self-concept that has been developed from his early family and school experiences.

IMPLICATIONS FOR PHYSICAL EDUCATION

The moment a child is born, his awareness of his new environment initiates responses that eventually evolve into a specific personality pattern. The responses elicited by the child are, for the most part, in the form of overt, physical movements that enable him to learn about himself in relation to his environment. These responses emerge in the development of the child's self-concept. Movement is one of the primary ways in which the child finds out about his world. Through movement the child is able to express emotions and learn that others share many of these same emotions. The child also learns to identify with a group and possibly develop ethnic pride through the movement experience. Cratty and Martin (1969, p. 156) believe that a child's total self-concept results from collective feelings about many things. ''. . . the child's self includes the manner in which he views his capacities to perform motor tasks. Basic to physical performance, of course, is his 'vehicle' for movement, his body.'' On the basis of Cratty and Martin's assumption that the child's conceptualization of himself is in many ways reflected in his attitude toward performance in physical activity, physical educators are becoming more cognizant of the cognitive and affective, as well as motor, domains within the child.

Teaching behavior and self-concept

Teaching is a process in which a dynamic interplay of human personalities takes place. These personalities center on the relationship of the teacher and student. Hamachek (1971) and Mixer and Milson (1973) think that a teacher's relationship with his students is a prime professional concern. This relationship can allow the teacher to become a ''significant other'' figure in the lives of students and, therefore, to influence personality development. Once the teacher has established himself as an important member of the students' social scheme, he must acquire and maintain a sensitivity to what the child feels about himself and the world. Mixer and Milson further stated that ''to the degree to which a teacher is able to predict how his students are viewing themselves, their subject, and their world—to that degree he is in a position to become a successful teacher'' (1973, p. 347).

However, Reisman et al. (1953) found that frequently when the teacher becomes the other-directed agent for the child, he continues to hold the reins of authority in his hands under the guise of ''reasoning'' and ''manipulation.'' With this kind of teacher the student can no longer be his forthright self, free to inquire and develop. Instead, he becomes defensive and reactive, concerned more with survival than with learning.

Watson (1973) believes that the prevention of negative self-concepts in children is a vital first step in teaching. Although few teachers profess to be insensitive enough to tell a child that he has below-average ability, Watson found that many educators do, in fact, tell them in numerous ways—red marks on papers, report cards and grades, after-school help, visits to a reading specialist, and various nonverbal gestures of teacher annoyance or disapproval. Watson also

found that as a result of these teaching subtleties low-ability children who receive both peer and teacher approval in nonacademic areas, such as a physical activity, in which they can excel develop and maintain a more positive self-concept.

Snygg and Combs (1949) clearly bring out the point that an individual acts in accordance with his concept of himself. If he is made to think of himself as inadequate and worthless, then he will tend to act in accordance with that concept. Jordan (1971) emphasized the need for teachers to realize the importance of their role in motivating a child to maintain a healthy self-image. The student's self-image can be changed by fulfilling his present needs in a way that supports his dignity and reinforces his strengths while dealing with his weaknesses. It has been shown that children's perceptions of their teachers' feelings toward them correlated positively and significantly with self-perception; in addition, the child's overall academic achievement and social class position were significantly higher when the perception of the teacher's feelings was interpreted as favorable toward him (Davidson and Lang, 1965).

The importance of the instructional process to self-concept has led to research into various teaching approaches and their effects on a child's emotional level. Research dealing with the effects of the open classroom or a more student-centered approach to education rather than the teacher-centered approach has yielded interesting results. Keilty and Green (1973) found that in the open approach in teaching— that is, when students have alternative activities to choose from—a more positive self-concept is manifested. It also was indicated that the students showed a more favorable attitude toward school in general. Significant increases in self-concept were also found when students were involved with a more student-directed teaching approach. However, it should be noted that a totally unstructured class could be a detriment to the child's ability to gain insight into his own self-awareness (Brown and MacDougall, 1973; Raimanis, 1972).

How individualized instruction affects self-concept has also been investigated. Powell

(1972) conducted a study with a group of elementary school children to see what changes occurred in levels of self-esteem as a result of individualized instruction. The children chosen were from a working class, ethnically mixed school, in which self-esteem was low prior to instructional treatment. These children were compared to a control group of students with higher IQ and achievement levels. From the results of the individualized instruction it was found that the ethnically mixed children had greater self-esteem than children from the control group. While more detailed analysis was needed to determine the effects on achievement, such striking effects on self-esteem in a population with heavy minority representation were considered of major importance.

Dauer (1971) and Mosston (1965) proposed a developmental approach to individualized instruction as a means of maintaining educational individualism. By modifying the degrees of difficulty for a specific activity or stunt a child is allowed to succeed in that activity. As a result of this approach the child could gradually experience the development of a positive self-concept. Both authors think that these values can only be obtained when the child is offered the type of program in which he can meet success and not be discouraged by failure.

Several educators have been able to utilize a student tutorial method of teaching as a means of developing self-reliance as well as self-concept in their students. This tutorial method is in many ways synonymous with Mosston's (1965) reciprocal teaching, in which one student teaches the other. From this peer-directed approach to teaching the "little teacher" gains self-confidence through his new authoritarian role. Lippitt (1969) recognized that there is a growing recognition among educators that having children help other children to learn may offer an answer to four educational challenges: providing individualized instruction; scheduling enrichment opportunities; increasing motivation; and helping build self-esteem. Lippitt also expressed that greater advantages are gained when older students become helpers for children younger than themselves. She found that academic achievement increased in those older children who were involved in the tutoring of younger children. A further rationale was offered for the use of cross-age reciprocal teaching:

They [children] are closer in age and can often reach a child who is having difficulty when an adult cannot; they provide more realistic models of behavior; and they offer opportunity for friendship within peer culture. Studies show a direct ratio between feelings of peer acceptance and ability. (Lippitt, 1969, p. 41)

Another direction of research has attempted to look at what goes on in the classroom and how it affects self-concept development. In looking at interaction patterns of an elementary classroom it was found that the type of behavior exhibited by the teacher had a significant effect on students' self-concept (Spaulding, 1965). Those teachers who were classified as "socially integrative" and "learner supportive," that is, people concerned with helping the learner and providing an adequate classroom environment, exhibited behaviors that showed a high degree of private and semiprivate communication with children, overt facilitation of task-directed behavior, attentiveness to children's needs, concern for divergent responses in students, and the use of control techniques involving humor.

Unfortunately, many teachers are still not fully aware of the tremendous influence that the teaching process can have on a child's development of self-concept. Combs (1962) believes that if the development of self-concept is the result of an experience, then a positive self-concept is teachable. Consequently, the children can learn about themselves in the classroom. The individualized approach to instruction provides a stockpile of personal meanings as a resource for guiding a child toward a positive realization of self. According to Combs, there are three basic principles or guides for a teacher to consider when encouraging full actualization of the child's self in the classroom:

1. Accept each contribution a child presents. Never belittle anything a child cares to relate to his group or the teacher.
2. Provide each child with an opportunity to make an important contribution to the activity in which the class is engaged.
3. Search constantly for ways of expressing the care for each child in my group.

The evidence presented clearly describes effective teachers on the basis of personal interactive characteristics. The effective teachers appear to be those who are humanistic in the fullest sense of the word. According to Hamachek (1971), these are the teachers who have a sense of humor and are fair, empathetic, and more democratic than autocratic. Their classrooms seem to reflect miniature enterprise operations in the sense that they are open, spontaneous, and adaptable to change.

What physical educators can do

Hellison (1973, p. 12) listed reasons why physical education plays an important part in the development of the child's awareness of his true self:

1. Physical activity and physical appearance are valued in the American culture.
2. Physical education has a visible affective component.
3. The body and self are related.
4. Physical education has a unique, although limited, potential for providing significant others who can influence the self-esteem of the participants in certain physical education programs.

The ability of a child to function well physically has important implications for manifestations of self-image. This is especially true with preadolescents, who are far more concerned with physical characteristics such as size and strength than with other aspects of the body. In general most people who are in good physical condition define a feeling of enhancement of the self as feeling adequate, competent, and in control of situations. Shaffer (1966) reported that bodily disturbances are especially evident during adolescence. During this period of biological turnover there is an onset of emotional stress, awkwardness, and greater feelings of inferiority. Since the evolution of the child's self-concept relies on the adjustments made to environmental changes, the development of the child's self-image can in turn be affected. Shaffer also stressed that the physical education program must be able to adapt to the emotional status of the individual if the student's self-concept is to be positively maintained.

Up until 1960 there was little research found relating to physical education and its effect on behavioral characteristics of the elementary-age child. Scott (1960) was one of the first to write on the topic of physical education as it related to emotional development in elementary children. Since then much research has been directed toward the psychological development of the child through the advent of various types of physical education programs.

Researchers have looked at the relationship between self-concept development and (1) physical fitness, (2) movement education programs, (3) perceptual-motor programs, (4) participation in physical education as opposed to no participation in physical education and (5) special children involved in physical education programs. Generally speaking the results of these kinds of studies have been equivocal, with some researchers finding that physical education programs produce positive changes in self-concept and others showing no significant differences. One consistent finding seems to be that children with special needs improve on measures of self-concept after involvement in a physical education program (Cary, 1963; Marshall, 1969).

Another seemingly consistent finding in the physical activity–self-concept research is that there is very little correlation between one's reported self-concept and one's motor ability (Erhartic, 1977; Martinek et al., 1977). That is to say that some children report low self-concepts and have good motor ability, whereas other children report high self-concepts and have poor motor ability. This does not mean, however, that motor ability does not influence the self-concept and vice versa. Our interpretation is that self-concept (in itself a complex phenomenon) is only one of a number of interrelated factors that contribute to motor ability. It is naive to think that self-concept is directly and causally related to motor ability. One's improved self-concept may not necessarily improve one's motor ability, and likewise improving one's motor ability may not necessarily improve one's self-concept.

Even though many studies derive conflicting results, it is fair to say that in many instances physical education participation has had positive effects on self-concept development for the students in the program (Lewis, 1972; Zaichkowsky et al., 1975). Therefore, to teach for positive self-concept development is a desirable goal. By allowing students the opportunity for social interaction in the physical education setting it is possible to give children chances to view themselves in a more positive fashion. One should, however, adopt the position that physical education classes can serve as wonderful vehicles for teaching self-concept development as an objective on its own. If this carries over to improving motor ability, all have benefited.

The style of teaching used in physical education, according to Mosston (1965), can determine how a child develops along an emotional, developmental channel. The crucial consideration is in the development of self-concept, in which the child acquires the ability to accept herself—whether in achieving excellence or in facing her physical limitations. The teacher's role is to aid the child in her emotional growth and in the development of her own physical image, rather than mandating an image created by the teacher.

Martinek et al. (1977) further found that when children were given a chance to share in decisions concerning the operation of a physical education class, they were able to develop a more positive self-concept. The researchers also found that because the child was allowed to interact freely with the environment, he was able to develop a helping relationship with the teacher and peer group members.

We feel that investigation into the effects of physical activity on self-concept must be carried out with continued refinements. This is especially true for those teachers, curriculum specialists, administrators, and other researchers who make claims regarding the psychological attributes evolving from various programs.

References

Anderson, J. E. *The psychology of development and personal adjustment.* New York: Holt Co., 1949.

Biller, H. B. Father absence and the personality development of the male child. *Developmental Psychology,* 1970, *2,* 181-201.

Bolea, A. S., Felker, D. W., & Barnes, M. D. *The development and validation of a pictorial self-concept scale for children in K-4.* Paper presented at the annual meeting of the National Council on Measurement in Education, Minneapolis, March 1970.

Brandt, R. M. Self: missing link for understanding behavior. *Mental Hygiene, 1957, 41,* 24-33.

Brown, J. A., & MacDougall, M. S. *The influence of interpersonal skill training on the social climate of elementary school classrooms.* Paper presented at the annual meeting of the American Educational Research Association, New Orleans, 1973.

Bryant, P. *Perception and understanding in young children.* New York: Basic Books, Inc., 1974.

Cary, R. A. *An investigation of the relationship between emotional problems and lack of motor proficiency with children in grades 4, 5, 6 and an attempt at remedial work with selected subjects.* Paper presented at Midwest District Convention of American Association for Health, Physical Education, and Recreation, Chicago, April 1963.

Combs, A. W. *Perceiving, behaving, becoming.* Washington, D.C.: Association for Supervision and Curriculum Development, 1962.

Coopersmith, S. *The antecedents of self-esteem.* San Francisco: W. H. Freeman & Co., Pubs., 1967.

Cratty, B. J., & Martin, M. *Perceptual-motor efficiency in children,* Philadelphia: Lea & Febiger, 1969.

Creelman, M. B. *The CSC test: self-conceptions of elementary school children.* Unpublished doctoral dissertation, Western Reserve University, Cleveland, 1954.

Dauer, V. P. *Dynamic physical education for elementary school children.* Minneapolis: Burgess Publishing Co., 1971,

Davidson, H.H., & Lang, G. Children's perception of their teachers' feelings toward them related to self-perception, school achievement, and behavior. In D. E. Hamachek (Ed.), *Self in growth, teaching, learning.* Englewood Cliffs, N.J.: Prentice-Hall, Inc., 1965.

Erhartic, M. *Stability of global self-concepts of children from three different elementary schools during their first year in a regionalized jr. high school.* Unpublished doctoral dissertation, Boston University, 1977.

Felker, D. W. *Building positive self-concepts.* Minneapolis: Burgess Publishing Co., 1974.

Hamachek, D. E. *Encounters with self.* New York: Holt, Rinehart & Winston, Inc., 1971.

Hellison, D. R. *Humanistic physical education.* Englewood Cliffs, N.J.: Prentice-Hall, Inc., 1973.

Horrocks, J. E. *The psychology of adolescence,* Boston: Houghton Mifflin Co., 1969.

Hurlock, E. B. *Child development* (4th ed.). New York: McGraw-Hill Book Co., 1964.

Jersild, A. T. *In search of self.* New York: Columbia University, Teachers College Press, 1969.

Jordan, D. C. The disadvantaged child. In D. W. Allen & E. Seifman (Eds.), *The teacher's handbook.* Glenview, Ill.: Scott, Foresman & Co., 1971.

Keilty, J. W., & Green, J. *The effects of an open experimental program on the attitudes and self-concept of graduate students.* Paper presented at the annual meeting of the American Educational Research Association, New Orleans, February 1973.

Lecky, P. *Self-consistency.* New York: Island Press, 1951.

Lewis, G. B. *An exploratory study of relationships of ap-*

paratus movement skills with selected physical and psychological characteristics of kindergarten-aged males. Unpublished doctoral dissertation, University of Michigan, 1972.

Lippitt, P. Children can teach other children. *The Instructor,* 1969, *78,* 41.

McCandless, B. R., & Evans, E. D. *Children and youth: psycho-social development.* Hinsdale, Ill.: Dryden Press, 1973.

McDavid, J. W., & Harari, H. *Psychology and social behavior.* New York: Harper & Row, Publishers, 1974.

Marshall, K. G. *The relationship between participation in a program of planned aquatic activities and changes in the self-concept of children with orthopedic limitations.* Unpublished doctoral dissertation, Texas Women's University, 1969.

Martinek, T., & Johnson, S. Teacher expectations: effects on dyadic interaction and self-concept in elementary age children. *Research Quarterly,* 1979, *50,* 60-70.

Martinek, T., & Zaichkowsky, L. D. *Manual for the Martinek-Zaichkowsky self-concept scale for children.* Jacksonville, Ill.: Psychologists and Educators, Inc., 1977.

Martinek, T., Zaichkowsky, L. D., & Cheffers, J. T. F. Decision-making in elementary age children: effects on motor skills and self-concept. *Research Quarterly,* 1977, *48,* 349-357.

Maslow, A. H. *Motivation and personality.* New York: Harper & Row, Publishers, 1954.

Maslow, A. H. *The farther reaches of human nature.* New York: The Viking Press, 1971.

Mixer, A. S., & Milson, J. L. Teaching and the self. *The Clearing House,* 1973, *47,* 346-350.

Mosston, M. *Teaching physical education.* Columbus, Ohio: Charles E. Merrill, Pub. Co., 1965.

Moulton, R. W., Burnstein, E., Liberty, P. G., & Altucher, N. Patterning of parental affection and disciplinary dominance as a determinant of guilt and sex typing. *Journal of Personality and Social Psychology,* 1966, *4,* 356-363.

Piers, E. V. *Manual for the Piers-Harris children's self-concept scale.* Nashville, Tenn.: Counselor Recordings and Tests, 1969.

Powell, M. M. *Changes in self-esteem as a result of an*

individualized curriculum. Project sponsored by Westinghouse Learning Corporation, New York, 1972.

Purkey, W. *Inviting school success.* Belmont, Calif.: Wadsworth Publishing Co., 1978.

Raimanis, G. *Teaching effectiveness and the interaction between teaching methods, student and teacher characteristics.* Project sponsored by Office of Education, Washington, D.C., Bureau of Research, 1972.

Riesman, D., Glazer, N., & Denny, R. *The lonely crowd.* New York: Doubleday & Co., Inc., 1953.

Rogers, C. R. *Client-centered therapy.* Boston: Houghton Mifflin Co., 1951.

Rosenthal, R., & Jacobson, L. *Pygmalion in the classroom.* New York: Holt, Rinehart & Winston, 1978.

Santrock, J. W. Paternal absence, sex typing, and identification. *Developmental Psychology,* 1970, *2,* 264-272.

Scott, G. M. The contributions of physical activity to psychological development. *Research Quarterly,* 1960, *31,* 307-317.

Shaffer, T. E. The adolescent's health and activity needs. In A. Patterson & E. C. Hallberg (Eds.), *Background readings for physical education.* New York: Holt, Rinehart & Winston, 1966.

Snygg, D., & Combs, A. W. *Individual behavior,* New York: Harper & Brothers, 1949.

Spaulding, R. L. *Achievement, creativity, and self-concept correlates of teacher-pupil transactions in elementary school classrooms.* Cooperative research project supported by the Cooperative Research Program of the Office of Education, HEW, 1965.

Thorne, L. P. *Child psychology and development.* New York: Ronald Press, 1962.

Watson, J. R. I'm just plain dumb. *Today's Education,* 1973, *62,* 26-27.

Woolner, R. B. *Kindergarten children's self-concepts in relation to their kindergarten experiences.* Unpublished doctoral dissertation, University of Tennessee, 1966.

Wylie, R. *The self-concept: a critical survey of pertinent research literature.* Lincoln: University of Nebraska Press, 1974.

Zaichkowsky, L. B., Zaichkowsky, L. D., & Martinek, T. J. Self-concept and attitudinal differences in elementary age school children after participation in a physical activity program. *Mouvement,* October 1975. pp. 243-245.

Student projects

1. Observe some children at play on the playground. On the basis of behaviors, identify those with a high self-concept and those with a low self-concept. Describe the specific behaviors that reflect the two levels of self-concept. Then observe these same children over a period of two to three days to see if these same behaviors appear. Are the "high" and "low" children still perceived the same as in the first observation? If not, tell what types of behavior patterns changed.

2. Interview three or four elementary physical education teachers and find out ways in which teachers identify whether a child is working up to her potential achievement level, below her level, or at an appropriate level in physical education. Ask the teachers to describe signs that indicate whether the standards set by the child are too high, too low, or appropriate.

3. Observe a physical education class and describe specific teacher behaviors that you feel have a positive or negative effect on the child's self-concept. Also, tell whether there were observable student reactions to the teacher behavior that further showed negative or positive effects.

Chapter 11

DEVELOPMENT OF ATTITUDES

A person's feelings or reactions to other people, objects, or concepts in the physical world have been and continue to be an interesting topic for discussion and investigation. Ever since the work of Thomas and Znaniecki in 1918 the area of attitudes has been considered a major component of social-psychological research. Even though there has been a great deal of attitudinal research, there is still much debate over the concept, primarily because of the abstractness of the construct.

Physical educators have for many years considered the development of positive attitudes a desirable outcome of the physical education experience. This thinking is typified by the following:

The importance of attitudes, how one "feels about" physical activity, and how attitudes can be changed cannot be overlooked by those interested in encouraging active physical participation . . . in school physical education programs and further physical activity throughout life. (Wessel and Nelson, 1964, p. 563)

When dealing with attitude development it is important to ask the following questions. What is an attitude? What is its importance for learning? How are attitudes formed? How are attitudes changed? How are attitudes measured? In this chapter we look at these questions and at age and sex differences. We then discuss their implications for physical education.

An attitude is commonly thought of as a feeling or a like or dislike for a particular object. A positive attitude is displayed when one likes a particular object, for example, the sport of football; and a negative attitude is considered a dislike of a particular object, perhaps the game of soccer. This knowledge of *feelings* does not really provide much information about what kind of behavior might be expected from the individual who likes football but not soccer. Our "common" definition of an attitude is not complete. Kenyon (1968b, p. 567) defines an attitude as a "latent or nonobservable, complex, but relatively stable behavioral disposition reflecting both direction and intensity of feeling toward a particular object, whether it be concrete or abstract."

From this definition it can be seen that a *behavioral disposition* is also an important part of

Fig. 11-1. Developing positive attitudes toward physical activity covers many aspects of the environment.

an attitude. This means that when a person is given a choice between participating in a football or soccer game, such as in the above example, we would expect him to play football, if all conditions were equal. There is one further component of attitude that we have not mentioned—cognition, a person's knowledge or belief about the attitude object. What the person knows or believes she knows about the attitude object has a relationship to the other attitudinal components.

All three components—affect (feeling or emotional aspect), behavioral predispositions (tendency to respond to the attitude object), and cognition (knowledge and beliefs)—of attitude are considered interrelated and dependent on one another. When there is consistency among the three attitudinal components, one is more likely to be able to predict a person's actual behavior. This theoretical definition of attitude, which hypothesizes the interrelationship of the three components, is depicted in Fig. 11-2.

It would be ideal to be able to predict that a person who has learned the value of physical activity and likes it would consistently participate in physical activity throughout her lifetime. Unfortunately, this kind of prediction is most

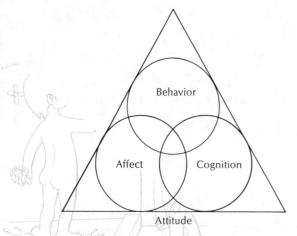

Fig. 11-2. Schematic representation of components of an attitude.

difficult because we find that at a particular time, in a particular situation, people may act or react differently when confronted with the attitude object. For example, Joe and Lorrayne think racquetball is a fascinating and exciting sport to play, but they may find themselves in a situation that does not allow them to participate. There is a racquetball court near their place of employment that they would like to use during the lunch hour. However, their work-mates consider the game silly and frivolous; this attitude prompts Joe and Lorrayne to curtail their participation in the activity.

Why are attitudes important in a learning environment? A learning environment connotes a positive situation that promotes the growth of people in that setting. In this situation positive attitudes are contributing causes to learning, not only in the present but also in the future. Mager (1968) would encourage all teachers to ensure that their students leave the classroom with as favorable an attitude toward their subject matter as possible. This, in theory, helps the student remember what he has been taught and makes him eager to learn more.

By creating a positive situation a teacher can encourage the development of positive attitudes. As teachers we wish to create an environment that allows people to do what they should do and discourages them from doing what they should not do. For example, in a physical education class Mary Slow has decided

she does not want to run a mile, which is one of the required objectives. The teacher, Sally Swift, has several options. One is to force Mary into running the mile; another is to run the mile with her. By creating a positive situation (running with Ms. Slow) Ms. Swift may have enhanced the learning environment and promoted the acquisition of more positive attitudes by her students.

How are attitudes formed? Most people who have studied attitudes would agree that they are not innate but are learned phenomena. This conclusion is reflected in the work of Bandura and Walters (1963) and Kelman (1958). These men basically believe that the influence of another person or persons plays a very important part in the social influence process, which in turn has a great deal to do with attitude formation.

Bandura and Walter's most famous experiment involved the learning of aggressive behavior. In this experiment children exposed to aggressive adult models demonstrated more aggressive behavior than those children who did not have any model. The terms ''modeling'' or observational learning are often used to reflect this type of behavior.

Kelman's work is based on a hierarchical model suggesting that there are three basic processes in acquiring an attitude or behavior. These processes are called *compliance, identification,* and *internalization.* Compliance deals with doing something because one hopes to receive a favorable reaction from another person. Identification occurs when a person adopts an attitude or behavior of another person or group because it is associated with a satisfying relationship to that person or group. Internalization refers to an individual's accepting influence because the resultant behavior is congruent with her own value system.

An example of this hierarchy in relationship to a person's attitude about jogging is demonstrated in the following example. Janet is a member of a fitness class in the school that she attends. As part of the exercise for this class she has to jog. This is not her favorite activity, but she does it because she wants to get a good grade in the class; if the instructor sees that she does not jog, her grade suffers (compliance). After school one day she sees her friends jogging and notices a particular male whom she would like to get to know better. She therefore decides to jog with this group after school to be with a particular person (identification). After jogging with this group for some time she finds that she really enjoys jogging and is now participating in the activity because it is her own wish to do so (internalization).

A person's contact with others plays a very important part in the acquisition of attitudes or behaviors. There are other theories concerning attitude formation; however, we believe the influence of others has a great amount of validity in education. We are staunch supporters of the belief that a teacher who demonstrates positive attitudes exerts a more significant influence on positive attitude formation than a teacher who merely talks about positive attitudes.

Although the process of forming attitudes is complex, a person can form an attitude without actual contact with the attitude object. This is illustrated many times over when a person shows tendencies of racial prejudice without having actually dealt with persons of the particular race. This same principle can apply to physical activity. Children can easily pick up a negative or positive attitude about physical activity simply by the manner in which parents approach the subject. Ideally, all parents would value physical activity as a result of their connection with physical education courses throughout their years of formal schooling. If this had occurred, the job of the physical educator in relation to developing positive attitudes would become simpler.

During infancy the home environment, which includes parent-child and other interactions, has a pervasive influence on the development of the child's affective behavior. By the time a child enters school she has already acquired desirable and undesirable attitudes. "It therefore becomes one of the major tasks of the school to change undesirable attitudes, to strengthen existing desirable ones, and to work toward the development of new attitudes by providing appropriate learning experiences" (Kahn and Weiss, 1973, p. 761).

How are attitudes changed? Attitudes can be changed in a number of ways. However, it is necessary to ask the corollary question, How important is the attitude object to the individual. The work of Festinger (1957), Rokeach (1968), and Sherif and Hovland (1961) sheds some light on this. All of these authors basically say that if a person has a very strong affect about the attitude object (either positive or negative), it will be a more difficult task to change the attitude than if a person has a more neutral opinion. Therefore, it would seem logical to start as soon as possible to develop favorable attitudes and thereby decrease the problem of having to change negative ones. Since this is more of a hope than a reality, we must know how it is possible to change the attitudes of individuals to make them more positive toward physical activity.

Any change in behavior is generally considered a result of learning. In order to alter an attitude it is necessary to set up certain conditions to promote change. According to Roedell et al. (1976), there are three basic ways in which children change and learn. They state that children:

1. Interpret events in the context of their own experience
2. Learn by observing others
3. Learn from the consequences of their behavior

Children make interpretations of their present experience based on what they have learned in prior situations. Those children who, prior to entering school, have been encouraged to participate in physical activity would view going to physical education class as an extension of prior good feelings about play, games, or sports. Those children who have been prevented from participating in physical activities or perhaps had "bad" experiences may resent having to go to "gym."

Because children also learn by observation, it is necessary that the teacher make an effort to ensure that what students observe is positive. This can be done through establishing a "model"; that is, a teacher may demonstrate by personal example the value of physical activity. There is some evidence to indicate a low but positive relationship between liking a teacher and the physical education experience and one's feelings about physical activity (Brumbach,

1968; Yandell, 1965; Zaichkowsky, 1973).

The fact that people learn from the consequences of their behavior allows the teacher to use experiences that are happening daily in the classroom as reinforcers. It would be possible to point out to students which kinds of behaviors are considered appropriate and which are not. This type of reasoning comes from the Skinnerian approach to learning.

Another point to consider in attitude change is the interdependence of the three components of an attitude. It would seem logical that if one tried to effect change in one area, a subsequent change would occur in the other areas, thus making the attitude consistent with itself. This indeed is what Festinger (1957) contends in his theory of cognitive dissonance. Therefore, one might try to give a person more information about the attitude object (cognitive component), allow the person to experience positive or negative feelings about the attitude object (affective component), or have a person exhibit the desired behavior (behavioral component).

MEASUREMENT OF ATTITUDES

Attitude measurement is one area in which it is difficult to derive valid and reliable information. Regardless of the technique or method used to construct a measure of any of the components of an attitude, it must be remembered that most of these instruments are self-report scales that have inherent problems. This means that a respondent could actually be stating her true feelings or giving the experimenter the answers that she thinks the investigator wants to hear (social desirability).

Some researchers try to alleviate this problem by disguising the true intent of their instrument (that is, they do not say that they want the subjects to fill out an attitude questionnaire), or they actually are able to disguise the measuring instrument so that the subjects do not know that it is an attitude scale. Others assure the respondents that their answers are anonymous and that the researcher is the only one to see the individual responses to the measuring instrument.

Another problem, particularly in physical education, is the fact that so many instruments have been used to assess attitudes in relation to physical activity. Some of these have been simply one question such as, Do you like physical education, whereas others are multidimensional scales that break affect down into several components. Except for the use of the Wear Attitude Inventory for Physical Education (1951, 1955) and, in more recent years, Kenyon's Attitude Toward Physical Activity (ATPA) scale (1968a, 1968b) few studies have used the same instruments to measure the phenomenon in question, and it is therefore difficult to make any generalized statements about attitudes and their development.

A scale that is typically used to measure affect is a Likert-type scale (Likert, 1932). It is probably one of the most commonly used techniques for attitude assessment in physical education. Using this type of procedure a researcher develops a number of statements to which he wants the subject to respond, usually on a five- or seven-point scale, with the five-point scale the most common. A sample item might look like this:

	SA*	A	U	D	SD
I think that physical education is a waste of time.	☐	☐	☐	☐	☐

The subject places a check mark under the statement that most closely represents her attitude. The tester, in tabulating the data, assigns a number to each of the responses and derives a total attitude score.

Another technique currently being used, although less popular than the Likert scale, is called the Semantic Differential (Osgood et al., 1957). This technique uses bipolar adjectives and has the subject respond to a particular concept by indicating his feelings on a seven- or nine-point continuum; usually a seven-point scale is used. For example:

Physical education

good __ : __ : __ : __ : __ : __ : __ bad
worthless __ : __ : __ : __ : __ : __ : __ worthwhile
pleasant __ : __ : __ : __ : __ : __ : __ unpleasant

The person places a check mark in the appropriate space on the continuum, and the re-

*SA = Strongly agree; A = Agree; U = Undecided; D = Disagree; SD = Strongly disagree.

searcher assigns a number to each space (generally a 7 for a positive response to a 1 for a negative response, with a neutral response assigned the value of 4). The researcher can then find a total score for the scale to determine how positive or negative a person's feelings are.

Attitudinal assessment of younger populations has always presented a measurement problem. A fairly recent technique in the attitude assessment of physical activity has been a nonverbal approach that allows flexibility in measuring the attitudes of younger children. The work of Cheffers et al. (1975) in constructing a nonverbal attitude scale to assess children's attitudes toward physical activity is noteworthy. This measuring device uses a picture of a particular situation related to physical education and gives the student the option of checking whether she likes, dislikes, or has no feeling about what she sees. Each response is then given a number on a three-point scale, and a total score is derived by adding up the score of each item. One representative item from this scale is shown in Fig. 11-3. It is hoped that further work can be done with nonverbal assessment of attitudes so that it is possible to investigate the attitudes of young children more effectively.

Other techniques are utilized in constructing attitude scales, but we will not deal with them in this text. It can be readily seen that there is a need to use similar assessment techniques so that statements made about attitudes toward physical education can be compared and contrasted across different populations as well as across age groups and sex groups.

AGE DIFFERENCES IN ATTITUDE DEVELOPMENT

In looking at affective responses Kahn and Weiss (1973) note that many personality theories hypothesize a rapid growth in different

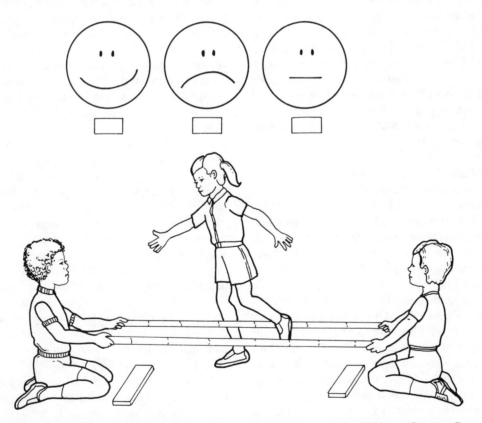

Fig. 11-3. Item from Cheffers and Mancini nonverbal attitude scale for children. (Courtesy Dr. John Cheffers, Boston University, Boston, Mass.)

personality characteristics during the early years of infancy and childhood, with marked changes during the adolescent period and small change in the postadolescent period. However, studies indicating stability and change of affective responses over time are scarce.

When age differences in attitudinal development are discussed, infancy is not considered a particularly important time. This may very easily be due to the fact that it is difficult, if not impossible, to acquire good data from children so young and not to the fact that attitudes have or have not been acquired. Some pediatricians are, in fact, saying that eating habits are well established by the age of 2, and one would certainly assume that attitudes about food are a part of these patterns.

For this section, as well as the one on sex differences, we find that in regard to physical education most attitudinal studies that have been conducted have looked at people in late childhood and adolescence. The reason for this, as mentioned earlier, is that there is a lack of instrumentation to adequately measure the attitudes of children toward physical education. Part of this problem is being eliminated through the work of Cheffers et al. (1975) and Simon and Smoll (1974). Cheffers and others used a nonverbal scale, while Simon and Smoll adapted Kenyon's ATPA scale to make it suitable for children in the upper elementary grades.

Although we have stated that there are three components of an attitude, most studies in education as well as in physical education do not attempt to measure all three, but rather deal with affect alone; therefore, most of the conclusions drawn are in reference to the affective dimension only.

The following generalizations can be made regarding attitudes. In general a student's expressed liking (affect) for school decreases over time (Dunn, 1968; Hogan, 1975). In the primary grades (late childhood) it is found that students generally have favorable attitudes toward school subjects, but as they progress toward and through adolescence they express less favorability toward subject-matter areas. In physical education we find the same type of trend, although there is not much research dealing with affect in the earlier years. Studies looking at the attitudes of children (Mancini et al., 1975; Zaichkowsky et al., 1975) have drawn conclusions similar to those in education—as age increases, a less positive feeling for physical activity is demonstrated. Studies done with persons in the adolescent stage do not indicate whether attitudes become less favorable with age either because the studies were not done cross-sectionally or longitudinally or because the results were derived from so many different measuring instruments that generalizations are very difficult to make. However, it should be noted that at all ages the subjects who were involved in the research studies held favorable attitudes toward physical activity.

The question then arises whether feeling positively about physical activity has any relationship to achievement in physical education or to actual participation in some type of physical activity. Several studies have indicated that a measure of success (final grade in physical education) was positively associated with favorable affect toward physical education (Carr, 1945; Vincent, 1967). Studies in other areas of education, however, have found equivocal results concerning the relationship between academic achievement and positive feelings toward school (Kahn and Weiss, 1973).

In reference to whether affect has any influence on behavior there are few studies that deal with this particular relationship. Kidd (1971), using a sample of college students, found a decrease in the amount of time spent in voluntary physical activity even though the affective measure of attitude indicated a positive feeling toward physical activity. Zaichkowsky (1973), also using college students, found some significant correlations between affect and actual participation in physical activity (self-report measure), but the correlations were low to moderate (.30-.50). Smoll et al. (1976) found a significant relationship between positive affect and participatory behavior in fourth-, fifth-, and sixth-grade boys and girls.

To say that there is a causal relationship between affect and actual behavior in physical activity is premature, primarily because the studies that have demonstrated a positive relationship have been correlational. Correlation does not necessarily mean causation. None-theless, the fact that some relationship does exist indicates that we need to investigate the matter more fully.

In summary, as age increases positive feelings toward school in general decrease. The same trend has been shown with physical activity. Most subjects, regardless of age, indicate positive feelings toward those things associated with physical education. There is some evidence (although quite meager) to indicate a positive relationship between actual behavior and positive affect toward physical activity.

SEX DIFFERENCES IN ATTITUDE DEVELOPMENT

Prior to the 1970s an apparent lack of interest on the part of most physical education researchers to study growth and development in children resulted in a scarcity of studies dealing with populations across time or looking at sex differences. This problem, however, is being alleviated by a growing number of people, involved in teaching children how to move, who feel that physical education should be based on sound psychological principles related to the manner in which children become adults.

Some researchers have investigated sex differences with a developmental emphasis. A study by Zaichkowsky et al. (1975) found that during late childhood girls respond more favorably than boys to physical education; a similar study by Mancini et al. (1975) did not find these differences in attitude with similar age and sex groupings.

Studies using Kenyon's ATPA scale found that men and women at the adolescent stage respond to physical activity on the various sub-domains of the scale differently at the high school and college level and also indicated differences among male and female champion athletes (Alderman, 1970; Kenyon, 1968c; Zaichkowsky, 1975). On certain scales men responded more favorably than women, and on others women responded more favorably, perhaps indicating that certain types of activities are more pleasing to one sex than to the other.

Studies in other areas of education have found that girls generally respond more favorably than boys toward school and teachers

(Jackson, 1968; Josephina, 1959; Leeds and Cooke, 1947). However, it is noted that even though girls are more positive about school than boys, a great percentage of all attitudes are positive.

IMPLICATIONS FOR PHYSICAL EDUCATION

We have repeatedly pointed out the inadequacy of meaningful research in the area of attitudinal development in physical education. This inadequacy is demonstrated in investigators' rarely applying a theoretical base to their research and in the difficulty in developing and acquiring valid and reliable data. This is most unfortunate. Although it has been stated that generally positive attitudes are held for physical activity, there has been little research that has pointed to a causal relationship between positive feelings and behavior. This is attributable, in part, to the complexity of the attitude construct and an inability to accurately assess attitudes with the research tools that are presently available (Kahn and Weiss, 1973). Triandis (1971) and Roedell et al. (1976) have suggested that we consider different variables in studying the attitudinal construct. Some of these are social norms, habits, and expected consequences of behavior.

One of the important goals of physical education, as we see it, is the promotion of life-long participation in meaningful physical activity. We consider it most important that the teachers of physical education investigate the area of attitudes, particularly attitude formation and change and its effect on actual behavior, in order to ensure that the types of processes utilized in the gymnasium enhance this lifetime-participation concept. Presently this goal has not been reached by physical educators. One needs to look only as far as one's own community to verify our failure. It is no problem to find instances of obesity, inadequate physical fitness, or people who are spectators rather than participants. How many of us have experienced the "hangover" of New Year's Day after watching four football games on the television set in one day? Let us use the information we have about human behavior and build upon it to initiate those actions which enhance habits of participation rather than "spectation" in some type of physical activity throughout a person's lifetime.

References

Alderman, R. B. A sociopsychological assessment of attitudes toward physical activity in champion athletes. *Research Quarterly*, 1970, *41*, 1-9.

Bandura, A., & Walters, R. H. *Social learning and personality development*. New York: Holt, Rinehart & Winston, 1963.

Brumbach, W. B. Effect of a special conditioning class upon students' attitudes toward physical education. *Research Quarterly*, 1968, *39*, 211-213.

Carr, M. G. The relationship between success in physical education and selected attitudes expressed by high school freshman girls. *Research Quarterly*, 1945, *16*, 177-191.

Cheffers, J. T., Mancini, V., & Zaichkowsky, L. D. The development of a non-verbal attitude instrument for children. *The Physical Educator*, 1975, *33* (March), 30-33.

Dunn, J. A. The approach-avoidance paradigm as a model for the analysis of school anxiety. *Journal of Educational Psychology*, 1968, *59*, 388-394.

Festinger, L. *A theory of cognitive dissonance*. Evanston, Ill.: Row, Peterson, 1957.

Hogan, T. P. *Survey of school attitudes: manual for administering and interpreting* (primary and intermediate levels). New York: Harcourt Brace Jovanovich, Inc., 1975.

Jackson, P. W. *Life in classrooms*. New York: Holt, Rinehart & Winston, 1968.

Josephina, C. S. J. A study of attitudes in the elementary grades. *Journal of Educational Sociology*, 1959, *33*, 56-60.

Kahn, S. B., & Weiss, J. The teaching of affective responses. In R. M. W. Travers (Ed.), *Second handbook of research on teaching*. Chicago: Rand McNally College Publishing Co., 1973.

Kelman, H. C. Compliance, identification, and internalization: three processes of attitude change. *Journal of Conflict Resolution*, 1958, *2*, 51-60.

Kenyon, G. S. A conceptual model for characterizing physical activity. *Research Quarterly*, 1968a, *39*, 96-105.

Kenyon, G. S. Six scales for assessing attitude toward physical activity. *Research Quarterly*, 1968b, *39*, 566-574.

Kenyon, G. S. *Values held for physical activity by selected secondary school students in Canada, Australia, England, and the United States*. Washington, D.C.: United States Government Printing Office, 1968c.

Kidd, T. R. An evaluation of a foundations of physical activity course. *Research Quarterly*, 1971, *42*, 35-41.

Leeds, C. H., & Cooke, W. W. The construction and differential value of a scale for determining teacher-pupil attitudes. *Journal of Experimental Education*, 1947, *16*, 149-159.

Likert, R. A technique for the measurement of attitudes. *Archives of Psychology*, 1932, *140*, 44-53.

Mager, R. F. *Developing attitude toward learning*. Belmont, Calif.: Fearon Pubs., 1968.

Mancini, V., Cheffers, J. T., & Zaichkowsky, L. D. A comparison of two decision-making models in an elementary human movement program based on attitudes and interaction patterns. *Research Quarterly*, 1975, *46*, 420-426.

Osgood, C. E., Suci, C. J., & Tannenbaum, P. H. *The measurement of meaning*. Urbana: University of Illinois Press, 1957.

Roedell, W. C., Slaby, R. G., & Robinson, H. B. *Social development in young children*. Washington, D.C.: National Institute of Education, 1976.

Rokeach, M. *Beliefs, attitudes, and values*. San Francisco: Jossey-Bass, Inc., Pubs., 1968.

Sherif, M., & Hovland, C. I. *Social judgment*. New Haven, Conn.: Yale University Press, 1961.

Simon, J. A., & Smoll, F. L. An instrument for assessing children's attitudes toward physical activity, *Research Quarterly*, 1974, *45*, 407-415.

Smoll, F. L., Schutz, R. W., & Keeney, J. K. Relationships among children's attitudes, involvement, and proficiency in physical activities. *Research Quarterly*, 1976, *47*, 797-803.

Thomas, E. J., & Znaniecki, F. *The Polish peasant in Europe and America*. Chicago: University of Chicago Press, 1918.

Triandis, H. C. *Attitude and attitude change*. New York: John Wiley & Sons, Inc., 1971.

Vincent, M. F. Attitudes of college women toward physical education and their relationship to success in physical education. *Research Quarterly*, 1967, *38*, 126-131.

Wear, C. L. The evaluation of attitude toward physical education as an activity course. *Research Quarterly*, 1951, *22*, 114-126.

Wear, C. L. Construction of equivalent forms of an attitude scale. *Research Quarterly*, 1955, *26*, 113-119.

Wessel, J. A., & Nelson, R. Relationship between strength and attitudes toward physical activity among college women. *Research Quarterly*, 1964, *35*, 562-569.

Yandell, K. M. *A study of expressed attitudes of freshmen women toward physical education during their enrollment in a required course in "Foundations of Physical Education" at the Texas Lutheran College*. Unpublished master's thesis, Texas Women's University, 1965.

Zaichkowsky, L. B. *A study of change in the affective, behavioral, and cognitive components of the attitudes of university students toward physical activity*. Unpublished doctoral dissertation, University of Toledo, 1973.

Zaichkowsky, L. B. Attitudinal differences in two types of physical education programs. *Research Quarterly*, 1975, *46*, 364-370.

Zaichkowsky, L. B., Zaichkowsky, L. D., & Martinek, T. J. Self-concept and attitudinal differences in elementary age school children after participation in a physical activity program. *Mouvement*, 1975, pp. 243-245.

Student projects

1. Select five people who like physical activity and five people who do not. Interview them to ascertain why they like or dislike physical activity. Discuss what the future physical educator can or should do to maintain the positive aspects of the comments and change the negative ones.
2. Take a random sample of people and ask them if they like physical activity, for instance, jogging. If they respond positively, ask them how often they participate in their liked activity.

a. Is there a relationship between the activities they like and how much they say they participate in them?
b. Observe as many of the interviewed people as possible to determine if they participate in the activity as they told you they did.
c. What types of comments can be made about what people say they do and what they actually do?

Chapter 12

ANXIETY AND AGGRESSION DEVELOPMENT

Stars and Stripes

Often we speak of emotional development in terms of behavioral changes resulting from conscious experiences of emotion. Many of these observable behaviors can deeply affect each and every member of society. Common but most important features of human emotional response are anxiety and aggression. Despite the varied theoretical assumptions concerned with anxiety and aggression, there is overwhelming agreement that the two have enormous impact on human life. The existence of trusting relationships among societies and countries relies heavily on the individual's ability to cope with the frustrations and inconsistencies of everyday life. Undue anxiety may prevent the child, youth, and adult from performing those essential human transactions needed for cooperative and prosocial behavior. Indeed, the focus of these social-psychological concepts is aimed at the improvement and perhaps the very continuation of human life. This chapter examines some of the theoretical aspects of anxiety and aggression and looks at developmental characteristics of girls and boys. We also discuss the implications for physical education in dealing with these two concepts.

Anxiety

Sometimes in our lives we all experience feelings of anxiety about something or somebody. These feelings can be felt as a result of our first date or the uncertainties facing us during our first year at college. In either case these anxious feelings can be experienced in various degrees of discomfort depending upon the circumstances involved, as well as the inherent differences in each human being. Whatever the causes there is no doubt that anxiety can be manifested in a number of different actions. Such actions are reflected in nervous forms of laughter at parties, the aggressiveness of the school bully, the child who is afraid to go to school, parents who continually abuse their child, or the child who chooses drugs and alcohol to provide some temporary cathartic relief.

But what exactly is anxiety? Certainly this concept is among the vaguest terms in psychological literature. The list of responses in which we claim anxiety plays a role is certainly imposing. Nearly every identifiable form of pathology—physical and social—is included. Almost every aspect of human endeavor is thought to be affected somehow by anxiety. Although there is debate as to whether anxiety is a measurable construct of physiological response or simply a set of drives or learned responses, there is common agreement that it is an unpleasant state of mind and body.

In order to minimize confusion about this multidimensional concept we have chosen to use Levitt's (1967) definition of anxiety. According to Levitt, anxiety is defined as a personal feeling of fear that results in heightened apprehensiveness and physiological responses. Many of the fears are caused by well-defined circumstances, such as hearing footsteps when walking home alone at night or thinking of being spanked for misbehavior. Frequently, however, there are ambiguous fears that the child is less able to explain. Such fears might be the vague feelings surrounding the quality of school work, or the undefined expectations of the teacher. Along with the great discomfort of anxiety, one tends to go to great lengths to reduce it, thereby reinforcing it. The way in which feelings of discomfort are mitigated varies from response to response. Many responses are undoubtedly learned because they bring some form of relief or self-gratification (like picking on the class weakling). Avoidance of stressful situations and also aggressive behavior are common responses to fearfulness and anxiety (McCandless and Evens, 1973).

The theoretical explanations of the origins of anxiety primarily come from two major sources—the psychoanalysts and the learning theorists (Levitt, 1967). The advancement of psychoanalytic theory was originally reflected in the early works of Sigmund Freud. During the early 1900s many of Freud's investigative efforts demonstrated that anxiety played a crucial role in personality development. He also found that it was a fundamental phenomenon characterized by three main types: *reality anxiety, neurotic anxiety,* and *moral anxiety.* He further contended that these anxieties were not necessarily formed from childhood or adult experiences but, rather, from lack of experiences, which failed to fulfill basic and psychological needs during the early stages of infancy.

Reality anxiety consists of those types of anxieties that the experimental psychologist has been able to isolate and study in the laboratory. Reality anxiety might be related to such things as physical abuse or financial deprivation. Neurotic anxiety is the fear that certain antisocial, sexual, or aggressive urges will become uncontrollable and cause individuals to do something that will eventually cause them to be punished. According to Freudian psychology, symptoms of neurotic anxiety are found in such anomalies as phobias, panic, and numerous forms of free-floating anxieties. It is with moral anxiety that we find individuals fearful of their own conscience. Similar to those feelings found in neurotic forms of anxiety are acute fears of being punished. However, even individuals who feel guilty about their actions still behave in ways that are contrary to their moral standards. Kohlberg (1966) maintains that an individual's moral standards are experienced in various identifiable stages of life and that fewer moral concerns occur at higher stages of development, in which the individual willingly conforms to avoid self-condemnation.

Later, many of the neo-Freudian theorists, like Karen Horney and Erich Fromm, changed the orientation of psychoanalytic theory from biological and instinctual to cultural and environmental. They believed that anxiety originates in the social process and that it therefore cannot arise before children develop an awareness of their status relative to the environment. Much of the child's security depends on the quality of parental relations, such as acceptance, discipline, and protection. According to Horney (1950), various strategies are developed by anxious, insecure children in an effort to cope with their anxieties. Children may become hostile or aggressive and develop a neurotic need for power over others. They may constantly reach out for affection, approval, or admiration from others; they may constantly strive for personal achievement or for perfection; or they may withdraw from any social contact and become totally dependent. In either case any one of these behavioral strategies may become permanent and take on the char-

acteristics of a need or drive. Such needs or drives are referred to as "neurotic" because they represent irrational solutions to the child's basic problem.

Experimental psychologists like Levitt (1967) and Miller (1948) regard anxiety as a learned drive. On the basis of laboratory investigation, learning theorists believe that anxiety results from a pairing of a conditioned stimulus with some unconditioned stimulus.

Loree (1965) illustrated the conditioning concept in an experiment with an 11-month-old girl, Christine. Christine at the beginning of the experiment liked most furry animals like rats, gerbils, guinea pigs, cats, and dogs. However, Christine did show fear responses to loud noises. The investigators conditioned the infant by first presenting a tame laboratory white rat and then striking an iron bar with a hammer to produce a loud sound. After a number of trials were given, the pairs of stimuli (rat and loud noise) resulted in Christine's showing clear signs of fear of the rat. Even when the rat was presented alone, Christine began to cry and run to avoid being near the animal. Fig. 12-1 illustrates this concept.

It was also demonstrated that the response to the rat could be generalized to other furry objects such as guinea pigs, Santa Claus's whiskers, or perhaps even to "Cookie Monster." This experiment helps to further explain how many of our irrational phobias such as fears of enclosed places, heights, or water may have their origins in unfortunate childhood experiences.

The authors emphasize the seriousness of classical conditioning in the child's early school and home experiences. Those individuals who have been exposed to intense fears in early life are more likely to manifest a higher tendency toward anxiety in similar circumstances in later life. In innumerable ways the home and school provide a unique setting for each child. Some of the fears a child learns are related to the failures of home and school to provide a secure environment that adequately meets the needs of the child.

Spielberger (1966) believes that anxiety is a transitory *state* or condition of the individual that varies in intensity and fluctuates over time.

Fig. 12-1. Classical conditioning. Child originally perceives rat as likeable, **A,** but dislikes loud noise, **B.** When rat is paired with loud noise, **C,** child learns to associate rat with loud noise. When rat is presented by itself, child responds as though expecting loud noise to follow, **D.**

He also contends that anxiety is a personality *trait* that can become permanent and thereby characterize the personality of the individual. For example consider the statement, "Jane Smith is an anxious child." This statement can be interpreted as meaning either that Jane is anxious at this very moment or that she is inherently an anxious child. It would appear, then, that studying anxiety requires that a distinction be made between anxiety as a transitory state that fluctuates over time and as a personality trait that remains relatively stable.

MEASUREMENT OF ANXIETY

Like most psychometric measures the assessment of anxiety has been historically elusive. The multitude of theoretical definitions, as previously mentioned, illustrates the complexity of this multidimensional construct and further underscores the need to critically examine the validity of a single measure.

From a researcher's viewpoint the development of assessment tools must be preceded by an abundance of theorizing about the variables to be measured. However, the professional practitioners who have to wrestle with everyday problems of human behavior may not be concerned with theory and may choose to use an instrument based on personal preference rather than on the theoretical foundation from which it was developed. Therefore, they rely heavily on those few researchers who study the problem of anxiety measurement and who are willing to spend years of research needed for psychometric development.

Unfortunately, the development of anxiety measures has been meager. A major problem has been the inability of researchers to translate theoretical concepts of anxiety into operational terms. Many think that, as one attempts to operationally define a theoretical concept by a written statement, the concept loses much of its related significance. Although this may be true initially, there is no reason in principle why much of this loss cannot be regained. Refinements based on systematic investigation and acute sensitivity to the differences of one's measure and the conceptual meaning under study are necessary (Sarason et al., 1960).

Problems in measuring anxiety in children

One of the many problems facing the teacher is trying to identify those children who may be experiencing (or at a later time would be experiencing) the disabling effects of anxiety. Unlike the clinician who works only with children who have some recognized "psychological disorder," the classroom teacher can only rely on behavioral observation to identify the hypertensive child from among a myriad of personalities. However, it is not always the anxious child who "acts out." Our experiences with teachers point out a possible source for this misconception. If children are good performers, highly motivated, and well-behaved in class, it is extremely difficult for the teacher to believe that these children are highly anxious about their ability or social relationships in the classroom. There are those children who exhibit "good behavior," yet may have a great number of fears known only to them. These may be the very same children who later on in life manifest antisocial behavior as a permanent pattern of their personality makeup.

From a developmental viewpoint research has further demonstrated that behavioral assessment by teachers becomes even more difficult because older children tend to become less overtly emotional during times of incidental stress than the younger children (Spielberger, 1966). It could be said that the young child is more reactive to a number of specific situations. Situations such as the first day at school, going to the dentist, contending with a baby sitter for the first time, or sharing toys with little brother or sister may result in overtures of kicking, crying, or pleading. However, as a child grows older such reactions are more infrequent because of the child's increased awareness of social standards emphasized and imposed by peers, teachers, and parents.

Another viable alternative for anxiety assessment is the use of psychological inventories. This type of objective measurement not only provides a more definitive psychological profile of the child, but it also allows the user to establish baseline data for future planning. According to Sarason et al. (1960), the use of valid measures enables teachers and researchers to negotiate three important practical problems:

1. To identify children who are unable to perform well in school
2. To identify children who are initally successful in the school environment but subsequently have problems indicative of personality disorders
3. To find ways in which the classroom can be utilized to assist children who are unable to perform in the school environment

There are also many problems found in the use of more objective forms of assessment. As previously mentioned the interpretation of a child's response to an anxiety inventory should take into account whether it represents a temporal measure (state) or a measure that is more permanent (trait) (Spielberger, 1966). Although there are only a few scales that attempt to measure these two conditions (Cattell and Scheier, 1961; Spielberger, 1966; Taylor, 1953), they nevertheless represent important concerns that should be considered in order to avoid misinterpretation of a child's score.

Another major problem in measuring anxiety is that children tend to fake "good." Many times the validity of a subject's report is doubtful because of the common use of denial as a defense against awareness of anxiety. Sarason et al. (1960) found that denial is especially evident in boys. Girls appear to be less inhibited about expressing their inner apprehensiveness. This hypothesis might imply that girls view anxiety admission as neither statistically nor psychologically deviant. However, the boy may feel that admitting to anxiety is not a sign of masculinity.

Test validity can also be affected by the testing situation itself. Many think that the administration of an anxiety inventory to young children especially only produces invalid results simply because of the unfamiliarity of a "testing'' situation. Although this may be true with the lower elementary–age child, it is quite apparent that because of today's ''test-oriented'' educational systems, most children are habitually conditioned to a variety of testing situations. This does not necessarily negate the child's sensitivity to a test situation, but the overall effect of test anxiety appears to be appreciably reduced.

We point out that these problems are fundamental concerns for both the researcher and the practitioner and represent ''stumbling blocks'' for future test development. Much of the research that has been done should serve to alert the teacher that anxiety in the classroom is, in fact, a teaching problem. At best the problems discussed in this chapter should sensitize the teacher and researcher to the nature of personality anomalies and possibly provide some clues to constructive ways of validly assessing the problems.

Anxiety measures for children

Projective measures. There are a number of instruments that are used almost exclusively by clinicians. Most of these are projective types, which essentially contain a combination of both structured and unstructured stimuli. The two best-known projective techniques are the Rorschach Ink Blot Test and the Children's Apperception Test (CAT). In the Rorschach, children are asked to respond to ten different inkblots. For example a child may be asked to describe what a particular inkblot reminds him of. The CAT consists of ten plates that depict cartoon drawings of animals. The child is asked to tell a story about what is being depicted in each picture. The Rorschach and CAT both have the advantage of being able to prevent children from faking ''good'' in their responses; however, overall they have limited value for educators because they can only be administered and interpreted by professionally trained personnel.

Inventory measures. By far the most popular and practical form of anxiety testing by the practitioner and researcher is the *inventory,* sometimes called a ''scale'' or ''questionnaire,'' though neither of these terms is precisely correct. An inventory consists of a series of statements or words that describe how children feel about themselves or their environment. The child responds by assigning a degree of agreement or disagreement to the items, each of which can be scored as either a positive or negative indication of the subject's personality makeup. The popularity of this type of test is based on its ability to be administered and scored quickly and easily by anyone. The valid use of the inventory, however, is questionable with lower age groups and poorer reading groups.

The Children's Manifest Anxiety Scale (Castaneda et al., 1956) represents one of the early inventories developed to assess anxiety in children. A few years after this appeared, Sarason et al. (1960) developed two anxiety scales for children: Test Anxiety Scale for Children (TASC) and General Anxiety Scale for Children (GASC). More recently, Spielberger (1973) developed a preliminary version of a children's anxiety scale that purports to measure both situational (state) anxiety and more pervasive personality-type (trait) anxiety. This scale is basically an extension of Spielberger's very popular adult STAI scale (1970), which is based on his widely accepted state-trait theory. Perhaps the most meaningful scale for those interested in anxiety as it relates to sports performance is that developed by Martens (1977). Martens' scale, which he terms the Sport Competition Anxiety Test (SCAT), has both an adult and children's form and purports to measure situation (sports)-specific anxiety. Martens' validating procedures for the SCAT are quite extensive and represent strong theoretical considerations in the scale's development.

Physiological measures. Many researchers and clinicians believe that the self-report method for determining anxiety may be somewhat doubtful because of the common use of denial as a defense against awareness of anxiety (Levitt, 1967). The use of instrumentation to measure physiological reactions has offered another means of measuring state anxiety. The four most frequent physiological measures are blood pressure, heart rate, respiration rate, and electrical skin resistance. These measures have been most popularized by law enforcement agencies through the use of the polygraph or "lie detector." Unfortunately, there are no conclusive data to show that its use produces consistent and valid results. A major source of this problem is that physiological measures are infrequently found to be related to each other or to other psychological indices.

Experiments in recent years have shown that when these physiological measures—that is, blood pressure, heart rate, respiration rate, and electrical skin resistance—are "fed back" to experimental subjects via a feedback machine, the subjects remarkably learn to control these physiological processes. This discovery has been termed biofeedback and is the most popular topic today in both psychology and medicine (see for example Green and Green, 1977). Although the principle of biofeedback has numerous clinical applications, one of the most popular has been in teaching clients to control anxiety. The principle of biofeedback is really quite simple. A biofeedback device picks up small electrophysiological signals from a particular biological system (for example, muscle system), amplifies them, and displays them back to the subject either by a sound or some visual display. The subject then uses this informa-

tion to learn to control the particular biological system (Fig. 12-2). Biofeedback thus not only serves as a possible objective measure of anxiety, but offers the exciting possibility of teaching children to control specific and general anxiety.

AGE DIFFERENCES IN ANXIETY
Infancy

Although we have found the definition of anxiety variable, one common conclusion among theorists is that its formation is organized around experiences to which individuals are exposed throughout their entire lives. Developmental views of anxiety are often formed from various sources of emotional responses that have been observed in longitudinal studies of children (McCandless and Evans, 1973). An earlier study by Bridges (1932) found that the initial emotional responses by newborns can be described simply as a state of generalized excitement. She further noted that newborns display this undifferentiated excitement with uncoordinated movements of kicks and crying, which show little relationship to any type of stimulation, internal or external. As the in-

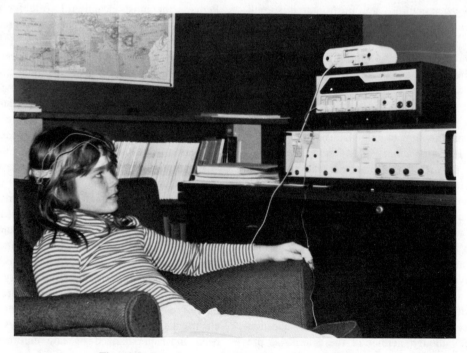

Fig. 12-2. Learning to control anxiety with biofeedback.

fant develops, reactions become more specific and more readily focused on certain kinds of stimuli. However, despite the presence of generalized excitement, it is also inescapably clear that other emotions appear in the older infant or child. Bridges further advanced this developmental principle by demonstrating that by about the age of 3 months the child begins to respond differently to situations that may be stressful or to those which are comforting. As the child continues to develop, the experiences of stress are further differentiated into anxiety and anger patterns. The validity of Bridges's theory rests on the fact that there is no distinctive pattern of physiological response according to the different emotions (Bridges, 1932).

As the infant reaches 7 to 9 months, one of the first reliable types of anxiety to emerge is *stranger anxiety* (Mussen et al., 1974). This usually appears when the infant cries or withdraws in the presence of a strange or unfamiliar person. By about 15 months this response usually has disappeared. The degree of stranger anxiety depends on the strength of the attachment to the mother.

Early childhood

The fear of abandonment or being unloved is probably the greatest source of anxiety by the age of 5 or 6 years. An early study by Spitz and Wolf (1946) showed that preschool children exhibit common reactions following separation from their mothers and subsequent placement in foster homes or institutions. The responses were found to occur in sequence, beginning with crying and strong protest and followed by progressive withdrawal from others. This pattern of detachment was in many instances a precursor to pathological personality and affectionless character.

Even the threat of separation of the child from the parent can cause worry in the child. One frequently overhears the desperate mother or father in the shopping center or street threatening the dawdling child that "if you don't come now, I'll leave without you!" Such a response sets up an immediate fear reaction that causes the child to fantasize about mommy's or daddy's leaving. This particular fear has powerful implications in today's society,

where separation and divorce are a common occurrence in the American family. Certainly the absence of the mother or father further crystallizes the fear of abandonment. In a more general sense these situations may reflect anxiety over possible physical harm, loss of affection from parents, or the inability to cope with an unstable home environment (Ginott, 1965).

Late childhood

On beginning the first years of school the child experiences concerns about peer acceptance or approval. Such concerns in children are reflected in their insistence on wearing similar clothes to those of their classmates. Although this consciousness appears to be especially heightened in later years of development, the initial concerns of peer acceptance prevail during the early school years.

Sarason and his colleagues (1960) found that early school anxiety is also related to behavior in academic progress, especially reading achievement. In a study of over 1,000 fifth-and sixth-grade children, four-fifths of the children admitted that they sometimes worried about a test, more than two-thirds worried about poor marks on their report card, and about two-fifths often worried about being hit by other children. Additionally, almost one-fifth of the children interviewed expressed concerns about being promoted to the next grade level (Jersild et al., 1941). An interesting extension of this study was that among the fears expressed, many were found to be unrealistic.

It also was demonstrated that although school anxiety apparently decreases during the middle years, children who show general increases in anxiety also exhibit slower academic progress. This is especially evident with children who have average or below-average intelligence. The majority of investigations done on academic achievement reveal significant relationships between anxiety and academic performance, usually to the disadvantage of the child who is the low achiever. It is therefore more tenable to assume that anxiety is a product rather than a cause of poor school performance. As the child approaches middle-school years, the fears begin to extend to sources outside the school

Fig. 12-3. Traumatic experiences during early years may lead to fears that persist through adulthood.

environment. It is during this time that many of the fears experienced are those which are carried over into adulthood. In an early study by Jersild and Holmes (1935) over 40% of the fears that children had were found to persist during their adult lives. Among the most commonly reported were fear of animals, of physical harm through such dangers as fire, illness, or drowning, of the supernatural, of the dark, and of being alone. The presence of these insecurities in adults presumably keeps alive these fears. Consequently, their persistence from childhood is an impressive indication of the importance of the emotional experiences during the middle-school years (Watson and Lindgren, 1973) (Fig. 12-3).

Adolescence

During the periods of early adolescence the youth experiences much concern about achieved identity. The individual struggles to identify with a variety of social roles. Erik Erickson calls this experience *role diffusion*. The adolescent vacillates between being dependent and independent, loyal and deviant, daring and timid. The feeling of anxiety comes about when the youth is unable to master these divergent trends and give up being a carbon copy of other people. Such diffusion may result in a serious personality disorder. However, if individuals come out of that period with some commitment

toward their future, role identity will most likely be achieved (Hilgard et al., 1971).

The individual's entrance into the pubescent period of adolescence offers new sources of frustration and anxiety. With an increase of hormonal output by the body the adolescent experiences new and sometimes awkward bodily changes. Accompanying the maturing bodily proportions are the secondary sex characteristics. The ability to negotiate newly acquired characteristics (such as pubic hair, enlarged breasts, deeper voice, and increased size of reproductive organs) depends on the adolescent's awareness of the normality of such changes.

But most important is the dramatic effect of these changes on the intensification of the sex drive. It is a well-established fact that a feeling of sexual desire is most often relieved through sexual activity (Dollard et al., 1967). In American society, however, one of the strongest taboos is on sexual activity. For example, the majority of the states in our nation prohibit marriage of the young couple under 18 without the permission of the parents, and yet there exists legislation, moral belief, and societal sanctions against sexual relationships between persons who are not married. It can only be expected, then, that adolescents become confused and anxious about their own sexuality. This pervasive dilemma for the adolescent is clearly demonstrated in the transition from child to adult. Even though the adolescent shows the physical characteristics of an adult, in other aspects of his world he is not treated as an adult:

His sphere of activity is circumscribed, his efforts to assert himself are suppressed, his possessions are definitely limited, his economic independence is not tolerated, his status as an adult is unrecognized, and many of the restrictions of his childhood remain in force. (Dollard et al., 1976, p. 95)

SEX DIFFERENCES IN ANXIETY

It is virtually impossible to imply differences between males and females without looking closely at a number of interacting variables. According to McCandless and Evans (1973), and Sarason et al. (1960) girls generally appear to have higher anxiety levels than boys because they are allowed freer expression of almost all forms of emotion and, accordingly, admit to more anxiety than do boys. This attitude is a result of a cultural concept, a reaction to expressed anxiety in boys and girls. The American culture indoctrinates both sexes with the belief that admission and expression of anxiety is a feminine characteristic not to be found in the male population.

With respect to age influence research has indicated that when school-related situations were plotted against age, there was little sex difference through various grades. However, boys did appear to reach the peak of their concern over school somewhat earlier than did girls. Additionally, there was a tendency for boys from high socioeconomic levels to be more anxious about school at an earlier age than boys from the lower class (Sarason et al., 1960). The normative data in Spielberger (1973) gathered on elementary school children in Florida show that females have slightly higher trait anxiety scores than males at the fourth- and fifth-grade levels.

Still, there are many studies that show little or no sex difference in anxiety. The classic study by Jersild and Holmes (1935) found that both girls and boys from infancy to 6 years of age showed remarkable similarities to situations that induced fear responses. A later study by these researchers also found that children 2 to 6 years of age showed no significant sex differences in fear of such things as snakes, large dogs, heights, dark unfamiliar places, strangers, and loud, unexpected noises. More recent studies have also found few sex differences in regard to stranger anxiety. Although girls may show at an earlier age some evidence of stranger anxiety, there is no consistent difference in stranger reactions after the first 2 years (Bronson, 1972).

The evidence concerning sex differences in relation to anxiety is inconclusive; however, one might also consider that in light of all that is known about the influence of anxiety on other variables, any significant difference that might exist may very well be negated by the interactions of outside factors. Therefore, we suggest that where the evaluation of a child is being implemented, the events and situations are far more relevant for explaining anxiety than is the sex of the child.

IMPLICATIONS FOR PHYSICAL EDUCATION

The need for physical activity is apparent through one's life span. The very nature of a child's psychological state is largely dependent on the amount of time and space provided for physical activity. In today's homes young children are often frustrated by a lack of space for motor activity. Cramped apartments and congested neighborhoods result in strict inhibitions on crawling, climbing, running, and jumping. In many instances these restrictions start early in the child's life. The infant may not be provided with the opportunity and stimulation to perform the basic motor functions so essential during the initial stages of development. As a result the child becomes frustrated and anxious.

Physical educators have become aware of the link between physical education and social and emotional well-being. Hellison (1973) contends that physical education should go beyond the education of the physical perspective and pay more attention to the possibilities of achieving psychological ends as well. Although it is commonly agreed upon by many that in learning or performing physical skills one should seek to avoid feelings of anxiety, the very act of skill performance may, in itself, produce a stressful situation. One of the major concerns educators have is that competitive sports for young children produces undue stress and, therefore, can be psychologically damaging. There are also those who argue that competition is good since it gets the child ready for the "dog-eat-dog" world that must be faced in the future. We believe that competition can be good and can be a growing experience for the child. However, the problem *is not* in competition itself, but in the way it is presented. As adults we have the option to choose what we would like to compete in. Unfortunately, children are often not given that choice but, rather, are thrown into competitive situations that they cannot physically or psychologically handle. Consequently, the avoidance of competitive circumstances is manifested in later life in order to circumvent feelings of fear and anxiety.

Lock et al. (1968) suggest three alternatives from which a participant can choose to cope with this situation: (1) leave the situation,

Fig. 12-4. Anxiety brought about by parental pressure to excel. Child is usually not capable of focusing attention on task at hand.

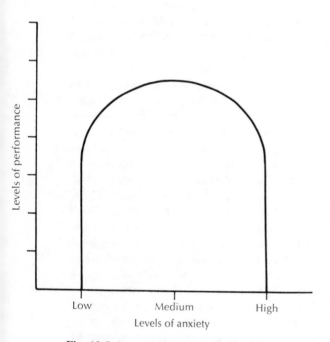

Fig. 12-5. Inverted U theory expresses hypothesized relationship between anxiety and motor performance.

(2) try to negotiate it, and (3) compensate for it. Leaving the situation obviously does little for the acquisition of the desired skills. However, attempts to overcome or compensate for the state anxiety might indirectly improve performance. For example, the little girl or boy who is concerned about getting a base hit in a Little League baseball game may do well to simply ignore the shouting mother and father in the stands. Attempts to overcome anxiety states then allow the child to focus more attention on the skill being performed.

Basically there are two major theories regarding the relation of anxiety to performance of motor skills: the *inverted U theory* and the *drive theory*. The inverted U theory is probably the most widely accepted one but has received less empirical support than the drive theory (Martens, 1977). Fig. 12-5 illustrates the U-theory principle as it applies to motor skill performance. As one can see, there is an improvement in performance as anxiety is increased from a low level to a point where anxiety is at an optimum. After this point is reached, there is a deterioration in performance with increased anxiety. Many theorists believe that this phenomenon is a result of various physiological and psychological forces.

Drive theory implies that increased drive multiplies habit responses. Habit responses mean dominant responses that may be correct

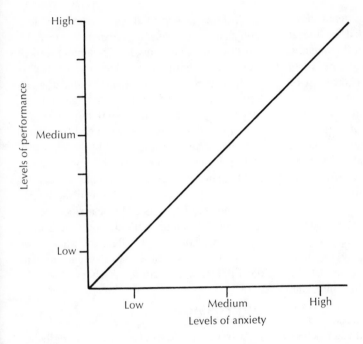

Fig. 12-6. Drive theory expresses hypothesized relationship between anxiety and motor performance.

or incorrect. It is hoped that as instructional and practice models are employed, these dominant responses are correct ones. The occurrence of correct dominant responses is evident as the skill is mastered. When the dominant response is correct, anxiety and performance have a positive linear relationship (Fig. 12-6).

Martens (1977) found that both theories are overly simplified. They do not adequately distinguish between inferior and superior motor performance and are not necessarily viable for predicting complex motor behavior. Although controversy reigns regarding the efficacy of drive theory and inverted U theory, one thing is certain: anxiety at a given level does impair motor performance. We have all witnessed children and adults who are skilled performers under normal practice conditions succumb to competitive anxiety. The response is usually decreased performance or failure, a condition that is very difficult for the young athlete to accept. Since it appears that children are entering high-level competition at younger and younger ages, it behooves teachers and coaches to learn more about the conditions that create anxiety and to teach young competitors techniques by which they can learn to control anxiety. Biofeedback, which we discussed earlier,

may serve as a useful device to teach anxiety control; however, there are other very useful techniques such as relaxation training, systematic desensitization, and meditation (Zaichkowsky, 1978).

Instructional considerations can also prove influential in the reduction of anxiety levels during physical activity. Controversy continues to exist over the implementation of *open* and *closed* instructional models in physical education. Some say that the open approach is of great benefit to both student and teacher—the student learns to make decisions, and teachers are less burdened with classroom "structure," so they have more time to spend with students individually. Others feel that the traditional teacher-directed method is the better of the two and insist that students need the rigid discipline and framework of the "closed" classroom. Unfortunately, many confuse the issue of open classroom teaching with those models of instruction that allow for chaotic, nondirected, and contraproductive learning. Cheffers and Evaul (1978) point out that there is a great difference between the classroom that is "student-centered" and the one that is "student-dominated." Because decision making is not always an easy task for the elementary-age child, attempts to implement a student-centered classroom too quickly have often ended in disaster for both the teacher and the student. Frequently, children become confused and anxious when confronted with a multitude of choices to be made within an instructional setting.

The majority of studies that have dealt with structured-unstructured characteristics have been equivocal in terms of their effects on the anxiety levels of elementary children. For example, Ford (1975) and Peterson (1976) found that there was a significant relationship between teacher autocracy and anxiety.

In an effort to further validate these findings Martinek (1978) investigated the effects of two decision-making models on anxiety in third- and fourth-grade children. In one model the teachers made all decisions concerning the operation of the class, while the other model encouraged students to share in the decision-making process. It was demonstrated that a teacher-directed model had more positive effects on lowering anxiety levels in fourth-grade males than a decision-sharing one. However, third-grade females benefited more from the decision-sharing approach. Anxiety scores for fourth-grade males in both treatment groups were significantly lower than the control (a group that received no physical education instruction at all). At least for that age and sex, this finding appears to support the contention that physical activity provides a cathartic outlet for anxiety and tension.

The search for generalization about anxiety and human behavior must take into account the complex interaction of variables in the human environment. Teachers and researchers seeking the "best" teaching method should be asking, "Best for whom?" and "Best for what?" We believe that these questions represent the main focal points of concern for teachers.

Aggression*

A frequent consequence of anxiety is aggression (Fig. 12-7). Although mankind has

*Parts of this discussion are taken from Martinek (1979).

Fig. 12-7. Frustration can many times lead to aggression.

been inherently aggressive throughout history, the psychological nature of aggressive actions has been rooted primarily in societal trends. Certainly one has only to look at the realism of violence on television and theater to see society's present-day attitude. It is no wonder one contemplates this impact on future generations.

The management of aggression, especially in children, is a major concern for teachers and parents. Historically, teachers have devoted their efforts to maintaining classroom order. Unfortunately, today's teachers are not merely preoccupied with order, but with physical abuse and psychological derogation as well. It is estimated that in the school year 1978-1979, 70,000 public school teachers were physically assaulted; this figure does not include assaults on other students. According to a study released by the Department of Health, Education, and Welfare, 11,000 junior high and senior high school teachers are robbed or physically attacked each year (Michaels, 1978). From a parent's point of view such behavior is most likely to be seen as either a danger to their child or a threat to themselves. In either case the very nature of home relationships greatly influences the level of success that the child has in learning to control overt expressions of anger.

In this section the definition of aggression is briefly examined, along with a theoretical overview of causes of aggressive behavior. Additionally, we look at age and sex factors as they relate to aggression. Finally, we discuss the role of physical education and the physical educator in the control of aggression.

What is aggression? Defining aggression is not easy. The term is used in many different ways, each unique to certain people and situations. For example, the "hillside strangler" who has made it a practice to rape and kill young women is obviously committing an aggressive act. The basketball player who pulls down 15 rebounds each game is called aggressive. The businessman who is not afraid of asking the boss for a raise is termed a "real go-getter." Aggressive behavior can also be epitomized by the child on the playground who refuses to let others play with her football. From a less obvious point of view aggressiveness can be seen in the child who constantly wets the bed in retaliation to home disharmony, or the

housewife who threatens suicide as a result of deep depression.

All these situations represent different forms of aggressive behavior, and yet because of the variability of their circumstances the definition of aggression becomes confused. In an effort to form a clearer picture of aggression we refer to Aronson's (1977) definition, which emphasized the intentions of the person committing the act. Thus he defines aggression as a behavior *intended* to cause harm or pain (Fig. 12-8). Consequently, by this definition, the basketball player is not considered to be performing an aggressive act if his actions are merely the result of his trying to be a top rebounder. However, if his intention is to give an opponent the elbow while executing each rebound, then the act is considered aggressive. To illustrate further, suppose a 4-year-old girl kicks her 12-year-old sister out of anger. Although the kick may be ineffectual and harmless, it nonetheless is considered an aggressive act. Similarly, if the same 4-year-old girl acciden-

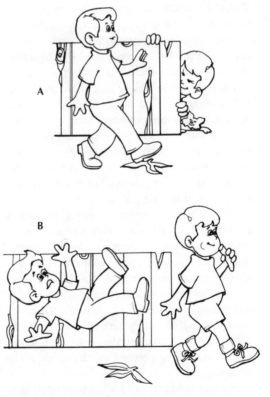

Fig. 12-8. Examples of aggressive behavior. **A,** Obviously intended. **B,** Not intentional.

tally slams the car door on her sister's hand and causes a number of fractured fingers, this action would not be considered aggressive, since the intention was not to do any harm.

The causes of aggression are many. The noted social psychologist Albert Bandura (1976) has postulated three main theories relating to the causes of aggressive behavior in children: the *instinct theory*, the *drive theory*, and the *social learning theory*.

The instinct theory relates aggressive acts to the innate nature of animals to protect themselves and those aspects of their lives that are important to them. Protection of the young, territory, and food supply are considered necessary for the existence and regeneration of the species. Because of rapid socialization of the human species, however, the evidence of inherent aggressiveness is only seen during the initial stages of infancy when social awareness is not as apparent. It will be remembered from our earlier discussion of Bridges's (1932) theory that the infant's emotional behavior is undifferentiated. This theory helps to explain the ill-defined nature of aggressiveness in early infancy; that is, emotional outbursts are generated by instinctive factors rather than social. Watson and Lindgren (1973) investigated this hypothesis and found that children's instinctive aggressive behaviors begin to be influenced by socialization at around 7 months. At that time children are exhibiting outbursts related to dressing, bathing, bedtime, and other routine child-care activities. Furthermore, aggression by infants was seen as obstacle-removing activities, often violent or strenuous, but not really oriented toward hurting another.

The drive theory postulates that aggression is caused by a set of conditions that result in frustration. Frustration is a term to describe an emotional state that results when an individual is unable to reach some desired goal. It can also involve physical discomfort and threats to one's self-esteem. According to Feshbach (1970), this frustration subsequently sets up an aggressive drive that is reduced by depriving or injuring others, expressing personal insults, or delaying rewards.

Another obvious way for teachers or parents to reduce aggressive drive is simply by avoiding prolonged frustrating circumstances in children. For example, teachers and parents should be aware of such conditions as trying to get children to sit quietly for long periods, insisting that they should "hurry up," not providing adequate rest periods, changing routines too frequently and unexpectedly, and inflicting physical punishment or discomfort (McCandless and Evans, 1973).

Certainly it is not necessary to eliminate *all* frustration. In fact, it is important for the youth to experience some degree of frustration in order to establish some level of tolerance. The important thing to remember here is the amount of guidance given by the adult. A key variable to effective guidance is the degree to which frustration is relevant to a given task. For example, many learning tasks in school may be too complex. The recognition of this complexity by the teacher is the key, along with providing various alternatives that the child may use in finding a solution to the problem. On the other hand, poor teaching strategies, poor planning, insensitivity to various ability levels, and distracting mannerisms are considered sources of frustration resulting from weak instructional concerns.

Social learning theory (Bandura, 1976) deals with those causes of aggression originating from three modeling influences: the family, the subculture, and symbolic modeling. As previously mentioned, much of the child's social behavior is initially developed through home experiences. Much of the information gathered about parental influence on violent behavior has been related to the three types of parental discipline discussed in Chapter 9: *power assertion*, which uses physical punishment or taking away material objects or privileges; *love withdrawal*, which includes nonphysical punishment such as ignoring or isolating the child; and *induction*, in which the parent reasons with the child about the required change of behavior (Hoffman, 1970). Induction along with parental affection appears to be most effective for those children who are old enough to reason. Parental power assertion appears to be highly correlated with aggressive behavior in the child. It is theorized that parents often act out their own aggression on their children and, by doing so, provide a model of aggression for their children that is later imitated. The deplorable incidence of "child abuse" is depressing evidence of this type of aggression modeling (McCandless and Evans, 1973). It is also interesting to note that children who are victimized by parental aggression generally direct their aggression toward others *outside* the family.

Although family influences play a major role in establishing the direction of social behavior, the subculture in which people live and have repeated contact provides a second important source of aggression. Environments in which aggressive models flourish are usually those settings in which aggressive behavior is condoned. Consequently, effective aggressors are considered prestigious models on whom members pattern their behavior. For example, Bandura (1976) believes the military establishment is effectively influential in transforming people who consider killing deplorable and immoral into combatants who feel little remorse and a sense of patriotism in destroying human life.

Much of our social learning is also derived from symbolic models. The majority of symbolic models are provided by the mass media, especially television. The child has little trouble observing a graphic presentation of brutal murders, stabbings, stranglings, sexual assaults, and muggings. Millions of dollars have been spent on studying violence on television and its impact on children. Bandura has shown that viewing violent action can lead to imitation and increased aggressiveness in a laboratory setting. Unfortunately, many of the studies have been done in a clinical setting and have looked only at short-term effects. In an extensive study recently reported by Muson (1978) it was found that long-term exposure increases the frequency with which children engage in serious kinds of violence, such as swearing, aggression in sport or play, threatening verbal assaults on others, and other misdemeanors. Some authorities believe that stories that present violence in a very realistic fashion tend to produce more actual violence. The recent story of a teenager who commiteed a murder and claimed TV addiction as a legal defense only highlights the problems we are facing when dealing with aggression.

Symbolic modeling can also be seen in the shaping and spread of new social styles and tactics of collective aggression. The turbulent sixties illustrate numerous examples of this. The campus protest movement at Berkeley served as a model for other similar forms of protest throughout the country. The rash occurrence of air hijacking illustrates another form of collective aggression that has spread in the United States and abroad.

Increased kidnapping of political dignitaries was a common form of political bargaining during the sixties and seventies. One has only to look back at the "Black September" massacre at the 1972 Olympics in Munich for a grim reminder of the unfortunate consequences of collective aggression. The present-day increase in student attacks on faculty members in our schools represents a more contemporary example of this type of aggression.

AGE AND SEX DIFFERENCES IN AGGRESSION

When dealing with aggression, it is very difficult to discuss age differences without discussing sex differences, because males are viewed as more aggressive than females. Therefore, for this chapter, we have chosen to combine these two aspects in one discussion.

Developmental changes in aggression are important concerns for the teacher trying to cope with unpredictable behavior of students. Preschool children appear to be studied more frequently than those in any other age group. Generally, physical aggression among preschool children gradually decreases from 2 to 5 years of age, while verbal aggression appears to increase (Feshbach, 1970; Walters et al., 1957). It could be said that because preschoolers have fewer contacts with others than do older children, they have fewer opportunities for aggressiveness.

During the primary grades most children become less inhibited in expressing both physical and verbal aggressive behaviors. Males, more than females, appear to sustain a stronger aggressive behavior pattern during this time. However, for many children these forms of aggression appear to operate more under competitive circumstances such as sports, free play, and academic pursuits.

The different kinds of social influences experienced by girls and boys in their primary years have a great impact on the types of aggressive behavior displayed during their entrance into adolescence. Girls generally enter adolescence with a repertoire of socially accepted behaviors, whereas boys show substantially higher levels of antisocial aggression. This statement is supported by the fact that juvenile delinquency occurs at an earlier age with boys than girls (Hurlock, 1966).

One can see that boys in general appear to be more physically aggressive through their development. These sex differences can largely be explained by the differences in cultural conditioning, motivation, opportunity, and the degree to which society tolerates aggressive behavior among males and females. Under most circumstances aggression in girls is not acceptable according to their sex-role training. This can especially be seen in competitive sports. As we stated in Chapter 8, despite the increase in women's participation in the sports world, it is still considered inappropriate for a woman to aggressively participate or excel in the sports arena where males have long predominated.

IMPLICATIONS FOR PHYSICAL EDUCATION

For years physical educators have claimed physical activity as a catharsis for aggression. Unfortunately, there is little support for this claim. Cheffers and Evaul (1978) clarify this by contending that frustration need not always lead to aggressive acts. Frequently, when frustration leads to anxiety instead of aggression, physical activity appears to provide some relief. Some authors think that in a sports situation, whether participation leads to aggression depends on the conditions of the activity. Some of these conditions as listed by Hellison (1973, pp. 25-26) follow:

1. The amount of frustration experienced by the participant in expressing aggression in reponse to a stronger opponent or rules of conduct which encourage sportsmanship
2. Whether the participant wins or loses
3. The degree of emphasis on winning
4. Whether hostility is carried over after the activity has ended

One common characteristic that appears consistently in studies on aggression reduction is

Fig. 12-9. Physical activity can foster control of aggression or can serve as a vehicle for learning and displaying aggressive behavior.

the structure of competition in sports. Several studies have looked at this relationship and have found mixed results. For example, Clausen (1968) demonstrated that the game of handball (considered highly competitive) was very effective in the reduction of anxiety. However, a later investigation by Ryan (1970) demonstrated that frustration and "winning or losing" in a variety of competitive activities were interacting factors that only supported the complexity of this issue. He found that the activity, the degree of frustration, and the outcome did not effectively reduce aggressive behavior (Fig. 12-9).

Another confounding variable to the catharsis assumption is a phenomenon called *perversion*. This applies to those individuals who intentionally commit aggressive acts to draw attention to themselves. The professional sports world typifies this type of individual in numerous ways. Throwing two basketball players out of a game for exchanging punches with one another is a meager reprimand when compared to the attention received by the players from the press and the crowd. The teacher may be well aware of this phenomenon when dealing with elementary-age children who consistently get into trouble through various acts of aggression. The

labeling by the teacher of the "naughty boy" or "naughty girl" of the class may only provide richer consequences for their actions.

We believe that a teacher's prime concern is not merely immediate control of children's behavior, but, rather, helping them establish their own control over their aggressiveness. One way of providing this opportunity is by being aware of the various instructional stragegies one chooses. It was demonstrated earlier in this chapter that the degree of decision making offered to the student can have a significant effect on anxiety reduction. It is also our contention that a similar relationship exists with teaching strategies and aggressive behaviors. This relationship is illustrated in Fig. 12-10.

The classic study by Lewin et al. (1939) provides an illustration of this hypothesis. The authors worked with three groups of 10-year-old boys under three conditions: authoritarian, democratic, and laissez-faire. In the authoritarian situation the leader was totally in charge of all decisions concerning the operation of the group. In the laissez-faire situation the boys were given total freedom in deciding how the group was to operate. Other than supplying materials, the leader in no way interfered with any of the group's decisions. The democratic

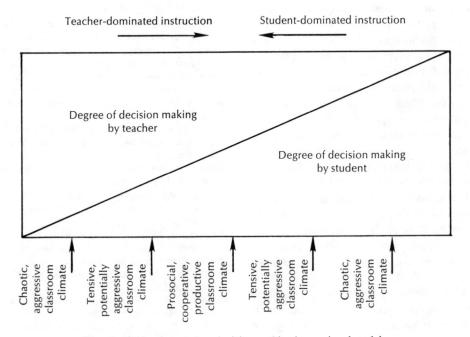

Fig. 12-10. Teacher-student decision-making instructional model.

group operated by having all decisions discussed among the leader and group members. The leader provided a framework from which the group could work and provided additional guidance and encouragement when needed.

From the results of this study it was found that the authoritarian group appeared to foster aggressiveness. It is interesting to note that within this group was a polarization of high- and low-aggressive groups, with the more aggressive children intimidating the low-aggressive children. Under laissez-faire conditions aggressive behavior appeared to be equally high. The democratic conditions appeared to have the greatest effect on reducing aggressive actions. These findings suggest that classes with some teacher guidance in self-direction and decision making have the best effect on controlling aggressive behavior in children.

The results of this type of study have far-reaching implications in physical education. The sudden shift to total individual freedom can have disastrous consequences in the gymnasium. In many instances frustration can result from having to make too many decisions with little or no guidance from the teacher. Especially where safety is a concern, or certainty of one's own physical capabilities is unclear, this frustration only nutures potential aggression.

The extent to which teachers can control aggression in the gymnasium largely depends on their ability to shift their teaching strategies according to the psychological needs of the students. It is disheartening to see that the issues of discipline have assumed negative proportions in our schools. Although there is no denial that physical education teachers face many problems with their class, it is, nevertheless, our contention that disciplinary problems are reduced when children are *interested* and *involved*. Highly motivated children tend to respond constructively to various techniques directed toward the control of disruption. On the other hand, poorly motivated children tend to be disruptive with disciplinary incidents. The child who likes his teacher tends to judge the actions of the teacher as "fair," while the child who dislikes the teacher judges the same actions as unwarranted and unfair. Once children have developed a positive or negative

relationship with their teacher, they tend to perceive and judge the behavior of the teacher in ways consistent with their attitudes.

References

Aronson, E. *The social animal.* San Francisco: W. H. Freeman & Co., Pubs., 1977.

Bandura, A. Social learning analysis of aggression. In E. Ribes-Inesta and A. Bandura (Eds.), *Analysis of delinquency and aggression.* Hillsdale, N. J.: L. Erlbaum Associates, 1976.

Bridges, K. M. A genetic theory of the emotions. *Journal of Genetic Psychology,* 1932, *37,* 514-527.

Bronson, G. W. Infant's reactions to unfamiliar persons and novel objects. *Monographs of the Society for Research in Child Development,* 1972, vol. 37.

Castaneda, A., McCandless, B. R., & Palermo, D. S. The children's form of the manifest anxiety scale. *Child Development,* 1956, *27,* 317-326.

Cattell, R. B., & Scheier, I. H. *The meaning and measurement of neuroticism and anxiety.* New York: The Ronald Press, 1961.

Cheffers, J. T. F., & Evaul, T. *Introduction to physical education: concepts of human movement.* Englewood Cliffs, N. J.: Prentice-Hall, Inc., 1978.

Clausen, J. A. Perspectives on childhood socialization. In J. Clausen (Ed.), *Socialization and society.* Boston: Little, Brown & Co., 1968.

Dollard, J., Miller, N. E., Doob, L. W., Mowrer, O. H., & Sears, R. *Frustration and aggression.* New Haven, Conn.: Yale University Press, 1967.

Feshbach, S. Aggression. In P. Mussen (Ed.), *Carmichael's manual of child psychology.* New York: John Wiley & Sons, Inc., 1970.

Ford, C. A. *An investigation of the relationship between dogmatism and anxiety as a prediction of performance on tasks of creativity.* Unpublished doctoral dissertation, University of Maryland, 1975.

Ginott, H. *Between parent and child.* New York: Avon Books, 1965.

Green, E., & Green, A. *Beyond biofeedback.* San Francisco: Delacort Press/S. Lawrence Co., 1977.

Haugen, G. B., Dixon, H. H., & Dickel, H. A. *The therapy for anxiety tension reduction.* New York: Macmillan, Inc., 1963.

Hellison, D. *Humanistic physical education.* Englewood Cliffs, N. J.: Prentice-Hall, Inc., 1973.

Hilgard, E. R., Atkinson, R. C., & Atkinson, R. L. *Introduction to psychology.* New York: Harcourt Brace Jovanovich, 1971.

Hoffman, M. Moral development. In P. Mussen (Ed.), *Carmichael's manual of child psychology.* New York: John Wiley & Sons, Inc., 1970.

Horney, K. *Neurosis and human growth.* New York: W. W. Norton Co., Inc., 1950.

Hurlock, E. *Child development.* (4th ed.). New York: McGraw-Hill Book Co., 1966.

Jersild, A. T., Golman, B., & Loftus, J. J. A comparative

study of the worries of children in two school situations. *Journal of Experimental Education*, 1941, *9*, 323-326.

Jersild, A. T., and Holmes, F. B. Children's fears. *Child Development*, 1935, *20*, 250-252.

Kohlberg, L. Moral education in the schools: a developmental view. *The School Review*, 1966, *74*, 1-30.

Levitt, E. E. *The psychology of anxiety*. Indianapolis: The Bobbs-Merrill Co., Inc., 1967.

Lewin, K., Lippitt, R., & White, R. Patterns of aggressive behavior in experimentally created "social climates." *The Journal of Social Psychology*, 1939, *10*, 271-299.

Lock, E. A., Cartledge, N., & Koeppel, J. Motivational effects of knowledge of results: a goal-setting phenomenon? *Psychological Bulletin*, 1968, *70*, 474-485.

Loree, M. R. *The psychology of education*. New York: The Ronald Press, 1965.

McCandless, B. R., & Evans, E. D. *Children and youth: psycho-social development*. Hinsdale, Ill.: Dryden Press, 1973.

Martens, R. *Sport competition anxiety test*. Champaign, Ill.: Human Kinetic Publishers, 1977.

Martinek, T. J. *Decision-making in elementary age children: effects on motor skills, body concept and anxiety* (Research Project). University of North Carolina at Greensboro Research Council, Grant no. 012, 1978.

Martinek, T. J. Aggressive behavior in children: new concerns for the physical educator. *Motor Skills: Theory into Practice*, 1979, *3*, 99-101.

Michaels, M. Our nation's teachers are taking a beating. *Parade Magazine*, 1978, February 26, pp. 4-5.

Miller, N. E. Studies of fear as an acquired drive: fear as motivation and fear reduction as reinforcement in the learning of new responses. *Journal of Experimental Psychology*, 1948, *38*, 89-101.

Muson, H. Teenage violence and the telly. *Psychology Today*, 1978, *11*, 50-54.

Mussen, P., Conger, J., & Kagan, J. *Child development and personality* (4th ed.). New York: Harper & Row, Publishers, 1974.

Peterson, P. L. *Interactive effects of student anxiety, achievement, and attitude*. Unpublished doctoral dissertation, Stanford University, 1976.

Ryan, E. D. The cathartic effect of vigorous motor activity on aggressive behavior. *Research Quarterly*, 1970, *51*, 542-551.

Sarason, S. B., Davidson, K. S., Lighthall, F. F., Waite, R. R., & Ruebush, B. K. *Anxiety in elementary children*, New York: John Wiley & Sons, Inc., 1960.

Spielberger, C. D. *Anxiety and behavior*. New York: Academic Press, Inc., 1966.

Spielberger, C. D. *Preliminary manual for the state-trait anxiety inventory for children*. Palo Alto, Calif.: Consulting Psychologists Press, 1973.

Spielberger, C. D., Gorsuch, R. L., & Lushene, R. E. *Manual for the state-trait anxiety inventory*. Palo Alto, Calif.: Consulting Psychologists Press, 1970.

Spitz, R. A., & Wolf, K. Anaclitic, *Psychoanalytic Studies of the Child*, 1946, *2*, 313-342.

Taylor, J. A. A personality scale of manifest anxiety. *Journal of Abnormal Psychology*, 1953, *48*, 285-290.

Walters, J., Pearce, D., & Dahms, L. Affectional and aggressive behavior of preschool children. *Child Development*, 1957, *28*, 15-26.

Watson, R. I., & Lindgren, H. C. *Psychology of the child*. New York: John Wiley & Sons, Inc., 1973.

Zaichkowsky, L. D. *Biofeedback and anxiety management in sport*. Paper presented at the Canadian Society for Psychomotor Learning and Sport Psychology, Toronto, November 1978.

Student projects

1. In which of the two teaching models—command and decision sharing—would you expect the high-anxiety child to do relatively poorly? What difficulty might a physical education teacher encounter with this individual in teaching at the elementary and junior high school levels? In which type(s) of physical activity might it be desirable for high-anxiety children to participate at the two grade levels?

2. Observe a physical activity class for a period of three sessions. Describe ways in which the teacher constructively aided the high-anxiety child who was experiencing difficulty in a given task. Also describe how the child reacted to the teacher's intervention.

3. It has been suggested that man is instinctively aggressive. Much of this aggression is exemplified in terms of territorial protection. Explore the existence of instinctive aggression by describing your experiences in the following situations:

   a. Ask a boy and girl what they would do if they were playing with a ball and someone came and took the ball away. Are there any sex differences in terms of their reactions?

   b. Walk through a dormitory until you see an open room of someone you do not know and then sit down on the bed and start reading a book. What are the other persons' reactions?

   c. What would the reactions of a fellow teacher be if you were to interrupt a class and start to help teach part of the class?

   d. Walk up to a person you do not know and place a tissue in his or her pocket. What are the reactions of that person?

GLOSSARY

accommodation Piagetian term that refers to a second form of adaptation; a child's understanding is changed by experiences (see *assimilation*).

actual self Self-perceptions of an individual that are true and realistic concepts of the self (see *ideal self*).

adaptation Piagetian term that refers to the continuing change that occurs in an individual as a result of environmental interaction.

aerobic power Amount of optimal work a person can possibly do for a period of 15 to 30 minutes resulting in the maximum delivery of oxygen to the working muscles; aerobic capacity of the individual depends on the heart and lungs to resupply oxygen to the blood and muscles during exercise.

affect Feeling or emotional component of a person; one of the components of an attitude.

aggression Any action that is directed to an object or person for the purposes of causing damage or harm.

anaerobic power Amount of exercise possible in an all-out effort for a period of approximately 45 seconds; this is dependent on the natural oxygen supply that is present in the blood prior to exercise.

androgyny Recently popular psychological term, which when discussing sex roles refers neither to femaleness nor maleness.

anxiety Personal feeling of fear that is accompanied by feelings of apprehension or physiological responses; many times the sources of anxiety are unidentifiable.

assimilation Piagetian term that refers to one form of adaptation; the child interprets experiences according to present level of understanding (see *accommodation*).

associative play Play that occurs when children start using social interaction as a part of their activity.

attention Focusing of perception that leads to heightened awareness of particular stimuli.

attitude Learned predisposition to respond in a favorable or unfavorable manner with regard to a specific object; attitudes are not observed directly but are inferred from the actions of the individual.

autonomous morality Piagetian term that indicates a stage in which a person's moral behavior is governed by experiences in society; right and wrong may now contain shades of gray depending on the intent of the action.

behavioral predisposition Tendency for a person to make an overt response; one of the components of an attitude.

cardiovascular function Specialized form of fitness that involves the function of the heart, lung, blood, and vessels. This is developed by continuous types of activities such as running, jogging, rope skipping, and so forth.

cephalocaudal development General phenomenon of development that describes a movement in rate of development from the head to the tail or peripheral region of the body.

chromosome One of the rod-shaped bodies in the nucleus of a dividing cell that carries the hereditary factors (genes); each human cell contains 46 chromosomes arranged in 23 pairs, one member of each pair deriving from the mother, one from the father.

client-centered therapy Approach to help an individual move through stages of self-evaluation and motivation in order to gain a greater self-awareness; client is questioned in order to synthesize possible solutions to various emotional problems.

conditioned response Learned response to a conditioned stimulus (see *conditioned stimulus*).

conditioned stimulus Stimulus that does not initially cause a response or causes a general response, but, as a result of being paired with an unconditioned stimulus and its response, causes the same response (see *unconditioned stimulus*).

coefficient of correlation Numerical index (between 0 and ± 1.00) used to indicate the degree of correspondence between two sets of paired measurements; positive correlation means that as the scores of one measure increase, so do the scores on the other measure; negative correlation means that as one measure increases, the other decreases.

cognition Knowledge or intellectual component of an individual; one of the components of an attitude.

cognitive flexibility Aspect of self-concept that pertains to the individual's ability to adjust to sudden changes in life and, therefore, maintain inner consistency (see *self concept*).

compliance In Kelman's hierarchy of attitude acquisition, a term that refers to a person's following instructions because a person who holds power is present.

concrete operations period Third period in Piaget's developmental theory (7 to 11 years); child begins to use elementary logic and to reason about size, volume, numbers, and weight.

control group In an experimental design, the group of subjects not given a specific treatment (treatment being tested for effect).

cooperative play Goal-directed play among children; one or two people may serve as the leaders in the group.

critical periods Theoretically, a point in the development of a specific behavior at which experience or training has an optimal effect.

cross-sectional studies Research that differs methodologically from longitudinal studies, rather than studying the same children for a period of years, children representing specific age groups are sampled and studied.

deoxyribonucleic acid (DNA) Large molecules found in the cell nucleus that are primarily responsible for genetic inheritance.

directionality Ability to identify and relate objects or people other than self to each other in terms of left and right, for example, ''Is the pencil to the right or left of the penny?''

distance curve of growth Recording and plotting of growth from one year to the next; each point is dependent on previous growth (see *velocity of growth*).

dizygotic twins Fraternal twins that develop from separate eggs; they are no more alike genetically than ordinary siblings, and can be of the same or different sex.

drive theory Implies that the level of performance increases as the degree of anxiety in the performer increases.

dynamic balance Related to the individual's ability to move in a linear direction along a beam while balanced.

dynamic flexibility Ability to perform spontaneous stretching muscular contractions.

dynamic strength Muscle's ability to exert repeated contractions, dynamic strength is often synonymous with the term muscular endurance (see *muscular endurance*).

ectomorph Third of three components in Sheldon's

categories of physique, prominence of tallness and thinness.

ego Freudian term that refers to the second stage of personality development; related to the individual's awareness of what the environment provides and excludes; also diminishing the forces of the id (see *id*).

egocentrism Characteristic of preschool children (Piaget) that refers to the fact that they can only relate to experiences in terms of themselves and cannot place themselves in someone else's position and make accurate observations.

embryo Technically describes an unborn child from conception to age 8 weeks.

endomorph First of three components in Sheldon's categories of physique; prominence of stockiness and obesity.

environmental effects Effects, other than heredity, on an individuals growth and development; include factors such as physical environment (enriched or deprived), nutrition, and learning.

epiphysis End of a long bone, separate from the shaft of the bone in young children, but at the termination of growth fused with it.

ex post facto studies Done after the fact; researcher has no control over many variables; although relationships may be demonstrated, caution must be exercised in making causal inferences, for example, using data from old school records.

experimental group In an experimental design the group of subjects that is given a treatment for the purpose of testing treatment effects.

explosive strength Type of strength used when one is performing an activity that requires spontaneous muscular energy.

extent flexibility Ability to flex the body in various directions.

factor analysis Statistical technique used for both exploratory and confirmatory analysis; commonly used for purposes of data reduction, but its most frequent use is in test construction; method enables the investigator to compute the minimum number of factors required to account for the intercorrelations between the scores on the test items—items that measure the same ''factors'' are grouped together.

fetal alcoholism syndrome Physical, mental, and emotional characteristics demonstrated by infants born to alcoholic women.

fetus Technically describes an unborn child from 8 weeks after conception to birth.

fine motor skills Skills that are distinguished by involving small muscles and limited activities of the body extremities, for example, typing, threading a needle.

flexibility Range of motion found for each joint of the body (see *extent flexibility* and *dynamic flexibility*).

formal operations period Final period in Piaget's developmental theory (11 years and beyond); child capable of the highest level of cognitive functioning—hypothetico-deductive logic.

gene Basic unit that determines hereditary characteristics; part of the chromosome.

genotype Group of individuals sharing a specified genetic makeup.

gross motor skills Skills incorporating large, usually several, muscle groups of the body; for example, running, throwing.

growth Observable step-by-step change in quantity, such as body size; changes may be due to maturation but also environmental effects.

heredity Set of qualities that are fixed at birth and hence predetermine certain individual characteristics.

heteronomous morality Piagetian term that indicates a stage in which a person's moral behavior is governed by rules that come from a "higher authority," generally parents.

id Freudian stage of personality development that is defined as all the urges that are instinctual and are antecedents to human motives.

ideal self Those self-perceptions that are considered unrealistic and inaccurate concepts of the individual's actual self (see *actual self*).

identification In Kelman's hierarchy of attitude acquisition, a person's demonstrating a certain behavior because a person or group she belongs to, or aspires to belong to, behaves in that manner.

imprinting Species-specific type of learning that occurs within a limited "critical" period of early development and appears resistant to forgetting, for example, young duckling's following an object other than its mother within 11 to 18 hours after birth and attaching to that object thereafter.

induction Discipline technique that involves the use of reason in trying to control behavior, an explanation of the consequences of the action is an essential component of this type of discipline.

instinct theory Relates aggressive acts to the innate nature of animals and man to protect themselves and those aspects of their lives that are important to them.

internalization In Kelman's hierarchy of attitude acquisition, a person's demonstrating a certain

behavior because it is her own wish or desire to respond in that manner.

inverted U theory Implies that there is an improvement in performance as anxiety is increased from a low level up to a point where anxiety is at an optimum level; after this point is reached, there is a deterioration in performance with increased anxiety.

lateral awareness Correct labeling of the two sides of the body, that is, left and right.

lateral dominance Development of a preference for using the left or right hand, foot, or eye.

laterality Developing the ability to distinguish between the two sides of the body or simply being aware that the body has two sides; one of the earliest body-awareness characteristics.

Likert-type scale Scale commonly used in measuring attitudes that asks a person to respond to a particular statement, generally using a five-point response scale; the response can indicate varying degrees of agreement or disagreement with the statement.

longitudinal research Research that is conducted on the same child or group of children for an extended period of time.

long-term memory (LTM) Relatively permanent component of the memory system (see *short-term memory*).

love withdrawal Punitive discipline technique that involves the use of nonphysical forms of punishment to eliminate undesirable behavior.

maturation Changes in body size, shape, and skill within an individual where timing and patterning are independent of exercise or experience.

menarche First menstrual period; indication of sexual maturation of the female.

mesomorph Second of three components in Sheldon's categories of physique; prominence of bone and muscle as exemplified by a typical athlete.

mitosis Process by which a cell splits into two new cells.

monozygotic twins Identical twins, having arisen from the same fertilized egg; always the same sex.

morpheme Smallest meaningful unit of language having a differential function.

morphology Study of how morphemes are put together to form words.

moral anxiety Anxiety created from fear of being punished for committing acts that are contradictory to moral standards.

muscular endurance Component of fitness that refers to the ability of a muscle or group of muscles to sustain repetitive contractions over a long period of time against a moderate resistance; generally related to strength.

myelin White fatty tissue that forms a sheath around neurons, thereby allowing them to transmit nerve impulses more effectively.

neurotic anxiety Anxiety created from fear of committing antisocial, sexual, or aggressive acts that result in punishment.

norm Expected or stereotypical behaviors that should be displayed by all people occupying the same status.

parallel play Play that occurs in the presence of other children but without any social interaction.

patterning Technique for treating children with inadequate neurological organization; method stems from Doman and Delacato's theory; calls for passive and active responses relating to crawling, creeping, and walking.

percentile Point in a distribution below which falls the percent of the cases indicated by the given percentile; thus, the twenty-fifth percentile (for example) refers to the point below which 25% of the scores fall.

perception Organization and interpretation of sensory information; influenced by prior experience.

phoneme Shortest arbitrary unit of sound in a given language that can be recognized as being distinct from other sounds in the language.

phonology Science of the phonemes of a language and the rules governing their combination.

power assertion Punitive discipline technique that involves the use of physical means to control a person's behavior.

prenatal Period of development that extends from conception to birth.

preoperational period Second period in Piaget's developmental theory (2 to 7 years); appearance of the ability to utilize symbols.

primary model Group of people consisting of the family and significant others outside the family that conveys the expectations and value systems of the culture and social setting.

proximodistal development General phenomenon that describes development from the midline of the body to the extremities.

reality anxiety Anxiety created as the result of fears of physical abuse or financial deprivation.

reflex Relatively simple response largely under the control of a specific stimulus rather than voluntary control; initial infant responses are largely reflex-ive; adult reflexes include knee jerk, sneezing, perspiring.

reinforcement contingencies Use of various types of rewards for increasing the chances of eliciting a desired response from an organism.

role Behavior a particular individual utilizes in carrying out the functions associated with a status.

role diffusion Inability of an individual to identify or establish a social role; usually experienced during early adolescence and subsequently results in feelings of anxiety.

schema Hypothetical construct that can be interpreted as a cognitive analogue of a bodily structure; small units of understanding.

secular trend Phenomenon whereby children at all ages are growing larger than their predecessors from earlier decades.

self-actualization Term coined by Abraham Maslow that refers to the process of becoming oneself or achieving an awareness of one's identity.

self-concept Multidimensional construct representing the total range of one's perceptions and evaluations of oneself.

self-esteem Individual's need to be held in high esteem by peers and others as well as maintain a high opinion of one's own behavior.

semantic differential Measurement technique in which a word or concept is presented and a person is asked to respond to it in terms of bipolar adjectives (for example, good-bad); generally a seven-point response scale is used.

semantics (1) Study of meaning in language that includes the relations between language, thought, and behavior; (2) study of the development of the meanings of words; goal is to account for the knowledge a native speaker has that enables him to judge some sentences as meaningful and some as ambiguous.

sensation Reception of stimuli by specialized receptors, for example, the reception of sound by the ears (see *perception*).

sensorimotor period First period in Piaget's developmental theory; infants' learning is limited to the simplest aspects of motor behavior and sensory perception.

seriation Ability to order objects or events along a single dimension, for example, largest to smallest.

short-term memory (STM) Theoretical view that certain components of the memory system have limited capacity and maintain information for only a brief period of time.

skeletal age or bone age Measure of age that takes into consideration how far given bones have progressed toward maturity, not in size, but with respect to shape and position to one another on an x-ray film.

socialization Process by which a person (from birth to death) learns to exist in a social system through changing behaviors and attitudes as a result of interacting with other people in a social environment.

solitary play Play that a child participates in by herself.

state anxiety Transitory anxiety, that is, one that may change over time.

status Hierarchial categorization of a person's position in the social system; some positions are deemed as having more prestige than others.

static balance Individual's ability to hold a stationary, balanced position for a period of time.

stranger anxiety Anxiety produced in infants (7 to 9 months) by the presentation of a strange face or person.

superego Third level of personality development according to Freud; sometimes referred to as the human moral conscience and, like the ego, in conflict with the id (see *id*).

symbolic representation Source of modeling found in animated forms such as television, movies, books, newspapers, records, and so on.

syntax Rules that dictate the acceptable sequence, combinations, and function of words in a sentence.

theory Summary of known ''facts'' and conjecture that serves to organize large amounts of information in a meaningful way; useful in the social sciences for explaining and predicting behavior and for guiding research.

Title IX Federal legislation that assures equal opportunity for girls' and boys' participation in school and other institutional sponsored physical education and sports programs.

trait anxiety Differs from state anxiety in that it is considered more permanent and, therefore, a part of the individual's personality makeup.

transformational grammar (1) Operation that changes configuration or expression into another, in accordance with a rule; (2) in linguistics involves changes, that add or delete symbols, make substitutions, or effect order changes, but that do not alter the meaning of the sentence.

unconditioned response Response caused by an unconditioned stimulus (see *unconditioned stimulus*).

unconditioned stimulus Stimulus that causes a response prior to conditioning; all reflexive behaviors are considered caused by unconditioned stimuli.

values clarification Process by which a person is helped in decision making about a values situation, that is, what is right or wrong for the person involved in the decision-making process.

velocity of growth Actual amount of growth in inches or centimeters during a given year (see *distance curve of growth*).

Appendix A

GROWTH CHARTS

BOYS FROM BIRTH TO 36 MONTHS

LENGTH FOR AGE

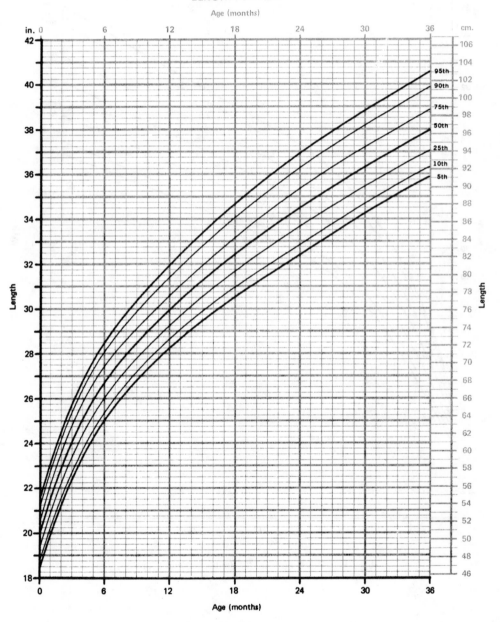

Fig. A-1. Boys, birth to 36 months—Length for age.

BOYS FROM BIRTH TO 36 MONTHS

WEIGHT FOR AGE

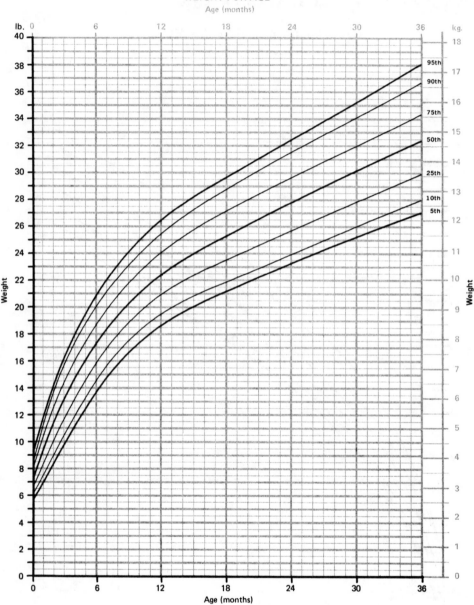

Fig. A-2. Boys, birth to 36 months—Weight for age.

BOYS FROM BIRTH TO 36 MONTHS

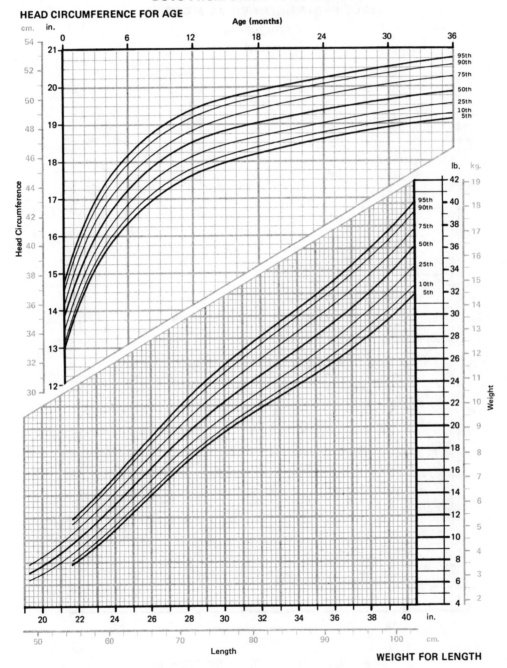

Fig. A-3. Boys, birth to 36 months—Weight for length and head circumference.

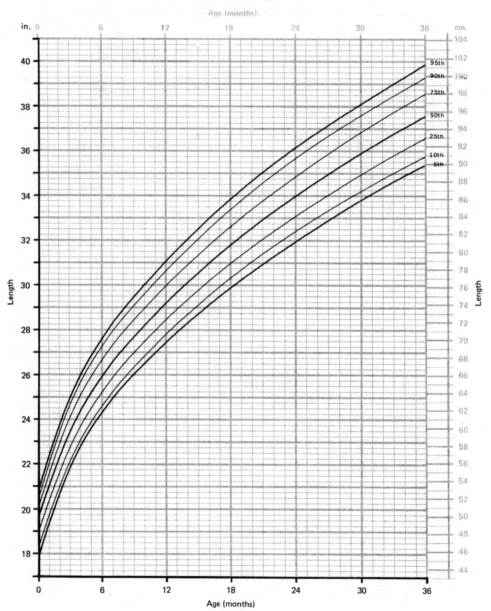

GIRLS FROM BIRTH TO 36 MONTHS

LENGTH FOR AGE

Fig. A-4. Girls, birth to 36 months—Length for age.

GIRLS FROM BIRTH TO 36 MONTHS

WEIGHT FOR AGE

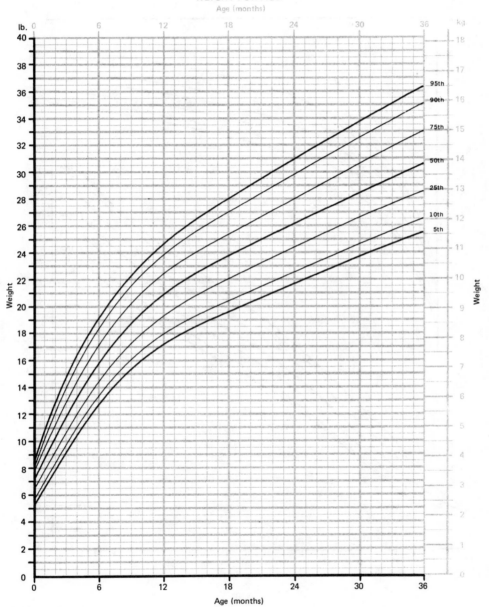

Fig. A-5. Girls, birth to 36 months—Weight for age.

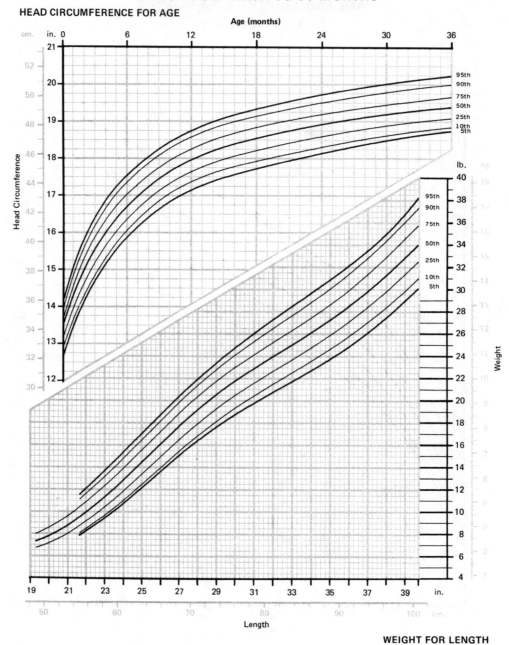

GIRLS FROM BIRTH TO 36 MONTHS

HEAD CIRCUMFERENCE FOR AGE

WEIGHT FOR LENGTH

Fig. A-6. Girls, birth to 36 months—Weight for length and head circumference.

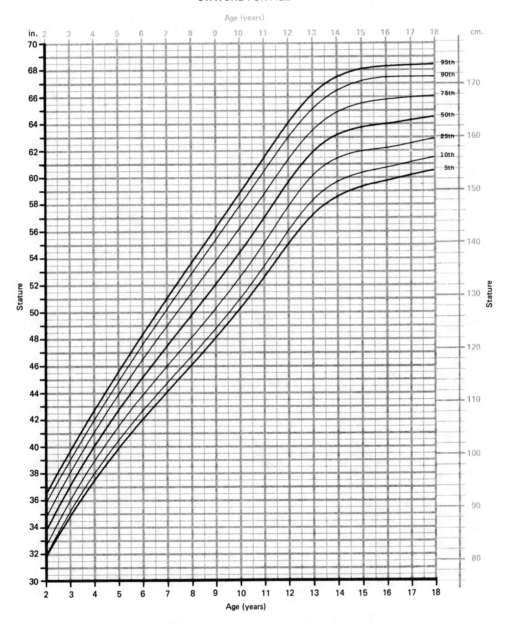

GIRLS FROM 2 TO 18 YEARS

STATURE FOR AGE

Fig. A-7. Girls, 2 to 18 years—Stature for age.

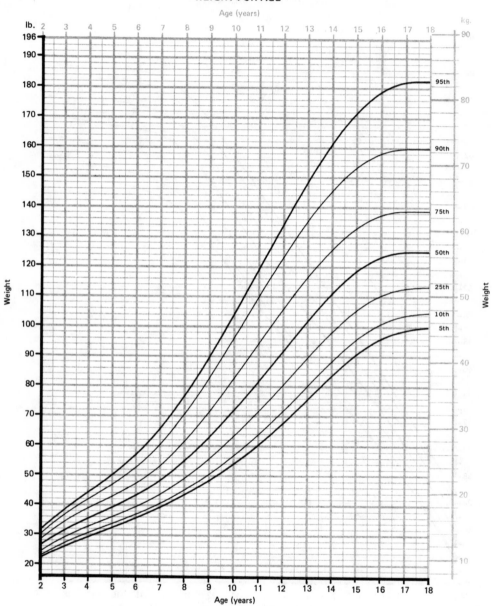

GIRLS FROM 2 TO 18 YEARS
WEIGHT FOR AGE

Fig. A-8. Girls, 2 to 18 years—Weight for age.

PRE-PUBERTAL GIRLS FROM 2 TO 10 YEARS

WEIGHT FOR STATURE

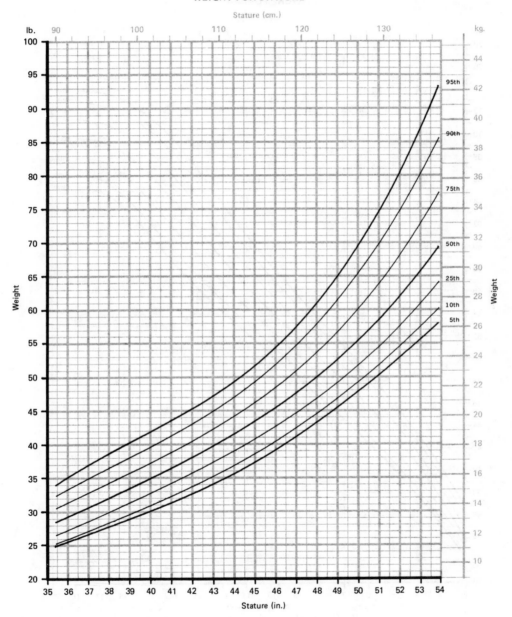

Fig. A-9. Girls, 2 to 10 years—Weight for stature.

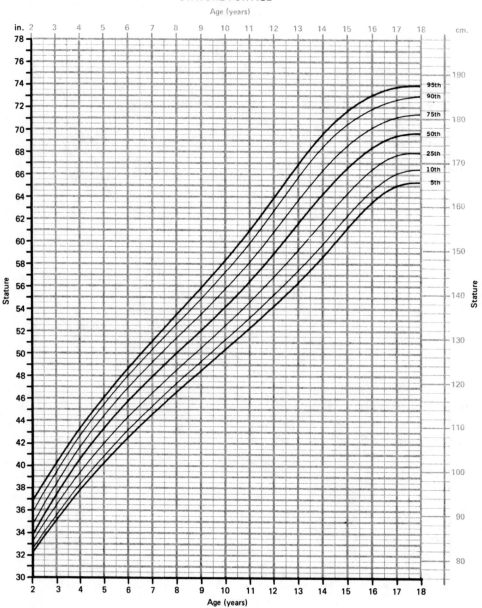

BOYS FROM 2 TO 18 YEARS

STATURE FOR AGE

Age (years)

Fig. A-10. Boys, 2 to 18 years—Stature for age.

BOYS FROM 2 TO 18 YEARS

WEIGHT FOR AGE

Age (years)

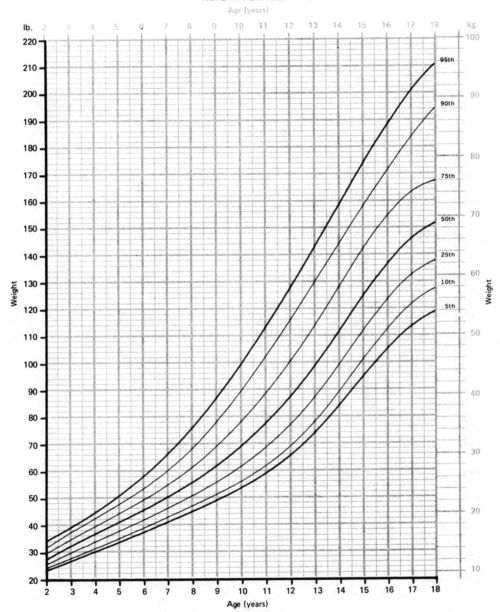

Fig. A-11. Boys, 2 to 18 years—Weight for age.

PRE-PUBERTAL BOYS FROM 2 TO 11½ YEARS

WEIGHT FOR STATURE

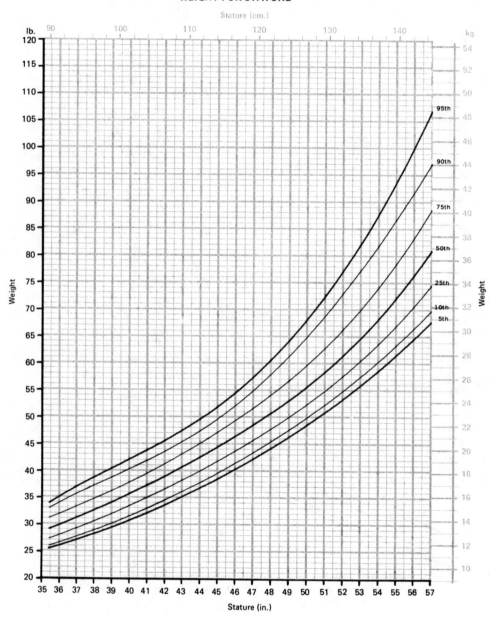

Fig. A-12. Boys, 2 to 11½ years—Weight for stature.

Appendix B

SUMMARY TABLES OF CHILD DEVELOPMENT

Table A-1. Summary of child development—infancy

Psychomotor	Cognitive	Affective

Brain near adult weight at birth
Birth weight triples in first year
Sensitive to sound from birth
Perception of moving stimuli:
  3 to 5 days old, responds to
    movement
4 months, notices arms and legs
Movement initially reflexive,
  gives way to purposive move-
  ment in the following chrono-
  logical order:
Rolling—stomach to back
  (3 months)
Rolling—back to stomach
  (4 to 6 months)
Sitting (5 to 9 months)
Crawling (7 months)
Standing (9 months)
Walking (9 to 15 months)
	Learning accomplished through
	  use of senses and basic motor
	  patterns
	Infant noises reflexive until
	  around 4 to 6 months
	First word appears about 1 year
	By 2 years usually able to make
	  two-word sentences
		Family is main source of interac-
		  tion and stimulation for child
		Early experiences have impact on
		  self-concept development
		Stranger anxiety appears at 7 to 9
		  months

Table A-2. Summary of child development—early childhood (2 to 5)

Psychomotor	Cognitive	Affective
Voluntary control of body is becoming more proficient Running ability improves with adult gait at 4 to 5 years Can jump on two feet at 28 months and for distance at 40 months 75% skilled at jumping by 4½ years Can hop short distances at 4 years Can skip and gallop by 5 years Can climb up and down stairs with foot-alternating pattern at 4 years Has beginnings of throwing patterns Can catch 20 cm (8 in.) diameter ball with a bounce 60% to 80% of the time by 5 years Hand and foot dominance established by 5 years Has developed concept of laterality by 3 to 4 years	Learning still accomplished through perceptual processes Uses trial-and-error to explore environment Doubles vocabulary between 2 and 3 years Increases in ability to use more parts of speech correctly in sentence construction Communication is characterized by questions, requests, and commands	Physical aggression decreases Verbal aggression increases Attitudes are formed through family and play group Basic moral foundation becomes established Children learn appropriate role for their particular sex

Table A-3. Summary of child development—late childhood (5 to 10)

Psychomotor	Cognitive	Affective
Can perform following skills with adult form: Running Hopping Galloping Skipping Throwing Catching Height, weight, and strength increases at steady gradual rate Has developed concept of lateral awareness by 7 years	Child able to use logic and reason about such concepts as: Size Volume Numbers Weight Able to manipulate symbols in thought rather than deed Child's communication has improved in elocution as well as use of the language Has adult abilities for precise speech production, auditory memory, and discrimination (8 years)	Beginning of schooling produces changes due to input from groups other than family School and peer group now become important factors in child's life Moral development sees most children at Stages 1 and 2 (Kohlberg) Self-concept shows general decline during this time period Child's self-concept starts to stabilize about 8 years Males appear to be more aggressive than females Child concerned about "separation anxiety" at 5 to 6 years

Table A-4. Summary of child development—adolescence (10 to 18)

Psychomotor	Cognitive	Affective
Time of great physical changes in: Height Weight Strength Attains mature adult figure Males show improvement in specialized skills through age of 18 Females improve in specialized skills until 14 and then level off or show decrease in performance	Child enters period of formal operations and is able to use abstract thought in problem-solving Able to apply general principles to specific situations—adult-level functioning Refinement of communication skills continues from this time on with an increase in vocabulary and complexity of sentence structure	Peer group has large amount of influence Standards of behavior set by peer group Self-concept, attitudes, and anxieties are subject to change as effort to enter adult world consumes a lot of time Moral development can range anywhere from Stages 3 to 6, with most people at Stages 3 to 4 during adolescence

INDEX

Numbers in italics indicate reference is to an illustration; t indicates reference to a table.

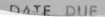